Brave
New
Ballot

Brave
New
Ballot

The Battle to Safeguard Democracy in the Age of Electronic Voting

Aviel D. Rubin, PhD

Morgan Road Books
New York

MORGAN ROAD BOOKS

PUBLISHED BY MORGAN ROAD BOOKS

Copyright © 2006 by Aviel D. Rubin

All Rights Reserved

Published in the United States by Morgan Road Books,
an imprint of The Doubleday Broadway Publishing Group,
a division of Random House, Inc., New York.
www.morganroadbooks.com

Morgan Road Books and the M colophon are trademarks of
Random House, Inc.

Book design by Chris Welch

Library of Congress Cataloging-in-Publication Data
Rubin, Aviel D.
Brave new ballot : the battle to safeguard democracy in the age of
electronic voting / Aviel D. Rubin. — 1st ed.
p.   cm.
Includes bibliographical references.
ISBN 0-7679-2210-7
1. Electronic voting—United States.   2. Electronic voting—Security
measures—United States.   3. Voting-machines—
United States—Reliability.   I. Title.
JK1985.R83 2006
324.6'5—dc22
2006041917

ISBN-13: 978-0-7679-2210-4
ISBN-10: 0-7679-2210-7

Printed in the United States of America

1   3   5   7   9   10   8   6   4   2

First Edition

TO ALL THE POLL WORKERS, ELECTION OFFICIALS, AND ELECTION
MONITORS, HERE AND AROUND THE WORLD,
WHO WORK TO GUARANTEE THE FUNDAMENTAL RIGHT
TO FAIR, SAFE, AND SECURE ELECTIONS

Acknowledgments

I am grateful to many people who helped make this book possible. First and always, I am indebted to my wife, Ann, for her patience and understanding. She not only supported my work on the book, but also provided valuable feedback on the manuscript as it took shape. My voting work was a great burden to Ann and our children, and the book only compounded the difficulty. Thankfully, she shares my belief in the importance of this work.

I owe a tremendous debt of gratitude to Adam Stubblefield and Yoshi Kohno, whose around-the-clock review of the Diebold code over several days in July 2003 sparked these events. I also thank Adam for providing valuable feedback on drafts of the book. Thanks, too, to Dan Wallach for his help on the Diebold analysis, as well as for pushing me to resubmit our proposal to the NSF for ACCURATE. Dan is largely responsible for the existence of that center, and he has contributed greatly to the public's awareness of e-voting security issues.

Special thanks to David Jefferson, who is an inspiration to me in the movement to ensure elections that are safe, secure, and auditable. He provided invaluable input on this book, and I had fun sending him each chapter for comments as I finished it. David often provided missing details and critical insights. Thanks, too, to David Dill, Doug Jones, David Wagner, Kim Alexander, Ron Rivest, and my other ACCURATE partners for all of their tireless work on securing elections. I would also like to thank Mark Benerofe for his feedback on the outline and early chapters in the book.

I am especially grateful to Cindy Cohn and her legal team from the Electronic Frontiers Foundation for providing us with free legal representation during the Diebold confrontation, as well as their continuing legal advice in the fight to protect personal liberties in the digital age. I also thank Mary Kiffmeyer for suggesting that I become an election judge, and to all of the poll workers in this country who volunteer on election day. Their hard work makes our democracy possible. I would also like to thank the EAC commissioners, with whom I have had the pleasure of interacting, and especially Buster Soaries, for giving me the final push to write this book.

I would like to thank David Pogue for introducing me to my fantastic agent, Jim Levine, who believed in my story, and did a tremendous job finding me the perfect match with Amy Hertz and Nathanael Brown at Random House. Jim, Amy, and Nate are the best possible team a writer could have. They recognized the importance of this story, and provided me with exceptional advice, editing, and feedback.

And finally, my heartfelt thanks to David Sobel, a phenomenal writer, who worked with me tirelessly to rewrite my entire manuscript so that it was not only accessible to the lay reader but a pleasure to read. In David I have found a true friend, collaborator, and kindred spirit.

The ignorance of one voter in a democracy
impairs the security of all.
—*John F. Kennedy, 1963*

I f I knew then what I know now, I might have recognized the
sound of the phone ringing on my desk as something like the
bell at the start of a wild horse race. My life, relatively calm on
that warm day in July 2003, was about to change in ways I could
never have imagined, and sometimes still can't quite believe.
Even so, if I knew then what I know now, I probably would have
answered the call anyway.

The call came from David Dill, like me a professor of computer science, a man I had never met but knew by reputation.
David was one of the leading voices in the computer science
community to speak up with concerns about electronic voting.
He was calling from his office at Stanford, and I was speaking
from mine at Johns Hopkins in Baltimore. He asked me if I
knew that Diebold's source code was available for download on
the Internet. I was a little embarrassed that my first thought
was, *What's Diebold?* until I told my wife the story and she
asked, "What's source code?" David explained that Diebold was

the country's leading manufacturer of electronic voting machines and that in the midterm elections of 2002 its Accuvote TS and TSx machines had been used in thirty-seven states.

"You mean the actual elections, where people go to the polls and vote?" I asked.

"That's right."

I hadn't realized that e-voting had already caught on to such an extent. I asked David if the code he was talking about was part of the back-end processing system, the code in the individual voting machines themselves, or some other part of the larger system. He told me that the source code for the individual terminals themselves, the machines that millions of Americans would use to cast their votes, was available for download from a New Zealand–based website. An activist named Bev Harris had found the files, completely unprotected, on Diebold's own servers and had posted them.

I couldn't believe it. The companies that make such machines are notoriously—and fanatically—secretive about their systems. Outsiders could never examine the source code except under ironclad nondisclosure agreements, and inside the companies very few people had access to the code. Even professionals like us had no idea how the systems were designed and developed, and we didn't believe there was much chance we'd ever find out. As unnerving as David's news was, it was also exciting. Conceivably, we could have our first glimpse into the inner workings of the machines at the heart of our electoral future. David let me know that he had called a number of computer scientists with this news but had been particularly interested in contacting me.

My special expertise is in computer security. I had become involved in electronic voting somewhat haphazardly in the late

1990s when a colleague enlisted me in an analysis of computerized voting commissioned by the government of Costa Rica. That project led to my appearance before a National Science Foundation (NSF) panel on the subject, after which I wrote up my comments for publication and began giving academic talks on the subject. When David Dill circulated a petition advocating *verified voting*—the simple idea that when people go to the polls to cast their votes, they should be able to verify with a receipt that their votes have been recorded correctly—I was among the first to sign. It wasn't that I had any special passion for politics, but the principle seemed straightforward to me, and the problems caused by computerized voting seemed obvious, as they did to most computer scientists.

I was already aware of several compelling arguments against electronic voting machines, notably that because the systems were proprietary, they hadn't been proven to be tamperproof; nor was the voting verifiable after the fact. If it were now possible to do a security analysis of the Diebold terminals, it would be an opportunity to address the first problem publicly. As for the second, it was the computer security community, ironically, that first recognized that achieving the goal of verifiability might involve old-fashioned, low-tech paper ballots.

There are several levels of code, that is, the instructions created by programmers to run computers. *Source code*, which is written in a variety of commonly used and readable programming languages, instructs the computer to perform specific tasks. Once source code is written, a program called a *compiler* is used to convert it into *object code*, also referred to as *executables*, the seemingly endless stream of ones and zeros that is comprehensible only to a machine and is what actually runs inside a computer. Professionals are trained to read source code, but even for us it can be profoundly difficult to decipher and understand a complete, complex program. Computer and software companies look upon their source code as their most precious asset and guard it like Coca-Cola guards its secret formula. That any company, especially one as sophisticated as Diebold, would allow such a basic breakdown in security that its source code would be available for all the world to see was unimaginable to me.

I had to see for myself. I opened up Google and typed in "Diebold source code." Sure enough, the very first hit was a website in New Zealand that appeared to contain all of the source code and documentation for an electronic voting machine. The documentation was password-protected, but the source code itself, the real treasure, was not. Apparently, whoever had set up the site had copied the code from Diebold's site before the company wised up and shut it down. If this was what it seemed to be, it was indeed a stunning discovery.

In that first phone call, David Dill suggested that we assemble a group of computer security experts to analyze the Diebold code. While David got busy contacting colleagues by phone and e-mail, I turned instinctively to Adam and Yoshi, the two PhD students who were working with me that summer. If anyone was going to get excited about getting their hands on this code, it would be these two guys.

I've worked with a lot of brilliant students, but none have impressed me like Adam Stubblefield. Adam was brought to my attention by Dan Wallach, his undergraduate adviser at Rice University. I introduced myself to Adam at a computer security research conference where, though only nineteen, Adam had presented a fascinating paper he co-authored with some well-established and accomplished researchers. His modesty, charm, and obvious intelligence immediately won me over, and on the spot I offered him a summer internship working with me at AT&T Labs. It was a remarkably successful and productive summer, with major national media taking notice of the work we did (professor-speak for the work *he* did). Adam was the first person to crack the security of the wireless networking protocol that was designed to protect Wi-Fi communication. And it took him less than a week. Adam and I had developed a great relationship, and I invited him to come with me when I went to Johns Hopkins.

A few years older than Adam, and equally impressive, Tadayoshi Kohno, who goes by "Yoshi," brought to our team experience and discipline that nicely complemented Adam's raw, untamed genius. Yoshi, who had been a PhD student in computer science at the University of California at San Diego, had approached me at a conference and asked if I was hiring any summer interns. This was just before I was to leave AT&T for Hopkins, so I jokingly told him he'd be welcome to come spend the summer with me, earning the lowly wages of an academic. Amazingly, Yoshi wasted no time, subletting an apartment in Baltimore and leaving his wife on the other side of the country for the summer. Later Yoshi even lived for a while in a spare room in our house. He was often off to work before we got up in the morning, and still out working by the time we went to bed at night, but somehow he found time to develop a strong and lasting friendship with our four-year-old daughter.

With Yoshi in my office and Adam at home connected by speakerphone, I described David Dill's phone call, suggested that the three of us form the core of the group doing the analysis, and asked if they were willing to drop everything else we were working on to concentrate on this project. Adam, who must have been sitting at his computer, replied that he was already downloading the Diebold code. Without missing a beat, Yoshi asked if he could go do the same. We hadn't even gotten started, and I could tell these guys were hooked.

Meanwhile, David Dill had assembled a formidable team of interested computer scientists and got about seven of us together on a conference call to discuss the logistics of a collaborative and distributed analysis. It's hard enough to work on a big project with people right down the hall. I couldn't imagine how a group this size, spread all over the country, could work effectively, but I was eager to get started and went along with things. It was agreed that results would all be shared on an e-mail list.

At Hopkins, Adam and Yoshi dove right in and spent the first few hours poring over the source code. They compiled the code and were able to run it on the Windows machines in our lab, literally creating a working voting machine. Adam began posting their results to the e-mail list, but only Dill responded. The pair made astonishing headway over the next several days, while we continued to hear nothing from any of the other members of the group. I decided to move ahead on the project as a small Hopkins team rather than keep up the pretense that it was the work of a larger group. It may have been a rash decision, and it was not without its cost. At least one of the people on the original call bore me a grudge for a very long time.

Also in that first conference call, someone raised the specter of the DMCA. The Digital Millennium Copyright Act, a law signed by Bill Clinton in 1998 that, among other things, makes it illegal to circumvent a digital copyright protection system, can be a great thorn in the side of computer security researchers, especially those whose work focuses on exposing the weaknesses in those very systems. In the past, the law has been interpreted broadly and has often been invoked to hinder the kind of research or analysis that I like to do. It reinforces the notion that companies like Diebold never need to disclose the code that runs their machines, not even to the government and not even when the machines serve critical public functions. A young Russian computer scientist went to jail in 2001 for demonstrating how to break one of Adobe's protection schemes. He was a young PhD candidate with two small children, presenting at an academic conference in Las Vegas, arrested for doing what he was trained to do. He was released on bail but not permitted to return to his family for six months. The DMCA is a sword hanging over our heads.

Knowing I needed to understand the legal risks better, I contacted Cindy Cohn, a sharp, tenacious attorney known as an effective defender of computer scientists against just this kind of legislation and legal trickery. Cindy works for the Electronic Frontiers Foundation (EFF), an organization founded in 1990 to help safeguard civil liberties in the age of digital communications technology. I brought her up to speed on our investigation into the Diebold code and asked if we needed to worry about DMCA. Cindy immediately—although already too late—said that she wanted to have a conversation with me, Adam, and Yoshi before any of us started looking at the code. When she had us all on the phone, she explained a point that should have been self-evident: since there was no protection scheme attached to the code, it probably wasn't relevant in this situation. The documentation, however, was another story. It was password-protected, and even though we had easily found the passwords online, she instructed us not to use them. The documentation would have saved us considerable time, but we chose not to look at it. Cindy added that she needed time to investigate whether or not the code represented a trade secret of Diebold's, like

Coca-Cola's recipe. If so, we would be upping the ante considerably if we were to publicly expose any flaws. Cindy offered to represent us pro bono, and I can hardly express how much her reassuring presence comforted me. I'm not sure we would have continued without her.

In the end, Cindy concluded that there was no real case to be made for the code as a trade secret. The code had been copied from Diebold's own website and had been available online for months. By checking with the host of the site in New Zealand and with that person's Internet service provider (ISP), Cindy established that Diebold had made no attempt to get its code removed. We could safely assume that Diebold knew about the online availability of its intellectual property, yet had made no effort to protect it. Cindy felt this pretty well deflated any trade-secret argument the company might ever hope to make, and she gave us the green light. The legal staff at Johns Hopkins confirmed Cindy's opinion: the documentation was off-limits, but the code itself was fair game.

Adam and Yoshi were consumed by the dissection of the code. Almost immediately, they flagged some serious problems. It seemed like every hour or two one of them would pop into my office and breathlessly tell me about a new wrinkle he had discovered. We were stunned by some of these discoveries and began to sense how big this thing might be. When I called Cindy after a few days to tell her that we would soon be ready to go public with our findings, she was amazed at how quickly we had moved. She mobilized the EFF legal team to be ready to review our drafts and come to our rescue if necessary.

I'll never forget what Adam and Yoshi put themselves through that week. They got almost no sleep, and Yoshi seemed to barely register the presence of his visiting wife, whom he hadn't seen in weeks. I've gotten most of the recognition for this work, but these two did the heavy lifting.

One other researcher soon joined our little core group. Dan Wallach, the professor who had been Adam Stubblefield's adviser at Rice, had been in on the conference call with David Dill and had also begun assembling a team of students to analyze the code. He had no way of knowing that Adam and Yoshi had moved like demons and were preparing a report by the end of that first week. When Dan e-mailed me with some thoughts on the project, I had to explain how far along we already were at Johns Hopkins. Dan didn't take it well that we had moved ahead unilaterally, but after hearing about the sacrifices, not to mention the discoveries, that the two grad students had made, he softened. The truth was that the project needed Dan, not only because he could help with the analysis, but also because he's a terrific writer and could bring much-needed clarity to the report, an invaluable contribution given how widely it was distributed.

Dan was also well acquainted with the legal issues surrounding security research, as were the lawyers at Rice. There had been complications relating to the DMCA with a controversial paper he co-authored about digital music, and now he correctly surmised that he would need clearance if his name was going on a report as explosive as ours seemed it would be. It was the middle of summer, however, and he couldn't get the attention he needed from the legal staff. This seemingly small roadblock would have unfortunate consequences for him down the road. Our work ultimately became known as the "Hopkins Report" instead of the "Hopkins/Rice Report."

2

As long as I count the votes, what are
you going to do about it?
—*William Marcy "Boss" Tweed, 1871*

Thomas Paine said that the right to vote is "the primary right by which other rights are protected." The vote makes democracy possible, and at the same time a healthy democracy ensures the possibility of fair and meaningful voting. And yet, preserving and protecting the integrity of the voting process has proven quite a challenge throughout our history. In the earliest elections, citizens cast their votes by voice, in public. Not only was there no guarantee of secrecy or privacy, but the voice vote was susceptible to any number of frauds and corruptions, from individuals casting multiple votes to the intimidation of voters.

It didn't take long for Congress to realize how insecure this system was, and in 1804 it ratified the Twelfth Amendment to the Constitution, which mandated voting by ballot. Paper ballots evolved throughout the nineteenth century. At first, there was no consistency in the ballots that voters used; as often as not, ballots were just random scraps of paper provided by the voters themselves, on which they had scrawled the names of their chosen candidates. These votes were unreliable, of course, as the ballots were open to subjective interpretation. Likewise, the protections against ballot-box stuffing and counting fraud were woefully inadequate. Quickly, candidates and political parties began making preprinted ballots available, but usually these ballots were designed to make it difficult, if not impossible, to vote for anything other than the straight party ticket. Moreover, since each party would print its ballot in a different-colored paper, voters often gave up the right of privacy or secrecy when they disclosed their votes simply by their choice of ballot. Although the ballots were gradually improved over time, it wasn't until the late 1880s that a uniform, standardized, preprinted ballot provided by the government—called "the Australian ballot"—came into common usage. The Australian ballot, combined with proper monitoring procedures, was designed to provide a high level of security and integrity in the voting process, although the problems of ballot-box stuffing and fair tabulating procedures were still present. As long as ballots were marked by hand, they could be said to be open to interpretation, and parties could "train" election officials in the favorable reading of unclear ballots.

Around the turn of the twentieth century, the first lever voting machines came into use; inventor Jacob H. Myers proclaimed that he had designed the machine to "protect mechanically the voter from rascaldom, and make the process of casting the ballot perfectly plain, simple and secret." But even though they became the dominant voting mechanism for decades, these machines posed their own problems. To begin with, at the time the lever voting machine was introduced it represented an extraordinarily high level of technology for its time. The machines were intricate and delicate, with hundreds of tiny moving parts that were subject to breakdown and malfunction. In fact, those little parts were vulnerable to an ingenious attack. While programming the levers, a technician could break off a pencil lead in one of the gears, creating a very small jam. The machine would fail to register the votes for a particular candidate, but there would be no obvious difference in how the machine operated. Eventually, the lead would wear away and fall out, leaving no evidence of the fraud—kind of like a bullet made of ice melting away after doing its damage. In addition, the lever machines did not provide a mechanism for maintaining an independent record of each voter's ballot. Even now, despite all the technological refinements to the voting process, this simple, critical piece of the puzzle continues to prove elusive.

As America's romance with computers took hold in the years after the Second World War, it seemed natural to apply this almost miraculous new technology to the election process. The most popular methods of registering votes by computer involved the use of either punch cards or a scanning process similar to the one used to record answers on standardized tests, like the SATs. Although these procedures went a very long way toward guaranteeing security from large-scale fraud or manipulation, there were still many problems at the local level, where improperly punched or filled-in ballots could lead to serious irregularities. The problems with punch-card ballots came under the harsh glare of public attention, of course, in the 2000 presidential election. The advantage to such systems, however, is that they naturally create a paper record of each vote for later auditing or recounting.

Most recently, as computers have become compact and portable, election officials have turned to direct recording electronic (DRE) systems. Congress helped this process along, in 2002, by passing the Help America Vote Act, a sweeping piece of legislation passed in a direct response to the election debacle of 2000. HAVA, as it is known, mandates wholesale reforms, including federal funding to states to improve election administration and update outdated voting systems. DRE machines, essentially personal computers running a special application, represent the digital equivalent of the old lever voting machines but lack the ability to monitor the settings of the levers. There are no ballots; voters make their selections from the list of candidates provided, using a touch screen, push buttons, or some other electronic pointing device. An onscreen keyboard is provided for write-in votes. Voters' choices are recorded and stored on a diskette, memory card, or some other electronic device. The DRE is familiar and recognizable to Americans, who have become so used to interfacing with computers. It's not purely coincidental that it reminds people of an automatic teller machine. Municipalities, counties, and even entire states have now adopted the machines. The security of DREs largely depends on the security of their hardware and software, and that is where computer scientists come into the picture.

After the 2000 election, the voting technology itself became the focus of large-scale public attention. The issue of electronic voting machines, particularly those that generate no paper receipts or other record that can be used in a recount, spawned a huge grassroots activist movement. At the core was Verified Voting, the organization founded by Stanford's David Dill. Dill's interest dated back to the moment when Santa Clara County, where Stanford is located, announced its intention to acquire Sequoia computerized voting machines. He was naturally curious about how the machines worked, and through his investigations he came to the realization that fully computerized, paperless voting poses enormous security risks. He set about trying to reason with county officials in early 2003 and launched a petition on his website. Dill mobilized people around the issue and contacted, among other people, Kevin Shelley, then secretary of state of California; Kim Alexander of the California Voter Foundation; David Jefferson, a secure voting advocate employed at Lawrence Livermore National Labs (LLNB); and me. He established Verified Voting, with an advisory board and a terrific executive director, Will Doherty. Dill actually created two separate legal entities: VerifiedVoting.org, a 501(c)(4) nonprofit lobbying organization, and the Verified Voting Foundation, a 501(c)(3) nonprofit educational group. VerifiedVoting.org quickly became the primary national resource on the issue, identifying its mission with a straightforward declaration:

> We advocate the use of voter-verified paper ballots (VVPBs) for all elections in the United States, so voters can inspect individual permanent records of their ballots before they are cast and so meaningful recounts may be conducted. We also insist that electronic voting equipment and software be open to public scrutiny and that random, surprise recounts be conducted on a regular basis to audit election equipment.

These two simple sentences form the basis of the intense debate that has rocked the electoral process over the last few years.

IT WOULDN'T TAKE long for a literature professor to determine if an uncredited manuscript had been written by a serious professional or by a hack. Likewise, a computer scientist can look at the source code for a computer program and know if it was developed by an expert or an amateur. We were struck almost immediately by the amateurishness of the Diebold source code. That was the last thing anyone expected from such an old and well-established company.

The Diebold brand name may not be as recognizable as Ford or Marlboro, but it's been around a lot longer and is probably vaguely familiar to most Americans. You can see it on everything from safes to alarm systems to cash machines. Founded in 1859 in Cincinnati by a German immigrant, Charles Diebold, the company's growth has been entwined with American history in odd ways. Diebold, a manufacturer of high-quality safes and vaults, got his first big break when, in the aftermath of the Great Chicago Fire of 1871, nearly one thousand Diebold safes were discovered with the contents intact, a feat that cemented Diebold's good reputation in the security business and brought the company a great deal of new business. Several generations later, after the company had become a large and diversified corporation, no less a personage than the legendary G-man Eliot Ness served for a time as its chairman of the board. Over the years, Diebold expanded from making locks and safes to designing sophisticated alarm and security systems for all manner of major industrial and governmental clients. Simply put, what Diebold sells is security. It's notable that in 2001 the company won the contract from the U.S. National Archives in Washington to secure the Charters of Freedom, including the Constitution, the Bill of Rights, and the Declaration of Independence.

In the late 1960s, Diebold began manufacturing automated teller machines (ATMs), a business that, in the words of Diebold's own literature, "could combine its security expertise and delivery system leadership with its metal construction and electro-mechanical device skills." It's only logical that such a company would be an early player in electronic voting machines, and in 2002 it entered what it called the "self-service elections industry" with the acquisition of Global Election Systems, an early leader in touch-screen voting technology. Previously, Global had acquired I-Mark Systems, the originator of the first DRE system, the Accuvote TS. An improved version of that machine, along with the Accuvote TSx, which ran the same software, became the anchors of Diebold's e-voting product line. These two machines were the subject of our analysis.

At its heart, an e-voting machine is a computer running a version of the Windows operating system. A touch-activated screen allows voters to tap the screen corresponding to the candidate of their choice. It's not much more complicated than voting by pointing. When you, the voter, arrive at your polling place, a poll worker confirms your registration status, then hands you a smartcard. The smartcard contains a computer chip that holds an electronic ballot corresponding to the races in which you are eligible to vote. You insert the smartcard into a slot in the e-voting machine, and your ballot is loaded onto the machine. The machine then displays a series of screens, allowing you to select your candidate in each race and to record your yes or no on each proposition on the ballot. When you've made all your choices, a confirmation screen lets you review all your choices and make any changes or corrections. When you're done, the machine stores your votes on a memory card, not much different from the removable cards found in digital cameras and other electronic devices. Then it spits out your smartcard, deactivated so that it cannot be used again until it is reprogrammed by a poll worker for the next voter. When the poll closes, the machine prints the total number of votes cast for each candidate, and the totals from all of the machines are combined. Finally, one of the machines is used to send the combined preliminary results, via modem and phone hookup, to tallying servers at the back-end processing center of the board of elections. Later, poll workers hand-deliver the memory cards containing the official results to the board of elections.

The designers of such a system would have had four basic points of focus. The first is the user interface, or the means by which a human interacts with the computer. The second is security, the means to survive an attack. The third piece is software engineering, the expertise that ensures that the programming can be updated to meet evolving needs. Fourth, and finally, they would take into account the established election procedures in place at the polling sites. Given that the system is supposed to safeguard the very foundation of our democratic system, you'd think that only the most seasoned experts would be assigned to any of these functions, but we kept turning up design problems that could only have been caused by inexperienced programmers. Moreover, the problems were so numerous that our report paid only minimal attention to the fact that the whole system ran on top of Windows, a platform notorious for its bugs and security flaws. That fact alone is probably enough to scare anyone whose Windows computer has ever been laid low by a hideous virus from the outside world.

The Accuvote programmers realized that the smartcards were vulnerable to tampering simply because they were removable. The card records the votes on a particular machine in the order in which they are cast, the equivalent of having a stack of paper ballots saved in sequential order. An observer who took the trouble to keep track of the voters as they used the machine would later be able to match up each individual voter with his or her vote. If nothing else, this could threaten voters' right to confidentiality. The programmers countered this possibility by designing a secure way to shuffle the votes, like a deck of cards, so that it would be impossible to reconstruct the voting order after the fact. The problem was that the procedure they chose, called a linear congruential generator (LCG), was not in fact secure, leaving open the possibility of reconstructing the voting order. Within the code itself, the programmers cite a book called *Applied Cryptography* by Bruce Schneier as the inspiration for this technique, yet in that very book the author says, "Linear Congruential Generators cannot be used for cryptography." As he told me later, after reading our report, Schneier himself was worried about "amateurs" misusing the techniques he describes in his book. As it happens, LCGs, as useful as they are in other areas of computer science, were broken back in 1977. We didn't like finding them used this way, but the worst part was that it seemed a symptom of a larger underlying problem. The question we kept asking ourselves was this: if you're programming machines to be used in public elections—any election, no less a presidential election—wouldn't you want to hire the guys who *write* books like this and not the guys who have to look things up in them?

We found this kind of sloppy mistake all through the code. Even when the programmers recognized that their code had a problem, they'd patch it up with a quick fix, a stopgap solution that we call a "hack," as though they were patching up the backyard hose with duct tape. They even left references to their shoddy workmanship with comments throughout the code:

```
/* Okay, I don't like this one bit. Its really tough to tell where m Audio-
Player should live. [ . . . ] A reorganization might be in order here. */
```

/* This is a bit of a hack for now */

/* need to work on exception *caused by audio*. I think they will currently result in double-fault. */

/* the BOOL beeped flag is a hack so we don't beep twice. This is really a result of the key handling being gorped */

/* the way we deal with audio here is a gross hack */

Cryptography, the art and science of protecting information, is as important to computer security as it is to intelligence work. A key component of cryptography is *encryption*, the process of converting data into a form that cannot be understood by unauthorized people, similar to the way a spy might use a secret cipher. Every encryption system relies on an algorithm that converts plain text into cipher text and back again (decryption), using secret keys. Naturally, computer scientists have developed staggeringly complex encryption techniques, but even the most sophisticated cipher is worthless once it gets broken, or worse yet, if the key is exposed. Every place we found cryptography used in the code, we found it used incorrectly. In several places where it was definitely needed, there was no cryptography at all. For example, the Diebold machines used totally outdated encryption to protect the vote tallies on the smartcards. In 1998 John Gilmore built a machine that could crack encryption keys, and he used it to break the most widely used encryption algorithm, called the data encryption standard, or DES. DES has subsequently been replaced by AES, the advanced encryption standard, and yet Diebold used DES instead of AES. Furthermore, the company used it in an insecure way. It was like giving a patient medicine that has passed its expiration date when there's a fresh supply at hand and when the expired medicine is known to do more harm than good.

A broken cipher can be replaced or repaired pretty easily, but there was an even bigger problem with Diebold's *key management*, the process of generating encryption keys and distributing unique keys to terminals or discrete machines. Proper key management is vital to any cryptographic system and represents one of the biggest programming challenges. It's particularly unwise, for instance, to use the same key in many different machines. Diebold's key management, however, consisted of one line of code, hardwired into *every* machine:

```
#define DESKEY ((des_key*) "F2654hD4")
```

In other words, the key used to encrypt the vote tallies in every single Diebold Accuvote machine is F2654hD4. Imagine if the front door to every house in America had the same lock, and the key was taped to every door. Later we were to find out that Diebold knew about this problem five years before we did our analysis and did nothing to fix it. This was arguably the most egregious of many security lapses.

We found another critical design flaw in something called the *ballot definition file*, which contains basic data such as the list of candidates, propositions or referenda for an election, and even information like the background color of the screen. The ballot definition file determines the candidates' order of appearance on the ballot—which is how they will appear onscreen to the voter—and how they will be tallied by the machine after the voting. If tampering results in the candidates being presented to the voter in a different order than they appear in the ballot definition file, votes will be tallied incorrectly. So if the red candidate appears on the ballot in position 1 and the blue candidate in position 2, but someone has gotten into the ballot definition file undetected and swapped those positions, red votes would then be counted as blue, and vice versa. It wouldn't take much to influence vote counts—just knowledge of a precinct's voting habits, physical access to the machines, and some minimal computer skill. This kind of tampering would be undetectable through normal procedures at the polling site, since the total number of votes would remain accurate. And by the time anyone noticed suspicious results, the voters would be long gone.

The ballot definition file had no cryptographic protection, leaving it completely vulnerable to attack. The problems with this file highlight a much larger issue, what David Dill calls the lack of voter verifiability. In fully electronic DRE machines—that is, machines with no redundant recording system using another medium or technology—there is no way for a voter to verify that his or her vote was recorded accurately. The machine provides a confirmation screen, but a display of the votes as cast does not necessarily mean the votes are stored or tallied correctly. In fact, an accurate confirmation screen wouldn't give the voter any clue as to whether the ballot definition file contains errors or has been corrupted.

This feature of DRE machines is particularly maddening, and it's important to examine this issue carefully, because it's a critical part of the larger e-voting debate that ensued. Diebold has in fact built three redundant storage systems into its machines. The problem is that each separate system stores the same votes as recorded by the machine, and based on the ballot definition file. If the file is corrupted, the vote is recorded incorrectly, and it doesn't matter if there are ten or one hundred redundant

systems; they'd still all store the incorrect votes. Without a
record that the voter can point to and verify, the systems are totally meaningless.

We found that in addition to this basic data, the ballot definition file contained more sensitive, security-critical information,
including the voting terminal's voting center identification
number, the dial-in numbers for the end-of-the-day tally reporting, the network address of the back-end processing server,
and a username and password. It was like finding somebody's
wallet: in this file you'd have everything needed to impersonate
the voting machine to the board of election servers. Since there
was no cryptographic authentication between the voting machines and the tallying servers, someone with a laptop and the
information from the ballot definition file could dial into the
board of elections computers from *anywhere* and send in fake
vote tallies. At the least, this could create serious confusion at
the board of elections when the memory cards with the true tallies arrived. After our report was confirmed, Diebold claimed to
have fixed this problem, but an independently commissioned
study found that it had not. Later still, the company claimed to
have *really* fixed it.

We found further problems in the smartcard. Recall that the
purpose of the smartcard is to prevent multiple votes, so it would
make sense that the voting terminal would need to know that a
voter is using a legitimate card. However, the developers of the
Diebold system did not provide any authentication between the
card and the machine. This means that nothing—at least no
design feature of the computer voting system—prevents someone from using smartcards they manufactured themselves. (It
would not take a massive amount of skill or knowledge to make
these cards at home.) Some simple cryptography on the smartcard could prevent this.

Besides the smartcard that a voter uses, the Diebold voting machines also utilize an administrator card that allows election judges and officials to manage the machines. The developers recognized the security value and sensitivity of these cards and established a PIN (personal identification number) code system for unlocking them, similar to the PIN that protects an ATM card. But the default PIN on every card was set to 1111. Diebold changed this once our report came out and disclosed the problem.

In addition to these and many other security flaws, we spotted breakdowns in established and accepted software engineering practices and a violation of the Federal Election Commission (FEC) standards for voting equipment.

IN THE 2002 election in Georgia, everyone who voted did so using an Accuvote TSx, the machine that uses code we analyzed. In fact, thirty-seven states used those machines that year. How did that come to be? It's not as complicated as one might think. If you think that the federal or local governments put these systems out for bid from manufacturers according to announced specifications and standards, you'd be wrong. If you think that the systems would face an arduous, multilevel approval process, with panels of impartial experts and institutional review boards, like the FDA approval process, you'd be wrong again. If a company wants to market an e-voting machine, it just builds one, using hardware and software engineers of its choice. No one outside the company is in a position to pass judgment on the quality or experience level of the system designer, nor, necessarily, should anyone be. It is natural and expected that any company making any product will want to do so as efficiently and economically as it can, which is why we say, "Let the buyer beware."

Once a system is completed, the company hires an independent testing authority (ITA) to certify it. If the ITA finds problems or declines to certify the system, the company can simply find another one that will, so there's some incentive for an ITA to generate favorable findings. The certified machines are then paraded in front of election officials, many of whom have little or no computer training, much less computer security expertise; although they may be well intentioned, these officials are ill equipped to make anything other than a cosmetic usability evaluation. If the machine meets the requirements and performs as advertised, and the manufacturer promises to hold their hands throughout the process, how could election officials, plagued by memories of rickety old voting machines or truckloads full of ballots, fail to be seduced by the promise of this gleaming new technology? Georgia, as it happens, went so far as to advertise its cutting-edge leadership and to proudly pronounce itself the first state to do away with paper ballots entirely.

The Federal Drug Administration's approval process for new drugs is grueling, and it takes years. Some drugs never make it to market. Everybody agrees that the risks are just too great. I argue that a reliable mechanism for electing our government is every bit as important, and yet in most states, putting a voting machine straight from the factory into use in a precinct requires no federal oversight as long as the machine qualifies under relatively weak FEC standards. This is a problem with far-reaching implications for our democracy, and at the time of our analysis of the Diebold source code, it had not entered the national consciousness, not to mention public debate. Our report was about to change all that and would later be called a "watershed event."

Before we could go public with our report, we had to send it out to colleagues for peer review. Peer review is a fundamental research practice. It helps with issues such as attribution, it lets different insights and perspectives come to light, and it ensures that more mistakes get caught. In addition, we were pretty sure our report was going to attract a lot of fire. The review process would help us get out in front of the criticism and either eliminate the cause of it or help us prepare to respond to it. Serious peer review is an example of the kind of rigor that was apparently so lacking in the Diebold development process and the voting machine certification process. With only a few days left before our self-imposed release date for the report, we sent it under strict confidentiality to some of the top computer security experts in the country, as well as to some computer scientists who had studied elections. Most people responded helpfully, enabling us to greatly improve the report. Many clearly caught a whiff of our excitement.

At least one, however, had some issues. Rebecca Mercuri, who had been on David Dill's conference call, really laid into us, posting a harsh criticism of the report to her website. Rebecca had pioneered the concept of a voter-verifiable paper ballot and had authority in the field. She attacked what she said were misconceptions or inaccuracies about election procedures, the growth of electronic voting in the United States, and the certification process. She cautioned us not to go public and demanded that, if we did, we make sure a link to her criticism appeared anywhere the report got published. Now, Rebecca is a serious and accomplished researcher with a legitimate claim to being the first computer scientist to focus on electronic voting. She has published prolifically in the field, and many even refer to the process of voting with voter-verifiable ballots out of an electronic touch-screen machine as "the Mercuri Method." It's possible that at least some of her criticism was triggered not by the content of our report but by the mere existence of such a report. After all, we were working in what arguably was her turf.

Rebecca's criticism stung, but not as sharply as the feedback from Steve Bellovin. Steve is one of the leading authorities on network security. Steve and I had worked together at AT&T, and he had honored me by inviting me to join him and his co-author, Bill Cheswick, on the second edition of their classic book *Firewalls and Network Security*. He is a member of the National Academy of Engineering, perhaps the most prestigious membership for a computer scientist. Although Steve's response was mostly positive, he too pointed out that we had greatly underestimated the role of election procedures in the process, and he predicted that we were going to get raked over the coals. He was right on both counts. If I regret anything about the way we released the report, it's that we didn't give it to Steve earlier or leave ourselves enough time to act on his feedback. By the time we got his comments, the report was already in the hands of a reporter, with the public release scheduled. If we had had more time, we would have accounted more accurately for election procedures, and maybe we wouldn't have ticked off so many election officials. Maybe. In the end, it's hard to say whether any such changes would have lessened the onslaught that was about to come.

3

Sarpy County election officials are trying to figure out how
they ended up with more votes than voters in the general
election. As many as 10,000 extra votes have been tallied
and candidates are still waiting for corrected totals.
—*NBC Channel 6, Omaha, November 2004*

I
t would be easy to say that I wasn't prepared for the storm
that our report created, but that wouldn't be completely true.
I've never been a firebrand, never been a crusader, but
throughout my career I've been attracted to problems and projects that go beyond the purely theoretical and have practical,
real-world applications.

I didn't start out as a computer geek. (And I like to think I
haven't ended up as one either.) My father taught me math at a
very young age, and later he had me doing physics experiments,
for fun. It was a fluke perhaps. He could have taken me fly-
fishing or taught me about literature (his own specialty), but he
settled on math, and I took to it. For years I assumed I'd go into
medicine, but my first chemistry course in college was enough
to make me rethink that plan. At the same time, I happened to
take a course in computer science. It was my first serious exposure to computers, and I never looked back.

I got my degree at a time when jobs in academia were few and far between, which was another lucky thing. My work in the private sector—three years at Bellcore followed by six years at AT&T Labs—was invaluable in many ways. The work I did developing secure systems brought me a fair amount of recognition, so that when I was finally able to make the transition into the academic world, I could do so at a relatively senior level, bypassing a lot of the unpleasantness of life as a junior professor. Even within the university environment, I kept working on real-world problems and was always up for the challenge of cracking a "secure" system designed to protect people's rights and information. My expertise in this sort of practical problem brought me to the attention of the general media.

By the time we got involved with the Diebold code, I couldn't claim to be naive anymore. I knew enough to know that the impact of our report was going to be significant and that the media were going to be all over it. I also sensed that it was going to be a public relations hot potato, and I was glad to have been involved with reporters before.

From the beginning, my plan was to break the story in the *New York Times*. I wanted this story in the hands of a reporter I could trust to get it right, someone who was comfortable with the technical details but also sensitive to the political ramifications. If the first major story doesn't get it right, any misinformation it contains is likely to be repeated countless times. The reporter I trusted most was John Schwartz, who covered technology for the *Times*. I had come to know John a few years earlier, when he did a story about a system I had helped develop for publishing information on the Web in such a way that it cannot be easily removed. The story was complex and subtle, involving controversial civil liberties issues, and I thought John handled it fantastically. I kept in touch with him over the next few years and developed a fundamental confidence in the fairness and accuracy of his reporting and writing.

John Schwartz and I coordinated a release date for the report. We would post the report to a website on the evening of July 23. His story would appear on the *Times* website that same evening and in the print edition of the newspaper the next morning, July 24, 2003. The waiting began.

I would have been bouncing off the walls under the best of circumstances, but only the day before another wrinkle had come to light, one that almost seemed like it came out of a bad Hollywood script. On the morning of July 22, I browsed the Diebold website, hoping to find a picture of the Accuvote TSx to use in our report. My eyes must have bugged out of my head like a cartoon character when I saw the home page, and as soon as I could get any sound out, I started yelling for Adam and Yoshi to get into my office. We all stood there staring at the Diebold site. That very day, Diebold was proudly announcing the sale of $55.6 million worth of Accuvote TSx machines to my own home state of Maryland! The machines were scheduled for use in the March 2004 primary and the general election six months later. We'd had no idea that this was coming, and yet our report would be public in less than two days, and it would look to all the world like we had timed the release deliberately.

Those hours were hard. We had given the story to the press, and there was no turning back. We had set something in motion, something we believed was important, and now the only thing we could do was to wait for the blowback. Would Diebold sue us? Would the university stand by me? Would the media play it up or just shrug and move on to the next celebrity scandal?

I couldn't sit still. For whatever reason, during those stressful hours it struck me like a good idea to let CNN in on the story as well. A friend of mine helped me contact the vice president at the CNN national desk, Nancy Lane. I explained I had a big story for her but would not be able to discuss it until ten that night. Ann and I put the kids to bed and waited to hear from John Schwartz. Around ten I got his very short e-mail: "It's up."

The *New York Times* had made our report the lead story on its website. John had done a great job with the story. He described how we had analyzed the code, and he detailed the vulnerabilities we had discovered. He quoted a Diebold spokesman defending the company and left it to several independent experts to speak about the significance of our findings. I quickly called Nancy Lane at CNN and explained the report to her in detail. She was seriously interested and got right down to business. The next morning, in a studio in Baltimore, CNN interviewed me and Cindy Cohn. Diebold provided a short comment, but clearly it had been caught unprepared. The company characterized the report as interesting, said it would look into it, and insisted that it took security very seriously.

4

There were disturbing, anecdotal reports of voters selecting
Kerry but then seeing the machine indicate a vote for Bush.
Poor calibration of some machines may well account for
these difficulties. Too bad we'll never know for sure. The
majority of this year's electronic voting machines had no
auditing system that most experts consider fully
trustworthy. They produce a result in their digital circuits,
and if you ask for verification,
they cough up the same result.
—San Jose Mercury News, *November 7, 2004*

I n my college days, I tended to feel more strongly about something like the seeding in the NCAA basketball tournament
than about political issues. Public controversy was somehow
someone else's concern, and crusaders, people whose lives were
driven by strong social or political convictions, tended to intimi-
date me a little. That began to change as my work became more
involved with public services and processes, but I can't say I was
prepared for the level of passion I encountered when I got close
to the world of politics.

The activist who triggered the Diebold firestorm was a
woman named Bev Harris. Bev, who has been called everything
from an obsessive conspiracy nut to a genuine American hero,

describes herself as a publicist and an investigative reporter. For years she has dug beneath the surface of corporate America to examine, and expose, inappropriately close relationships between corporations and government. In early 2003 she put it together that one of the senior officers of Elections Systems and Software (ES&S), the second leading manufacturer of voting systems, was the brother of the president of Diebold and that the two companies together controlled 80 percent of the electronic voting market. Alarmed by the discovery, Bev kept digging, and her search eventually brought her to a website, apparently hosted on one of Diebold's own servers, where she found what appeared to be the source code that operated Diebold's voting machines. She also found a great many internal memos that later raised concerns about ethical lapses and even possible illegality. But let's not get ahead of ourselves.

Knowing that Diebold's CEO, Walden "Wally" O'Dell, was a prominent fund-raiser for the Republican Party, Harris thought she might have hit the jackpot; that is, she could examine the very guts of the company's voting machines and see if they had been, or even could be, rigged unfairly. But Bev Harris is not a computer scientist, and so she was in no position to analyze the code. She passed the code along to some contacts of hers with technical expertise and, through their analysis, found what she believed to be proof that the machines were rigged. The media, however, did not find her assertions credible enough to follow up. Bev may have had the proof she claimed, but since she was unwilling to produce it, no news outlets were prepared to run with such an explosive story.

In 2004 Bev Harris published *Black Box Voting*, a book that examines the intricate relationships between politicians and manufacturers of voting equipment. The book delves into the history of vote rigging and describes the ways in which an electronic machine can be maliciously manipulated. Much of the information in the book is right on target, but a fair amount describes things that only seem suspicious. The *appearance* of foul play is presented with the same level of accusatory hysteria as the provable problems, and unfortunately, the indiscriminate nature of her attacks weakened the credibility of the book's many valid arguments.

Bev's shotgun approach occasionally put me in an uncomfortable position, particularly when I had to respond to reporters' questions about information that Bev claimed to have uncovered about e-voting machines and their code. More than once I found myself at a loss in these situations. The most telling example of her style sometimes hurting the greater cause was her handling of the vulnerability she and her colleagues discovered in the Diebold global elections management system (GEMS). GEMS is the central tabulating program that combines the vote subtotals from all of the precincts to produce a regional total, usually at the county level. Harris pointed out that even though the tallies were stored in a Microsoft Access database on a Windows computer and the data were protected by a password when logging into the Diebold application, the same data could be manipulated directly through the operating system's file access. I found out about the GEMS problem when reporters started asking me to verify Bev's discovery. If the data could indeed be manipulated outside of the application, it really was a security vulnerability. This would be an important observation, and I said so. I was surprised when the reporters moved on to ask me what I knew about monkeys. Monkeys?! It seems that in the effort to demonstrate how easy it would be to tamper with an election, Bev had hired a chimp and filmed him "hacking" a voting machine. Less than two months before the presidential election in 2004, she held a press conference where she showed the video. It was unfortunate that other people who supported Bev's work felt the need to distance themselves from this kind of circus stunt in order to be taken seriously by the press and the public.

Although her unorthodox tactics occasionally caused problems, Bev Harris performed a great service to this country. She was on to the problems with e-voting from the start and worked hard to bring the issue to the public's attention. Without her, we would never have analyzed the code in the first place. There wasn't much chance that anyone would have forgotten our debt to Bev, and if by chance we did, she was there to remind us. When our report first came out, Bev was the first to stand up and cheer, publicly referring to us as the "Hopkins Heroes" and doing what she could to push the story. It wasn't until the press started coming to me instead of her as the authority on insecure e-voting that Bev got her back up. She fired off an angry e-mail to me and others demanding that we give her clear and specific credit as the person who first found the source code, understood its implications, identified the security lapses, and published these findings. I can't speak for anyone else, but it had never crossed my mind to steal anyone's thunder. I appreciated Bev's desire to have her work recognized and the fact that she raised her objections privately so as not to distract attention from the real issues, but I was taken aback by the level of her anger and antagonism.

The private ill will became public when an AP reporter asked me my opinion of Bev and, wisely or not, I gave it. The wire story, picked up all over the country, quoted me: "I worry that sometimes her arguments sound farfetched, and I have been told on more than one occasion that she is hurting the credibility of all of us with her wild theories. On balance, though, I am grateful for the work that she does. We each have our own style." Bev let me know, in no uncertain terms, what she thought of my characterization of her, but the truth is that I *am* grateful for the work she does, as should anyone else be who values fair elections.

COMPUTERS ARE NO longer a novelty. In the developed world at least, there is no aspect of our daily lives that hasn't been changed by computers. Travel, manufacturing, banking, communications, education, even entertainment have all been radically reconceived through digitization. Any large-scale number-crunching task is made immeasurably easier and faster by computers, so it was only a matter of time before people thought to apply them to voting—a relatively simple process made complex by its sheer size. The 2000 election, with results too close for comfort in several states with outdated voting technology, made the switch to computers feel that much more urgent.

Nobody knows more about how computers really work than the people who design, build, repair, and program them for a living. It isn't exactly that familiarity breeds contempt, since we still all love the machines, but familiarity does sweep away the mystery. If some people regard it as miraculous that they can sit in front of their computer in Maryland and watch a live picture of traffic on the Golden Gate Bridge, we professionals know exactly how the tangle of circuitry makes it happen. We understand and appreciate the potential of the computer, and with the knowledge of its strengths comes knowledge of its weaknesses. In fact, the more one knows about computer technology, the more reluctantly one relies on computers for critical functions.

Don't get me wrong. We can build robust and reliable high-tech systems. NASA has managed to land a probe on a comet hurtling through space, the equivalent of a quarterback hitting a receiver running a couple of hundred thousand miles an hour, a few millions of miles away. Computers make that possible, the same way they make safe travel possible for millions of airline passengers every day. We are willing to let computers diagnose our heart disease, manage our bank accounts, and microwave our food. Computer scientists believe that e-voting is a logical and beneficial development. We also believe that the country is plunging ahead too quickly and too carelessly. If airplane systems were built the same way as today's voting systems, I doubt that planes would even get off the ground, much less get to where they're going.

A long time ago, the companies that built burglar alarms were smart enough to ask actual burglars to help design and test the systems. Remember the movie *Catch Me If You Can?* It tells the true story of Frank Abagnale, the master forger and check kiter who eventually became a consultant to both law enforcement and the banking industry because he knew more than anyone about getting past bank safeguards. In the same way, computer scientists, and specifically security experts, become intimate with electronic security schemes by trying our hardest to break them. And because voting, like global finance, for example, is a security-critical application, security expertise must be a critical component of the design of voting machines. Systems that depend on security have different requirements than systems that do not. Their architecture must match the threat. The incentives to tamper with election results are so high as to be almost irresistible to some, whether their interest is financial, political, or ideological. History has shown how far people will go to advance or protect their interests, and voting systems must be built with this in mind. Software is as much a part of that architecture as hardware is, and software is a funny beast.

Software is worrisome, in terms of security, because it is not always wholly contained within one machine. A program can govern a group or network of machines, or it can manage the communications between machines. With more traditional voting technologies such as lever or optical-scan machines or punch-card ballots, someone wanting to defraud an election must compromise every machine individually. We call this *retail fraud*. It requires considerable physical access and effort, and the risk of getting caught increases with each instance of tampering. By contrast, the ability to corrupt multiple machines in multiple locations, or to influence the aggregate results of multiple machines with a single action, constitutes what we call *wholesale fraud*, where the smallest effort causes the greatest damage. Software-based, paperless voting makes wholesale fraud possible.

THE DAY BEFORE the Bush-Dukakis election in 1988, when DREs were first being introduced in New York, journalist Ronnie Dugger published an exhaustive article in *The New Yorker* about computerized voting. He interviewed many computer scientists who had been looking into voting systems throughout the 1970s and 1980s and was able to identify some key issues that are still familiar to anyone involved in the e-voting debate. Among his assertions was that most state election officials had accepted the manufacturer's claims that its code was proprietary and had not sought to independently analyze those claims. Thus, Dugger didn't think it was possible for these officials to credibly certify election results from these machines.

Dugger's article gave many examples of people manipulating information by hacking into computers and concluded that it was logical to assume that somebody would try to hack an e-voting system. Moreover, because of the way elections were run using these machines, recounts would be impossible. The chief assistant attorney general of California at the time, Steve White, was quoted in the piece saying, "It could be done relatively easily by somebody who didn't necessarily have to be all that sophisticated. Given the importance of the national election, sooner or later it will be attempted. There is a real reluctance to concede the gravity of the problem." Dugger also quoted a report from Price Waterhouse, commissioned in 1970 to evaluate a new electronic voting system: "It is possible to write a program in such a way that no test can be made to assure that the program works the way it is supposed to work."

COMPUTER SOFTWARE IS unique in the world of science and technology. There's no exact equivalent in higher-level mathematics or theoretical physics or molecular biology, even though each of those disciplines has its own unique set of rules and its own obscure language. You can explain software to someone who's never programmed a computer about as easily as you can explain a 3-D movie to a blind person. The language barrier and the lack of critical background knowledge lead otherwise sophisticated people to insist that the current e-voting machines are both secure and reliable and make it hard for computer professionals to make their case. Even seasoned programmers who aren't used to thinking in terms of defending their code from determined attack are likely to completely misunderstand the security ramifications.

Much of the debate centers on one question: can the manu-

facturer of an electronic voting machine imbed malicious software in the terminal so that it is undetectable, even in a search
by a trained computer expert? Security specialists who work
with software for a living all say yes. The manufacturers, not to
mention some prominent election officials, say no. Those officials, whether or not they have any technical understanding,
have a powerful reason for believing in e-voting machines. The
Florida troubles left a bad taste in everyone's mouth, and no one
can bear the thought of more dimpled chads, more endless recounts, or more dueling lawsuits. The Help America Vote Act of
2002 stated as its purpose:

> To establish a program to provide funds to States to replace
> punch card voting systems, to establish the Election Assis-
> tance Commission to assist in the administration of Federal
> elections ... to establish minimum election administration
> standards for States and units of local government with respon-
> sibility for the administration of Federal elections, and for
> other purposes.

Among other provisions, HAVA released huge amounts of federal dollars ($1.4 billion in 2003, $1 billion in 2004, $600 million
in 2005) for states to upgrade their voting equipment. Anybody
who's ever relied on government or other outside funding knows
that anything that doesn't get spent right away can easily disappear or be redirected. Suddenly, state officials all over the country were scrambling to get their hands on the latest voting
machines, and vendors were more than happy to fill that urgent
need. It was at this time that Diebold purchased Global Election
Systems and dedicated itself to becoming the industry leader in
e-voting technology.

5

The Pennsylvania Department of State said Thursday that
Beaver County's $1.2 million electronic touch-screen voting
system is unreliable and can no longer be used, even in the
primary election that is only five weeks away.
—Beaver County Times *and* Allegheny Times, *April 8, 2005*

On the morning of July 24, 2003, the *New York Times*
story "Computer Voting Is Open to Easy Fraud" appeared, not on the front page, as I had secretly hoped,
but about midway through the front section. John Schwartz had
done an admirable job. His article described the flaws we had
found clearly and accurately, quoted Adam and Yoshi, and provided the Web address where the full report could be found. His
story included a noncommittal response from Diebold: the code
was "about a year old," and the company would decline to comment further until it had read and evaluated the whole report.
Significantly, Schwartz had gotten a comment from Doug Jones,
a name I should have recognized. Jones expressed shock that our
analysis had found these flaws, but what shocked him most was
not the flaws themselves but the fact that he had brought these
same problems to the attention of the system's developers *five
years earlier* when he had served as a state election official in

Iowa. Jones went on to speculate that software designed by other voting machine manufacturers might also be flawed.

I had prepped Adam and Yoshi the day before, passing along what I had learned when I underwent media training at AT&T. The main idea is to boil your information down to no more than three short, simple, and memorable messages that reporters can quote and broadcast news organizations can replay and that will stick in the minds of readers and viewers. We set up mock interviews, and I grilled them for hours. When we were done, we had filled several large white wallboards in my office with pithy statements, and we practiced ways to work these quotes into our answers, even if they didn't directly answer the question asked. The fact that many of these quotes turned up verbatim in news stories over the next few weeks both amused and gratified us. When the *New York Times* quoted Adam saying, "This isn't code for a vending machine, this is the code that protects our democracy," the line had come directly from the office wall.

Before going to my office that morning, I went to a television studio in downtown Baltimore to tape the CNN interview. I sat alone in a dark studio, bright lights and a camera trained on my face. I couldn't see anyone, but I could hear the interviewer in my earpiece. For about ten minutes I answered questions about our findings and the implications for the elections the year after, and then headed over to Hopkins. The interview offered me a little escape from the stress of the day. With no television in our department, Yoshi and I dropped into a local greasy spoon in the mid-afternoon and convinced them to switch their set from the soaps to CNN; when I came on, I was raucously celebrated by the daytime regulars. CNN had also done a thorough job, including some footage of Cindy Cohn of EFF on the broader implications of our findings and more insubstantial comments from Diebold.

In my office the red voice-mail light on my phone was shining brightly. Strange as it sounds, that's unusual for me. I could go for weeks without receiving any phone messages at the office, but today there were ten or so, and several more came in as I was sitting there listening to the first batch. Clearly, it would take all of us to field these messages, so I called Yoshi into my office and got Dan on the phone. (Adam was away camping for a few days.) We prioritized the calls that needed returning and divided them up between us, but as it turned out, most of the press wanted to speak to me and get quotes from me.

Around midday the camera crews started arriving. Phil Sneiderman, from Hopkins media relations, had helped us prepare for this media onslaught and was camped out at my door, moving the crews in and out. By lunchtime I had more than twenty calls to return and an equal number of e-mail queries from reporters, and the West Coast was just getting to work.

And it wasn't just reporters calling. The most unexpected was from Representative Marcy Kaptur, a Democrat from Ohio. I wasn't used to picking up my phone and finding a United States congresswoman on the other end. Kaptur's call made me realize that this was going to be trickier than I had thought. Diebold's base of operations was in her home state, and she was using the revelations in our report to point an accusing finger at the Republican Party. An alarm went off in my head. Anyone who saw this as a partisan issue was somehow missing the point. I collected myself and explained to the congresswoman that our belief was that the flaws we found demonstrated incompetence on the part of the developers, but that we had not seen even the slightest indication that the voting machines were rigged to favor one party over another. In fact, we hadn't seen any evidence of tampering at all. Our point had to do with *potential* fraud. My concern about partisanship grew throughout the day as I received calls from several other Democratic politicians and was even invited to join the technical advisory board of the Democratic National Committee (DNC). I declined, but now started to worry that only one party was calling. In our minds, insecure and unreliable elections threaten everybody, without regard to party or ideology, and the moment it became a partisan issue, we would lose the attention of at least half the nation. As easy as it was for some people to generalize about the conservative business tycoons who golf with Republican politicians when they aren't busy making rigged voting machines, one could also paint an opposite picture of long-haired, red-eyed programmers planning for the revolution while they program the machines to only register votes for the Green Party.

I also got calls from all kinds of conspiracy nuts and agitators, people who were convinced that Diebold had consciously designed its machines to make cheating easier. Schwartz's article made it clear that I did not share this view. "Mr. Rubin called such assertions 'ludicrous' and said the software's flaws showed the hallmarks of poor design, not subterfuge." Opponents of electronic voting took exception to that "ludicrous" remark, but once you're in the middle of a public debate, pretty much anything you say is going to get you into trouble with someone. A friend pointed out that if the flag-wavers and bomb-throwers on both sides of a question are criticizing you, you must be doing something right.

One call really shook me, at least at first. The man told me he was a computer scientist at the University of Iowa, and he made it crystal clear that he was furious. Maybe I had already fielded too many calls from crazies, or maybe I was just tired, but I assumed his anger was directed at me. I guess I wasn't listening that carefully, hearing only an angry diatribe about Diebold and encryption keys being hardwired into all the machines. I broke in and explained that the fact that all of the voting machines had the same encryption key and that the key was hardwired into the code was exactly the kind of serious security problem our paper addressed.

"I know!" he interrupted, sounding agitated and confused. "I was a state examiner, and I not only pointed this out to them as a serious security flaw five years ago, but I published it as well. I can't believe they still haven't fixed it. They knew about this five years ago! I raked them over the coals for it. It's a disgrace." For a moment I was speechless. It wasn't me he was furious with, it was Diebold. This was Doug Jones, who I've come to believe is the most qualified person in this country to talk about the security of voting machines. Not only is he a computer science professor specializing in operating systems, but he has worked as an election official for many years. He has written the most detailed and comprehensive analyses of electronic voting developments. Once we realized we were both on the same page, our conversation took off. Today I view my relationship with Doug as one of the great rewards of this whole experience.

As the volume of calls and e-mails mounted throughout the day, this question of partisan politics grew more and more volatile. I got a call from the secretary of state's office in Ohio and another from a state senator there. One seemed ready to string me up, the other wanted more information. Another call came from Tom Iler, the head of information technology for Baltimore County, Maryland. He told a story about a state election-technology committee that had voted five-to-one against obtaining Diebold equipment for the county but had been overruled by the Republican chairman of the committee. He even faxed me corroborating documents.

One of the media relations people at Johns Hopkins had told me that the second day after a news release is the big day for media coverage. That's when all the stories that follow on the original one appear. July 25 certainly bore that out. The *Baltimore Sun* featured insecure voting machines as its lead story on the front page, above the fold. Under the headline "Defects Reported in Voting Machines," the article detailed how our team had identified "serious software flaws that could allow voters or poll workers to tinker with election results." Reporter Michael Stroh further explained that Diebold's systems were "vulnerable to subversions ranging from multiple voting to vote switching," which, according to our report, "could be accomplished with little expertise, using inexpensive, widely available equipment."

That Sunday the *Sun* put the story on the front page again, with the headline "Computer Voting System Assailed: Scientists Say Machines Are Inherently Subject to Programming Error." The story seemed a little weightier and included comments from a number of other computer scientists, not just me. The *Washington Post* ran a story on July 25 on the front page of the metro section that took a more local angle, framing the story in terms of Maryland's recent agreement to purchase Diebold machines. The only trouble we had with local media came when a Baltimore NPR program on state politics mocked our institute and stated that our report was full of unproven results and wild theoretical speculation. Hopkins complained, and the station retracted the comments on the air and invited me on to set the record straight.

The media coverage continued unabated for several weeks, with almost daily wire stories and regular broadcast pieces on both the local and national levels. I was starting to understand that I would be fighting two distinct battles. The philosophical question of safeguarding a credible democracy through fair and verifiable voting procedures was going to be the subject of national debate. But the practical question of what to do right now was going to be fought locally, and Maryland was going to be the main, or at least the first, battleground. At home, state officials reacted harshly to criticism of the voting equipment, and for days Baltimore television news depicted me going head to head with David Heller, who worked for the director of elections for the state, Linda Lamone. He'd express complete confidence in the machines, and I'd contradict him, or vice versa. Heller seemed like a decent guy who just happened to be dead wrong on this issue, an impression that was borne out when we eventually got a chance to meet. Like too many other people who would get involved in the debate, he simply didn't have the technical expertise to back up his point of view.

Although it seemed like Maryland officials were uniformly critical of our study, political figures at the national level were more receptive. Dennis Kucinich, the Ohio congressman who was then running for the Democratic presidential nomination, had his office call me that first week. I was invited to Capitol Hill to meet with staffers of several House members, hence my introduction to the halls of government in Washington. At the time, *NBC Nightly News* was putting together a story on electronic voting. Its team happened to be interviewing me in my office when the trip was being arranged, and they asked if they could follow me to the Hill and get more tape. When the piece aired a few days later, there I was, walking down the halls of the House office building in my gray suit and red tie, wide-eyed like Jimmy Stewart in *Mr. Smith Goes to Washington*, until I walked into an office where all the staffers were waiting for me in blue jeans. (Congress wasn't in session at the time.)

The staffers asked me to explain the threats in layman's terms and then asked me the million-dollar question: what can be done to improve the security of electronic voting? My short answer was that fully electronic voting machines can be rigged, even if they are designed and implemented more skillfully than Diebold's machines. I emphasized the difference between retail and wholesale fraud and explained that electronic voting machine manufacturers (or anyone with access to their code) can control the behavior of tens of thousands of machines, constituting wholesale fraud. The solution I proposed, with which many in the computer science community agree, is to use a paper ballot, verified by voters, with any technology used in public elections, at a minimum. It doesn't matter whether the ballots are generated as a record by a machine or filled out by hand, or whether they get counted by machine or manually. As long as each voter's intent is captured in tangible form, votes can be counted—and *recounted* if necessary—in a publicly observable manner, eliminating the risk of wholesale fraud. This idea—the voter-verifiable paper trail, or VVPT—became the most hotly debated topic in both the news media and public hearings on electronic voting. VVPT sparked a grassroots activist movement and forced most of the DRE manufacturers to offer products with paper trails.

VVPT has not been fully or accurately understood, partly because the misleading term "receipt," used to describe the paper backup we were advocating for DREs, crept into the public discourse. A receipt is something you retain for your own records after a transaction, but if you somehow retain physical evidence of how you voted, it opens the doors to vote-buying and intimidation. The idea behind VVPT is that the paper record is maintained at the polling site, available for later analysis if needed.

I don't remember how many reporters, activists, and politicians I spoke with in the days just after our report became public, but in the following months I would become intimately familiar with the red voice-mail light on my phone. It was winking at me when I came to work in the morning, when I returned from lunch, even when I'd just stepped out to the bathroom. It was my direct line to the world outside that was still digesting our report and waking up to the problems threatening our election system. Or so I thought. Soon enough, I was to find out that it wasn't just Diebold and the state legislators (some of whom had egg on their faces after having purchased the Diebold machines) who were unhappy with the report. As I learned the hard way, once your voice hits the airwaves and the news pages, the landscape quickly becomes crowded with people just waiting to tell you, personally, why you're right, wrong, or irrelevant.

6

The right to search for truth implies also a duty; one must
not conceal any part of what one has recognized to be true.

—*Albert Einstein, inscription on the outside wall of the*
National Academy of Sciences, Washington, D.C.

I can't imagine finding a better professional home than Johns Hopkins, where I've never felt anything less than the complete support of everyone around me, from support staff to department heads. When my assistant, Jackie Richardson, poked her head into my office to tell me that some irate guy on the phone was trying to get me into trouble at Hopkins, it seemed somewhat improbable.

"This guy from Georgia called, and he asked to speak to the director of the Information Security Institute," she elaborated. "When I asked him if it was about electronic voting, and if he'd like to speak to you, he got even angrier, and he was practically yelling, 'No! I want to speak to his boss!' "

Jackie knew as well as I did that, as a professor, I didn't really have a boss, at least not in the way most people think of a boss. The person who most closely fit that description, Gerry Masson, was one of my biggest supporters. "So who is this guy?" I asked.

"I don't know, but you really seem to have upset him."

I can't say that it upset me too much. I didn't think about the caller again until Gerry showed up in my office. Gerry Masson has been at Hopkins for more than thirty years, having founded not only the computer science department, which he chaired for many years, but also the Information Security Institute, my bailiwick. Having understood the importance of information security very early on, he had the vision to establish the first center devoted to multidisciplinary studies related to information security and privacy. He had secured $10 million in private funds and recruited faculty specializing in computer security, cryptography, and privacy. Gerry manages to keep most of us convulsed in laughter while doing everything he can to support our work. The institute is his baby, and his enthusiasm is infectious. The expression on his face when I told him about our report was almost by itself sufficient reward for our efforts. The report and the attendant publicity were just what Gerry needed at a time when wider recognition and long-term funding were his top priorities. He followed the story in the news the way a parent tracks a child on the school team, tacking press clippings all over the walls of the department and forwarding copies to our department chair, the media relations people, and just about anyone else he could think of. The thought of someone calling Gerry to get me into trouble wasn't about to make me nervous.

So there he was in my office a few hours later, with a big wry smile on his face. The caller had demanded that I be reprimanded for my "irresponsible" report and suggested that Hopkins consider firing me. I couldn't imagine what I might have done to get so far under this individual's skin. It seemed a disproportionate response, as well as underhanded and malicious. I wondered aloud if he perhaps worked for Diebold, but Gerry didn't know anything one way or the other.

My accuser in this case was Brit Williams, a computer science professor who ran the Center for Election Systems at Kennesaw State University in Georgia. The center at Kennesaw State oversaw the design and implementation of the procedures, using Diebold Accuvote TS machines, for the 2002 elections in Georgia. The victory in that election of a gubernatorial candidate who had trailed in the pre-election polls had sparked considerable controversy, including heated accusations that the voting machines were to blame. Williams had worked closely with the office of the Georgia secretary of state and perhaps felt his personal expertise and recommendation were somehow under attack. But we knew none of this at the time, and even if we had, it wouldn't have explained what seemed to be a mad rush to silence me and quash the report.

Brit Williams wasn't the only one after my head. The president of Johns Hopkins, William R. Brody, received from a man named Stephen Burger a letter that sought to undermine me in a more subtle but potentially more damaging way. Burger held the position of chair of the Standards Coordinating Committee 38, a vendor-controlled voting standards committee sponsored by the Institute of Electrical and Electronics Engineers, or IEEE. Burger wanted to use his connection to this respected organization to stop the onslaught of bad publicity these vendors were receiving. His carefully worded letter asked if our study had been "peer reviewed or published in any refereed journal" and requested a full accounting of the "nature and extent" of that review process. Now, the IEEE publishes several major scientific journals and regularly sponsors scientific conferences, so Burger must have known that a paper takes at least two years from the time of submission to get published in a refereed journal. In addition, peer review is a cornerstone of the scientific process by which objective and often anonymous professionals with qualifications equal to the author's examine the procedures and results described in a paper. It is appropriate when the author of a paper is putting forth a new scientific theory—compelling new research—or a breakthrough solution to a long-standing problem. But if a mathematician discovers that a company has a product that assumes that two plus two equals four and writes a critical report to that effect, the report does not require peer review. The demand for peer review is a common delaying tactic when a special-interest group anticipates that analysis by independent scientists could cause them problems. Burger's questioning was disingenuous at best.

We had submitted our paper to the most important and competitive computer security conference, the IEEE "Symposium on Security and Privacy," known in our circles as "the Oakland conference," although it's actually held at the Claremont Resort in Berkeley every year. After going through twice the usual number of reviews, our paper was accepted with high marks. Not long after, Dan Wallach and Stephen Burger both received invitations to speak to government officials in Austin, Texas, about the e-voting controversy. Burger took the opportunity to introduce himself as a member of the IEEE and to start scathingly criticizing our work, saying that our paper wasn't properly peer-reviewed. Dan protested, and Burger countered that sending our paper out to a few "friends" did not constitute peer review. Dan was able to announce that not only had the paper been peer-reviewed, but it had been accepted to the discipline's premier conference, sponsored by Burger's own organization, the IEEE. Burger slunk back into his chair and did not say another word.

Ted Pohler, vice provost of Johns Hopkins, called me one day on behalf of the university president and asked me to brief him on the situation. He explained that the president supported our efforts, but that he could not ignore the letter from Burger and had asked Pohler to look into it. It briefly crossed my mind that I had to have a complaint lodged against me to rate a call from someone so high up in the school. I hadn't been there very long, and this both scared and annoyed me. However, I got the impression that Pohler was merely covering his bases and gathering whatever information he could. He listened for a long time and ultimately congratulated me for our efforts. He let on that he'd been following the story avidly in the press and was glad to finally make my acquaintance.

It unnerved me a little that some people were coming after me directly. So far, Williams and Burger had taken their best shots without doing any real harm. In an odd way, their attacks had given other people a chance to reaffirm their support, making me feel that much more insulated. When I began to notice quotes from Brit Williams cropping up in the same articles that quoted me, it occurred to me to reach out to him and try to clear the air. However, colleagues and friends warned me that the potential risks of calling Williams far outweighed the benefits. He clearly had something at stake, and he'd butted heads with many others in the e-voting world before. Engaging him more directly could complicate things further.

I ultimately met Brit Williams, a white-haired emeritus professor, in December of that year at a landmark symposium titled "Building Trust and Confidence in Voting Systems." Sponsored by the National Institute of Standards and Technology (NIST), this symposium marked the first time that election officials, computer security experts, members of the Election Assistance Commission (EAC), activists, and vendors had come together to discuss the many issues surrounding electronic voting. Several people I first met there would figure prominently in my life and in the e-voting debate. In addition to Williams, there was Linda Lamone, the director of elections for Maryland, and Kathy Rogers from the Georgia secretary of state's office. Kathy politely challenged me, asking if I had ever offered to help my home state election officials, since I was so public with my criticism of e-voting machines. I must have disappointed her when I explained that not only had I done so, but I had done so live on the radio, directly addressing Maryland governor Robert L. Ehrlich. (On the air, Ehrlich thanked me profusely for our "excellent" work, but I never heard from him again.)

Undeterred, Rogers had gone on to let me know that, in Georgia anyway, people saw me as someone who had driven a bulldozer through the beautiful rose garden represented by their modernized election equipment. My protestations that I was only the messenger, and that Diebold was driving that bulldozer, fell on deaf ears. Several months later, after refusing to debate David Dill and myself directly, Kathy followed us on an NPR show and argued that the Georgia voters loved their e-voting machines and that Georgia had never had a security incident. She made no effort to explain how she could possibly have known that, not being a computer scientist. This was neither the first nor the last time that officials with no computer security training were allowed by the media to expound on the subject as if they knew what they were talking about.

The NIST symposium was broken into four sessions, with all the leading voices of the elections community present for the discussion. These sessions grew quite heated at times. Brit Williams and I were scheduled to speak at the security session, along with David Dill, Donetta Donaldson, secretary of state for Colorado, and Jim Adler, the CEO of VoteHere, a company that develops e-voting software. Williams seemed to go out of his way to avoid me before our session, not even looking up to make eye contact. Over the next year I grew familiar with the state of high anxiety brought on by finding myself in a roomful of people who would have rejoiced if I were to somehow simply disappear. The panel went about as expected. David and I spoke about the insecurity of the machines, the potential for vendors rigging elections, and the necessity of paper ballots. Davidson opened up about the challenges of running an election when even the experts couldn't agree, and Adler proudly explained why his company had the answer.

But it was Brit Williams who surprised the room. If a vendor tried to rig an election, he said, or if an outside party tried to tamper with the results, their chance of success was one in a billion. Williams emphasized that people should not reject technology just because it is complex. After all, he said, people fly on airplanes all the time, so there was no reason to fear electronic voting machines. The kicker came when he stated that he had developed techniques for detecting Trojan horses in computer code. I heard some audible laughter in the audience, which I assumed came from computer experts.

In computer jargon, a malicious program hidden within an otherwise legitimate program is referred to as a Trojan horse, after the mythical wooden horse the Greeks bestowed as a gift on the city of Troy. The horse, of course, secretly contained Greek soldiers who snuck out in the night and opened the gates of the city to the Greek army, giving rise to the expression "Beware of Greeks bearing gifts." In computer terms, an example of a Trojan horse might be a little self-contained program that erases a computer's hard drive if someone hits the ESC key three times in a row. It would be alarmingly easy for a hacker to hide or disguise this malicious code in another, more common program, such as Microsoft Excel, so that it still works but remains virtually invisible to someone reading the code for the larger program, even an expert. Code could be hidden inside the data for a picture or other graphic, for example. Sometimes a hacker only needs to alter a single character in thousands of lines of code to create a ticking time bomb. Users of that copy of Excel would have no way of knowing about the Trojan horse, at least not until they happened to hit the ESC key three times and suddenly lost all their data.

Trojan horses are among the most serious threats to computer security. And yet a generally applicable technique for finding Trojan horses in other programs cannot exist. You can't get an undergraduate degree in computer science from a reputable university and not know the theorem that proves this. It isn't that Trojan horses can never be found; it's just that we can't ever say with certainty that none exist within a given program. This concept is difficult enough for laypeople to grasp; for someone like Williams to make such an improbable claim, it was clear that either he didn't understand that such a tool is impossible or he was being deliberately disingenuous. Either way, his statement was troubling. Williams had given me plenty of ammunition with which to take his credibility apart, but that wasn't what I was there for. Instead, I was able to find an opportunity to make a joke about it, which proved to be the right way to handle it. Everyone laughed, including Williams. He was still chuckling when he came up, offered me his hand, and introduced himself.

Afterward, against the better judgment of pretty much everyone I knew, I decided to take advantage of the little opening Williams had given me and try to start a productive dialogue with him. After serving as an election judge in Maryland on

Super Tuesday, I posted an account of my experience on the Web and sent Williams the link and asked for his thoughts. In his response, which he copied to several people, including Kathy Rogers, he sarcastically expressed amazement that I would be interested in any opinion of his. He went on to say that I had now completed my "freshman" education in the subject and that, were I a sophomore, I might have learned that Diebold does not designate an accumulator machine. The machines are all identical, and the poll manager is free to use any machine as the accumulator.

I couldn't recall having said anything one way or another about accumulator machines, especially in Georgia, and when I checked with the chief judge where I was a poll worker, she told me that in fact Diebold had designated the accumulator machine. Williams wasn't just condescending; he seemed to be wrong. Again. I could only guess that he construed any attack on Diebold as an affront to his personal operation. I wrote back to that effect, ending my message with another plea for civility:

> You and I are on completely opposite sides of this issue, but I hope that if we decide to continue this dialogue that we can maintain a respectful tone, otherwise I will drop it.

Williams's response was more of the same. "The fact that you did not know who I am speaks volumes about the difference in our methods of operation," he began, going on to imply that, if I were more like him, I would have worked quietly for two decades to develop my expertise and demonstrate my commitment to improving our voting systems. "But, alas, there would have been no publicity." He concluded by declining to enlighten me regarding my "many incorrect assumptions" about election

administration. His lordly condescension annoyed me, as did his
inexplicable bitterness. At one point I even considered taking
him up on an invitation, of questionable sincerity, to come visit
his center at Kennesaw State to learn from the master how elections work. He seemed genuinely committed to the promise of
e-voting, and in the end, I was most bothered by the realization
that people in my camp as well as his were too ready and willing
to believe the worst about those on the other side.

HAVING TAKEN THE criticism that I didn't know enough about
election procedures very much to heart, I took steps to learn
about the process from the inside, as a volunteer. That experience led to my being called upon to testify before the U.S.
Election Assistance Commission as well as several other congressional panels. Each time I was followed by Brit Williams, who
continued to go on about the safety of air travel, as if the fact
that airplanes didn't fall out of the sky meant electronic voting
was secure. At the EAC hearing, I found myself with Williams
sitting stonily on one side of me and Stephen Burger, who had
written the letter to President Brody, on the other. The hearing
also gave me the opportunity to meet the EAC chairman, DeForest "Buster" Soaries; only a few weeks later I would find myself
sitting in Soaries's office in Washington, across from none other
than Brit Williams. We had both come to Capitol Hill for House
subcommittee hearings, and Soaries had managed to corral us
for a powwow. I felt very much at ease with Soaries, having
spent twenty minutes before Williams arrived chatting with
him about the fact that we both were fathers of twins and that I
had lived in New Jersey when he was serving as secretary of
state there.

When the meeting began, Soaries got right to the point. "I

find it incredible that two people who know so much about computer science and who are so respected by their communities could disagree so fundamentally on the issue of electronic voting security. I wanted to sit you both down and find out what it is that you agree on. There must be some things you agree on." He stood next to a large easel with a marker in his hand and started firing questions at us.

Williams and I quickly fell into our usual sparring. He berated me, calling me "irresponsible" for publishing my "terrible report." I shot back that I couldn't understand how he could defend such obviously flawed machines. I asked him if he had ever examined the code himself, and he admitted that he hadn't. I looked up at Soaries and said that in any other industry a vendor who tried to market a product like that wouldn't survive. Soaries stepped in quickly, told us to knock off the sparring, and forced us to focus on areas of agreement.

Williams made the first effort, asking if I agreed that, with proper procedures, an election could be secured even with insecure machines, but I said no. I ventured a question about the extent of the threat, whether the incentive for tampering with elections was in fact high. Williams said yes, and Soaries jumped up and wrote it down excitedly on his big paper pad. "Now we're getting somewhere! What else?"

We continued in this vein for over three hours. Soaries lamented that his commission was formed so late and so close to the election. He asked what he could do in his position to give people confidence in the election process. I responded that people shouldn't have confidence in the process if it was insecure and suggested that voter-verifiable ballots represented a quick and obvious solution. Soaries had a real problem, though. If he were to come out with a mandate for voter-verified paper ballots on a national scale, he explained, he would immediately lose credibility with election officials all over the country. Williams added that such a mandate would lead to rioting in the streets after the election, when the loser would inevitably point to Soaries's statement condemning DREs, which were still in use in so many precincts. Soaries thought Williams's scenario a likely one, but I wasn't convinced. When Soaries asked what I would do in his position, I repeated my call for voter-verified paper ballots for all voters.

"I told you, I can't say that," he said.

I held firm. "In that case, if I were in your position, I'd get another job." I couldn't quite believe what had just come out of my mouth. Soaries was a presidential appointee, and even though I felt so comfortable with him, I was pretty sure I had just stepped over the line. In fact, he burst out laughing.

"Don't think I haven't considered that. I consider that every day. I'm in an impossible situation. My commission is grossly underfunded. I have the security experts telling me that thirty percent of the voters will vote on insecure machines, and I have election officials telling me that they cannot handle paper ballots." Listening to Soaries, I realized how lucky we were to have someone so clearheaded and fair-minded and willing to learn in that position—when it would have been easy to appoint someone with a partisan agenda—and I told him so. I also complimented him on the clever tactic of bringing Brit Williams and me together to find common ground, a sentiment that Williams seconded. It really seemed like Soaries had a handle on how to move things forward.

In July 2004 Brit Williams and I went at it again, this time at a hearing for the Committee on House Administration. I spoke about how I would design an electronic voting machine, suggesting a touch-screen machine not unlike those made by Diebold.

My machine, however, would not count any votes. It would simply be used to capture the voter's intent and print out a paper ballot with the votes recorded. I called it a ballot-marking machine. It would be accessible to blind voters and non-English speakers, and it would have all the advantages of a DRE machine. Overvotes—a voter invalidating his or her ballot by marking too many choices—would be prevented. Similarly, the machine could alert the voter about an undervote (not marking enough choices). The paper ballots could be counted in different ways, including by hand or by an optical scanner (from a different manufacturer). I outlined what I believed to be the main security issues and my main criticisms of DREs:

- There is no way for voters to verify that their votes were recorded correctly.
- There is no way to count the votes in a publicly viewable fashion.
- In a controversial election, meaningful recounts are impossible.
- The machines must be completely trusted not to fail, not to have been programmed maliciously, and not to have been tampered with.
- In the Diebold machines, we found gross design and programming errors. And yet the current certification process resulted in these machines being approved for use and being used in elections.
- We cannot determine the quality of other vendors' machines because their code is proprietary and they won't let anybody examine it.

By way of example, I explained the system we have at school for turning in grades. Professors log in through the Internet and upload spreadsheets with their students' grades. It would, of course, be a lot easier for a student to write a little computer virus, hack the process, and alter his or her grade than it would be to do a semester's worth of work, but we have secured the system with a very simple procedure. After each term, our secretaries hand-deliver a sheet directly from the registrar's office that shows all the grades that were recorded in the system. The professors then check these against the submitted grades. It's a straightforward, out-of-band, paper backup system. Electronic voting machines that do not create a paper audit trail do not provide even this level of protection or verification. Our system requires that ballots remain secret. A voter can verify his or her vote only at the time that it is cast; once it is received by the system, it must remain forever anonymous. Logically, people need to see a physical (paper) record of their vote, as they cast it, and to know that the physical record is safely and securely preserved.

Brit Williams spoke after me and countered my arguments without ever directly addressing them. He acknowledged that my dream voting machine was great, but he wanted everyone to see that in the "real world" the Diebold machines were what we had and that there was nothing wrong with them. He bolstered his usual airplane analogy by pointing out how simple the operations in a voting machine are. It accumulates votes and adds up the totals, whereas an airplane computer has to constantly recalculate variables like velocity, trajectory, wind speed, weight, and so on. I wanted to ask him why, if it was all so simple, the Diebold machines needed 45,000 lines of code on top of Windows' millions of lines of code. I also wanted very much to point out that if an adequate security analysis had been part of the design process, or even if our analysis had been done and implemented a year earlier, Williams's "real world" might look a lot different.

After the hearing, Williams mentioned that he would be unable to attend a hearing later that month at which we were both scheduled to testify. He had a primary that day in Georgia. "Do you think you'll be able to manage without me?" he asked wryly. "It'll be challenging, but I'll do my best," I laughed. We shook hands and parted, both of us smiling.

7

As California rolls toward a train wreck with federal and
state laws, voting activists told state elections officials that
Diebold and its voting machines aren't welcome along for
the ride. Witness after witness . . . called on state officials
Thursday to block Diebold's voting machines from the
nation's largest elections market, casting the firm as
synonymous with lost trust and vote "theft"
in the 2000 and 2004 elections.
—Oakland Tribune, *June 18, 2005*

Nobody was very surprised when the letter came from
Diebold's lawyers in late August. In fact, Hopkins's legal
team wondered what took them so long. Dan, Yoshi,
Adam, and I each received an identical letter from the law firm
of Jones Day:

> . . . We want to advise you to exercise caution in your use of
> the Content [our report] and your discussions with the media.
> Statements that contain material inaccuracies or are based on
> factual inaccuracies, especially when they appear designed to
> improperly impair and impede Diebold's existing and future
> business relationships, may give rise to legal causes of action.

> . . . Failure to exercise appropriate discretion in how you
> choose to present your limited and qualified study and how you

otherwise characterize Diebold, its employees and its products may result in legal consequences.

. . . Finally, this letter will also serve as Diebold's demand that you cease and desist all uses of the Code, including the reproduction of, distribution of, or creation of derivative works from the Code, and that you send to me, at the above address, all copies of the Code in your possession or subject to your control.

The letter went on in this vein and at one point seemed to lapse into nonsensical gibberish. When our attorneys asked for a clarification, they learned that some of the text had been accidentally deleted, prompting a few wisecracks about how Diebold's lawyers didn't seem much sharper than its programmers.

Johns Hopkins' legal staff responded with a strongly worded letter, stating that we had done nothing wrong and that the university stood behind all its researchers and would continue to do so. That was the last we heard from Diebold's lawyers, whose letter is still the only direct communication I have ever had from Diebold at all.

Knowing that Cindy Cohn and the Johns Hopkins legal team—not to mention my wife, Ann, a lawyer with litigation experience—were in my corner made me feel better about having incurred the wrath of a multibillion-dollar corporation. Maybe I'd seen too many thrillers about evil corporations, but one episode in particular helped me realize we were a little more concerned than we admitted. One day Adam and I were standing outside a restaurant in California, where we were attending a conference. A windowless white van with the blue Diebold logo on the side pulled up in front of us and came to a sudden stop. I don't know if we thought a Diebold SWAT team was going to jump out of the van and haul us away to some mysterious island prison, but there was that split second when we looked at each other, both wondering if we should run like hell. Nothing happened, of course, but at least later we were able to entertain our colleagues with this story of our own goofy paranoia.

Diebold's public statements on the subject were a litany of denial. The company claimed, among other things, that we had analyzed an old discarded version of the code, not the version actually used in production. At the same time, it claimed that not only was it aware of the problems we had identified, but it had fixed them all. Indeed, some of the problems we found could be fixed, but a great many were far beyond repair. The code had been built on a foundation of terrible software engineering and could be fixed only with a top-to-bottom rewrite by better programmers. You can't fix such poorly written software by tinkering with it or patching it up. It's not something that can eventually be refined into high-quality code. That's tantamount to trying to save a piece of spoiled meat by overcooking it. In the end, it's still inedible.

Part of Diebold's public posture was to take every opportunity to discredit computer scientists like us as technological doomsayers. NPR's *All Things Considered* interviewed me for a story on the flaws we had found in the Diebold machines. As I listened during my drive home from work to my own comments in the final report, I got steamed when a Diebold spokesman, who had the last word, compared the whole flap to the "hysteria" about Y2K. "They made such a big deal about it, and in the end, 2000 arrived and nothing happened." I wanted to drive right to a radio studio to rebut that point. In fact, Y2K had caused plenty of very real problems, and the fact that nothing disastrous occurred was due to the fact that billions of dollars and countless man-hours went into preparation and prevention. I only wish we were able to focus that kind of attention on election technology.

Diebold Election Systems fought doggedly on to counter the flood of negative publicity. In one feeble effort at damage control, Walden O'Dell, the CEO, told *Newsweek*'s Steven Levy that Diebold hadn't gotten into the voting game just for the money; to him, it was all about patriotism. If some of Diebold's comments were a little hard to believe, others made no sense at all. For example, when we first obtained the code, we did wonder if it was the real production system or perhaps an unused prototype, as Diebold claimed. There was evidence that the system was the real thing. Embedded in the code were comments from the developers about various phases the code had undergone, and we found names of previous products that showed that the software had evolved. But what really convinced us that the code was a real commercial product was that we were able to compile it and run it so easily. Anyone who works in software development knows what it takes to get code to the point that it compiles and runs successfully. We could run the code on a Windows 2000 machine in our lab, despite the fact that Diebold deployed it over Windows CE in the Accuvote TS machine, because the various Windows platforms contain the same operating system core. It was clear to us that the code was designed to run on other versions of Windows. Experience told us that this was a fairly sure indicator that the code was probably real, and we said so in our report. Diebold, of course, saw the opening here and used the statement to point out to the media that our analysis was flawed. After all, we had run the code on Windows 2000 when it had been written for Windows CE.

Too many reporters printed this uncritically, displaying their own lack of technical understanding. Our analysis, in fact, was based entirely on manual inspection of the code. We read the code and drew our conclusions, actually running it later only to confirm that it executed. We began to see that many journalists hadn't read our report and were perfectly ready to believe Diebold's claim that the integrity of our report depended on the version of Windows we had used. Nothing could have been further from the truth. The errors in cryptography, the poor software engineering, the 1111 PIN values, the unauthenticated smartcards, the hardwired key—none of these critical flaws had anything to do with the operating platform, and Diebold knew it. And yet, it repeated this bogus defense repeatedly to the press, exploiting the lack of technical sophistication in the mainstream media.

Looking back, I think it was that cynical and combative attitude that most angered and saddened me. Our intention was never to stick it to Diebold but to try to fix a dangerously flawed process. It was unsettling that the company couldn't come at it with the same spirit.

Additional evidence emerged that the code was genuine. *Wired News*, an online news service ·that is widely read within the technical community, ran a story about the Diebold code problems, including the following:

A Diebold representative confirmed that the source code Rubin's team examined was last used in November 2002 general elections in Georgia, Maryland and in counties in California and Kansas.

Here Diebold acknowledged that what we had examined was the right code. But a few days after the story ran, Dan Wallach and Doug Jones both e-mailed me to point out that the text of the article had changed, while the Web link had not.

> Diebold spokesmen said the code Rubin downloaded and examined was more than a year old. The code he obtained was "less than 5 percent" of the whole application, they said. In addition, the application Rubin examined "on the whole is not the same" as applications in machines used in elections in places like Georgia and Maryland, said John Kristoff, Diebold's director of communication and investor relations.

The new text painted a very different picture. Dan Wallach got in touch with the writer and asked why the story had changed. The response wasn't exactly comforting. The writer said that the first Diebold rep he had spoken to confirmed that the code we analyzed was indeed the code running on their machines in the 2002 elections. But apparently another rep called back after the story ran and retracted that statement, saying that the first spokesperson had misunderstood the question. The writer said that the change had been made reluctantly, and he regretted that the magazine had not told its readers about changing the text from the original version.

I never understood why *Wired News* meekly changed its story instead of investigating Diebold's contradictory statements. They never made any mention of the fact that they had revised their article. Later studies of the Diebold code confirmed most of our analysis, and in time it became accepted by all concerned that the code we had examined was the real code, the "live" code that ran in the Accuvote TS and the Accuvote TSx.

ON JULY 30, one week after we posted our report to the Web, Diebold released a twenty-seven-page "technical" response entitled "Checks and Balances in Elections Equipment and Procedures Prevent Alleged Fraud Scenario," although it read much more like the work of the public relations staff than of technical professionals. Indeed, the paper was nothing short of embarrassing from a technical perspective. The number of egregious errors highlighted once again the ineptness of Diebold's technical staff. The Diebold paper listed the key points from our report—or as its writer called them, "allegations"—and offered a response or rebuttal to each. The paper provided a fair amount of amusement for many academics and professionals in computer science, but it was difficult to be entertained for long when you realized the subject matter under discussion.

Here's a little sampling of Diebold's response:

Allegation #8 (p. 4): "Cryptography, when used at all, is used incorrectly."

Response: This statement is based on the presumption that there is a single correct means of using cryptography. This is not accurate. The software is designed with the realization that subsequent versions will be released to address any needed improvements or requested changes; but the cryptography in the software is used as the developers intended, taking into account the possibility of future development.

This is essentially like building a house out of straw instead of bricks and, when someone points out that a straw house won't stand up, claiming that the straw was used as intended. The errors in cryptography that we found were fundamental.

At times Diebold's responses seemed to misunderstand or misuse basic technical vocabulary.

Allegation #44 (p. 15): "Even if proper key management were to be implemented, many problems would still remain. First, DES keys can be recovered by brute force in a very short time period [Gi198]. DES should be replaced with either triple-DES [Sch96] or, preferably, AES [DJ02]."

Response: There are stronger forms of compression than DES . . .

If any students in my security class ever said something like that, I'd probably make them take the class again. There certainly are better compression functions than DES. Then again, there are better cleaning solutions than grease. DES is for encryption, not for compression, which is the process of compacting data so that they use less computer memory, like music in a compressed MP3 format or pictures in a compressed JPEG format. In fact, encryption functions generally enlarge a given block of data slightly, the exact opposite of compression.

Some of Diebold's points could only be explained by laziness, sloppiness, or total insincerity. The following comment referred to an account of testimony from Doug Jones of the University of Iowa, released in 2001, which we cited in our original report.

Allegation #45 (p. 15): "Jones reports that the vendor may have been aware of this design flaw in their code for several years [Jon01, Jon03]. We see no evidence that this design flaw was ever addressed."

Response: We were not able to find such a claim in the Jones paper.

As Doug Jones states on his website,

In additional discussion at the first Iowa examination of the AccuTouch system on November 6, 1997, it had come out that neither the technical staff nor the salespeople at Global Election Systems (subsequently acquired by Diebold in 2002) understood cryptographic security. They were happy to assert that they used the federally approved data encryption standard (DES), but nobody seemed to understand *key management*. In fact, the lead programmer to whom my question was forwarded, by cell phone, found the term unfamiliar and needed explanation. On continued questioning, it became apparent that there was only one key used, companywide, for all of its voting products. The implication was that this key was hardcoded into the source code!

The Iowa examiner's minutes of the meeting reflect this discussion but do not mention the cell-phone conversation:

Dr. Jones also expressed concern about data encryption standards used to guarantee the integrity of the data on the machine. DES requires the use of electronic keys to lock and unlock all critical data. Currently all machines use the same key. Dr. Jones stated that this is a security problem. However, the use of a single key for all machines is not a condition that would disqualify the system under Iowa law.

Dr. Jones further stated: "The Iowa Secretary of State's office routinely forwards the minutes of these meetings to the vendor in question, so they did have both written and verbal notice of this serious security flaw; in addition, I wrote several paragraphs on this topic to the Elections Division of the Secretary of State's office on December 23, 1997.

Unfortunately, a number of journalists treated Diebold's paper as a legitimate source of technical information and quoted it in their stories. It certainly had the veneer of legitimacy. The sheer volume of responses gave the impression that our report was full of holes and inaccuracies. As amusing as the report could be, it could also be dangerous, and we decided that some kind of rejoinder to their response was necessary. The paper we issued kept to the technical facts and falsities, which may not have served us so well since Diebold had been sidestepping these facts in favor of a public relations campaign. The press, however, got it right, although I'm sure our paper made most of their eyes glaze over. Maybe our credibility won out over Diebold's spin-doctoring, but its response went largely unnoticed by the media and the public in the end.

Diebold spent a lot of time and money refuting our study and doing its best to spin the attendant publicity, but it refrained from coming after me personally. It didn't have to. That dirty work fell to one Harris Miller, the president of a lobbying and trade organization, funded by technology vendors, called the Information Technology Association of America, or ITAA. Miller is a front man for a powerful industry group, and like the spokespeople and lobbyists for everything from tobacco and firearms to hospital chains and pork farmers, he serves his clients by making them look saintly and pushing their agendas with the public and inside government. *Wired News* reported that one month after we released our report, the ITAA proposed a lobbying campaign on behalf of voting machine manufacturers, at a cost of between $100,000 and $200,000 per vendor. Many of Miller's efforts ended up backfiring. Reporters almost always gave me a chance to rebut on the record, and more often than not the resulting story reflected badly on him.

I was starting to understand that pretty much anything goes when you're fighting issues out in public. You can distract people from the facts by raising irrelevant issues, or you can frame the discussion in any way that's advantageous to you. This is what Miller did. In one egregious example, he claimed that my colleagues and I were merely zealots from the open-source movement. "Open source" is a collaborative software development philosophy based on making source code publicly available so that qualified members of the computer community can freely access it and contribute enhancements. It was convenient for Miller to tar e-voting critics with the open-source brush in his statements to the press, suggesting that the e-voting vendors were innocently caught up in our blind pursuit of our agenda. Of course, our criticism had absolutely nothing to do with open source. I do believe that voting machinery should be transparent and that the code must be available for public scrutiny, but I am not, in general, a proponent of open source for all systems. Neither are a large number of my colleagues. I said repeatedly, in public, that open source is not enough to secure voting machines because Trojan horses can be hidden in programs in an undetectable manner. But Miller clearly believed this would be a good way to discredit computer scientists and was able to focus the media's attention on this bogus argument for a while.

Miller and the ITAA put out several press releases designed to discredit me, sometimes attacking me personally. Princeton professor Ed Felten told me encouragingly that when the attacks get personal, it's a sign that the other side is getting desperate. Although he had never met me and knew next to nothing about me, Miller generally tried to imply that I was naive and unsophisticated, an upstart unschooled in the way of elections and a publicity hound. "To anyone who has used, or is familiar with [electronic voting], Dr. Rubin's fifteen minutes of fame is starting to feel like fifty," one release proclaimed. "It is time to start listening to the election officials who are responsible for running elections and the voters, and tuning out the 'experts' who do not even understand what they are criticizing." You have to love a guy who can publicly advocate, with a straight face, tuning out the experts.

To reinforce the idea of my callowness, Diebold and the ITAA liked to refer to our study as a "homework assignment." At a tense hearing of the Voting Systems and Procedures Panel advising the California secretary of state, which eventually resulted in the decertification of the Diebold TS machines, Bob Urosovich, president of Diebold Election Systems, Inc., stated in his testimony that our study was not to be taken seriously because it was no more than a homework assignment. My colleague David Jefferson was involved in the hearing and e-mailed me that night about Urosovich's comment. I replied that if our results were what we had uncovered in a simple homework assignment, imagine what a serious analysis might have revealed. The next day another reference to the "homework assignment" was made at the hearing, and Jefferson seized the moment to read my e-mail out loud and into the record. The room erupted in uproarious laughter, to the great embarrassment of the Diebold officials. Someone else testified that what I had actually said was that it was so easy to find security vulnerabilities in the code that I could have given such a search to my students as a homework assignment.

To me, Harris Miller represents the sacrifice of the public good in the name of private interests. Diebold is guilty of developing flawed technology and defending it to the death, but it is possible that it doesn't understand the weaknesses of its own product and is defending the interests of the company and its shareholders. Miller, however, is a hired gun. He'll do whatever he has to do and say whatever he has to say to protect his clients. Fairness and objectivity are not part of his equation. His clients' interests always get top priority. In the context of electronic voting, that means those interests take precedence over the public interest, and to me that seems simply unconscionable.

8

Whenever the people are well informed, they can be trusted
with their own government.
—*Thomas Jefferson, 1789*

Harris Miller and his insinuations turned out to be only
the warm-up act, but I didn't know that at the time. In
August I found myself in southern California, heading
toward "Crypto," an annual conference at the University of
California at Santa Barbara, where top academic cryptographers
meet and present the latest developments in their field while en-
joying the blue Pacific and golden sunshine and indulging in
great quantities of food and drink. Cryptography is the science,
or art, of protecting information, usually with advanced mathematical processes.

I myself, though not a cryptographer, have attended Crypto
almost every year since 1993. The information presented there
is invaluable to me—assuming, of course, that I can understand
it. When the material gets far enough over my head that I can't
make use of it, I can usually find a kindred spirit with whom to
share a swim or a game of tennis. I was in a good mood as I

waited at LAX for the shuttle to the rental-car lot. I pulled out my BlackBerry and saw several messages from reporters. Not being the kind of person to let idle time remain idle, I started calling them back. The first call I returned was the one flagged as "urgent." It's not a call I'll forget.

"Hello?"

"Hi, this is Avi Rubin from Johns Hopkins. I received a message to call this number from a reporter. Is that you?"

"Yes, this is Lynn Landes." She announced her name in a way that made it clear she thought it would be familiar to me. It wasn't.

"I'm sorry, I don't think I know you. Can you tell me who you write for?"

"You don't know me? *Lynn Landes?* Are you serious?" I was beginning to be sorry I had called. "Come on. We've exchanged e-mails before. I write for *EcoTalk* and *Conspiracy Planet.*" Now I was *really* sorry I had called. She was clearly furious. Later I learned that *EcoTalk* is a one-woman operation (Landes being the one woman), and *Conspiracy Planet*, well, the title says it all.

"Lynn, ever since my report came out, I get hundreds of e-mails every day. I apologize, but I can't keep track of everyone, and I just don't remember you. I'm sorry if you are offended, but did you have any specific questions?"

She paused a beat and then asked, "What is your relationship with a company called VoteHere?" She waited. "Avi, are you there?"

I was, in fact, speechless, and my heart had started racing. I knew something was wrong, but I wasn't quite sure what it was yet.

"Uh, I am on their technical advisory board."

"That's right. Do you see a problem with that?"

Collecting myself, I answered carefully. "Actually, it's a defunct position. I haven't heard from them in years. I am not actively advising the company."

"Do you think I don't see the conflict of interest here?" she asked.

"There is no conflict of interest. Several years ago, I agreed to join the technical advisory board of VoteHere because a friend of mine was on it and because I was on a panel at a conference with their CTO, and that's the last I ever heard from them." That was no lie, and it was lucky that I had been able to even remember that much on the spur of the moment.

Lynn raised her voice another notch. "Do you think I'm stupid? Clearly, you wrote your report to discredit Diebold so that VoteHere could swoop in and provide an expensive fix. You'd then profit from that with a kickback from VoteHere. It's totally transparent." Now I was angry. This was a direct accusation, based on a couple of facts spun together in one person's feverish imagination. But Landes was a reporter, and I knew she was likely to print a story about this, whether it was true or not.

"Look, Lynn, I know that you feel you've scored a great scoop and that you have a big story here, but I'm telling you, you're making a big mistake." The mere fact that I had to be defensive now was adding to my anger, but I tried to stay calm. "I'm on seven or eight advisory boards right now. I can't keep track of them. I was not even conscious of my relationship with Vote-Here when we wrote the Diebold analysis. If you print what you are accusing me of, you'll be printing something that is simply not true."

As Lynn continued to hammer away at me, I realized that she was convinced that she had a story bigger than Watergate, a score for *Conspiracy Planet*, and that nothing I could say would change her mind. It took a while, but I eventually managed to hang up.

I felt a tremendous headache coming on as the implications of the call with Lynn Landes started to sink in. The phrase "conflict of interest" is a land mine. Reporters can't resist it, and this one was clearly going to treat it like a dog with a bone. The public is ready to believe this kind of accusation about virtually anyone even tangentially in the news. We have almost come to expect it, to some degree, of our politicians, sometimes our journalists, and especially our corporate leaders. But for a research scientist, whose career is predicated on a commitment to seek objective knowledge, even the appearance of a conflict of interest is intolerable and unthinkable. Our product is our research—the untainted data and our evenhanded analysis of that data—and if the integrity of our product is questioned, our work is meaningless.

I had been feeling pretty good about myself, fighting the good fight against a callous corporation, standing up for truth, justice, and the American way. But now I could see that it was going to be me on the wrong end of the media coverage. My integrity was going to be questioned in a public forum. The American way, I was learning, was the way of the big story, and now that big story wasn't going to be about voting machines and computer programs. It was going to be about me, and I had no idea how ugly it was going to get.

IN FEBRUARY 2001, I had attended a conference called "Financial Cryptography" in the Cayman Islands. I divide the world of cryptographers and computer security researchers into two basic groups: those who treated this conference like a wild Caribbean boondoggle, and those who took it seriously, as it deserved. I already had a reputation as an opponent of Internet voting and was invited to speak about the risks of such systems as part of a panel on the business of electronic voting. Among the other panelists was Andy Neff, the chief technology officer of VoteHere. Despite disagreeing with most of what he said, I found Neff to be both very sharp and reasonable. He approached me after our session and said he wanted to talk.

We met several times over the course of the conference. Andy knew that he and I had legitimate disagreements on many issues, but he explained that he believed that a dialogue with confirmed skeptics could only benefit his company's technology. He invited me to join his company's board of advisers. At first I resisted, concerned that my participation as an adviser would be seen as an endorsement of the company. VoteHere had developed, and was trying to sell, Internet voting technology, something to which I was fully, and publicly, opposed. Neff persisted, suggesting that I speak with Dan Boneh, a famous cryptographer at Stanford, for some additional perspective. Dan was a friend, and one of the brightest people I had ever met.

When I returned from the conference, I called Dan, who filled in the picture. Andy Neff had a PhD in computer science and had papers published at the Crypto conference. Of all the electronic voting machine manufacturers, Dan felt that VoteHere was the one that actually had legitimate technology and real security expertise. VoteHere's CEO, Jim Adler, was also a scientist. The software VoteHere produced could run either in electronic voting machines, such as Diebold's, or over the Internet. Andy Neff had developed special mathematical techniques by which voters could, after an election, verify that their votes had been counted without revealing to anyone else how they voted. The technology was novel, but I still had reservations about the security of the system. In particular, I had reason to believe that it wasn't feasible to secure the Internet portion for public elections. Dan Boneh told me he enjoyed his interactions with the company and said that, other than reviewing a few documents, the time commitment was negligible. Still, I wasn't convinced.

VoteHere contacted me several times over the next few weeks, repeating the invitation to become an adviser. I finally agreed to join, under one condition: our contract needed to state explicitly that my participation on its advisory board did not constitute an endorsement of the company, and that it would get my permission before including my name in any company publicity. Vote-Here agreed and asked if it could list me on its Web page as an adviser. I said sure; in hindsight, I realized that this was really all they wanted in the first place. I signed the advisory agreement, which included a handful of stock options. Although I was now officially affiliated with the company, it never asked me to review any documents, never asked me to participate in any advisory meetings, and in fact never contacted me again for any reason. Eventually, I simply forgot about VoteHere.

MY BLACK MOOD on the drive up to Santa Barbara contrasted harshly with the brilliant sunshine of the California coast. I knew that I had done nothing wrong. I knew just as surely, though, that perception is everything and that, if they wanted to, the media could have a field day with this. The explanation, while it seemed obvious to me, was subtle enough to be irrelevant to an ambitious reporter. There was really no way that criticizing Diebold could benefit VoteHere. The two companies were not, in fact, competitors. Diebold sold voting machines, while VoteHere hoped to sell software to companies like

Diebold. Diebold was an enormous international conglomerate. VoteHere was just a tiny start-up with a handful of employees. It had hardly even sold anything. It was like saying Ford was a competitor of a company that was developing new pollution control devices for its cars.

I wanted John Schwartz's thoughts on the problem. He had handled the original story so well, and I trusted his instincts about public relations. Just as important, I wanted John to hear this from me, rather than hearing it "on the street" and wondering why I hadn't been straight with him. I worried that it would make him look bad and discredit the story he had written. Sure enough, he took the news fairly coldly, telling me I could have, and should have, avoided any problems by resigning from Vote-Here before releasing the report. I explained that I would have done exactly that, but that I was on many different boards, and this situation hadn't even entered my mind. John warmed up and started to think constructively. I floated the idea, which John supported, of issuing a press release resigning from VoteHere's board and returning all the stock options. John predicted that even with that gesture things were going to get pretty uncomfortable in the short term, but that I could ride it out and it would blow over in time. Before we hung up, John told me to hang in there, and I was grateful that our relationship was strong enough to survive this kind of misstep.

I was shaking and sweating. I pulled off the road and got out of the car to let my nerves settle. The beautiful scenery still didn't lift my mood any, so I decided to call Darren Lacey of the Hopkins legal team before getting behind the wheel again. There's a slightly larger-than-life quality to Darren Lacey, and not just because he stands a solid six-foot-four. Darren played football in college and then went on to get a law degree from

Harvard. His career took some unusual turns until he ended up as executive director of the Johns Hopkins University Information Security Institute, or JHUISI (pronounced "juicy"). He had played a role in recruiting me to Hopkins, and we had a good working relationship, but I knew that he was all business in this kind of situation. Today was no different, and his matter-of-fact response to my problem made me that much more worried. No university wants to deal with a conflict of interest, but for Hopkins, whose primary reputation is as a medical school and research center, it was a particularly sensitive subject. The school is constantly on guard against tainted research funding, such as when a pharmaceutical company is connected to an independent trial of one of its drugs. Darren believed that I had no ulterior motive in the Diebold analysis and that the VoteHere relationship had simply slipped my mind, but he nonetheless questioned my judgment and said it was "very unfortunate" that I hadn't considered this important factor. I shared my plan for issuing a press release immediately, and we decided to go to Dennis O'Shea, executive director of communications and public affairs at Johns Hopkins, to get him involved.

Reaction to my press release was mixed. In it, I explained the situation fully and honestly, resigned from the advisory board of VoteHere, returned all stock options, none of which had been exercised, and asked Hopkins to review all of my outside consulting activities. Some reporters wrote back saying that they understood completely and that it didn't change their take on the underlying story about security flaws in Diebold's code. Others were less forgiving. Kim Zetter, a *Wired News* reporter with whom I'd spoken several times during her smart and professional coverage of the Diebold story, sent a note that really stung. Her thoughtful rebuke put the problem into clear perspective and deepened my already profound regret:

Avi,

This is very unfortunate news. This is the kind of "disclosure after the fact" that corporations and politicians engage in on a regular basis that produces cynicism and apathy in the public and that causes people like you and your colleagues to criticize them.

While I appreciate that you have now disclosed this information (and that it came from you rather than from Diebold or a third party), you can probably understand that it places the story that I or any other journalist wrote about your report into question. It also puts a small stain on our professional integrity, as well as the integrity of your colleagues who participated in the report. Readers will rightly want to know how you could have forgotten stock options and membership on the board of a Diebold competitor, no matter how dated that membership is, and they will want to know how I as a journalist failed to uncover that connection. You emphasized to me that you had made the study of electronic voting systems a primary part of your research. It is therefore hard to believe that in the time that you have been criticizing these systems, you failed to recall a relationship that you established with the manufacturer of one of them. . . . The fact that you never profited from Vote-Here is irrelevant. A formal relationship existed, which you did not disclose at the time when it was most necessary to disclose. The suggestion of impropriety is just as harmful as actual impropriety.

Kim

The upsetting things about Kim's note were that everything she said was true, and that she, too, had the misperception that Diebold and VoteHere were competitors. The next day virtually every major news outlet carried a story about it, most with some variation on the headline, "Author of Study Had Link to

Competitor." My voice-mail box back in Baltimore filled up, and I spent most of my time at the Crypto conference answering reporters by phone and e-mail. VoteHere helped out greatly, confirming that we had had no contact since I signed on as an adviser. And even though Jim Adler stated for the record that my stock options had been rendered worthless, we went ahead and signed an agreement nullifying them and terminating our relationship.

Because I had issued the press release so quickly, before Lynn Landes or anyone else could "break" the story, the first wave of news articles presented the information using my own words, which was ideal. A day later Diebold issued a press release, describing itself as "extremely disappointed" by this latest development, which, it said, raised the question of bias in the Hopkins study. Where Kim Zetter had stung me with the truth of her words, other outlets, such as the *Atlanta Journal-Constitution*, riled me with their outright falsehoods. The article in that paper sought to discredit our report rather than address the subject of my behavior and stated that our research had been "funded" by VoteHere. I couldn't even imagine how they came up with that one.

The damage control that was taking up all of my time had nothing to do with correcting the record or airing the truth. I found myself responding to statements in the press that were either beside the point or completely unconnected to reality. Some reporters, for example, described me as "on the board" of VoteHere, implying that I was a director and not just an adviser. The coverage and the debate were spinning out of control, and I found it more and more difficult to contain my frustration with the whole process. I can't count the number of knee-jerk, defensive answers that I gave to stupid questions and would give a lot now to be able to take back. During a live national interview on CNN, the reporter set me up with some softball questions and then asked me to comment on whether my financial link to a Diebold competitor biased me and my study. I responded instinctively, like a cornered animal, snapping that it was a lie that Diebold had been feeding the press. I told the reporter that I was a technical adviser to a software company that did not compete with Diebold, and rather than attacking innocent academics, maybe Diebold ought to have been fixing its insecure machines. Of course, I didn't do myself any good by losing my cool when I could have just calmly explained the origin of the story. Amazingly, this business about my being "on the board" of VoteHere still comes up—mostly from reporters who have had Diebold or the Georgia secretary of state's office whispering in their ear—but these days I'm better able to give a quick, matter-of-fact answer and move on.

The public questioning of my honesty and integrity struck at the heart of my sense of self. I was hurt and insulted when articles suggested that I might manipulate research for personal financial gain. In the weeks following the revelation about VoteHere, I received all manner of awful, hurtful correspondence from all over and learned the hard way that sometimes the harder you try to argue, the worse the situation becomes. One Hopkins alumnus wrote Darren Lacey demanding I be fired. A man named Jim Gessner went even further and sent a letter to the university claiming that my critique of Diebold had devastated not only his daughter, who worked for Diebold, but their entire community. He went on to imply that the university was itself to blame and that in addition to being fired I should be immediately arrested for fraud. "This criminal activity cries out for atonement . . . and *punishment!*" Mr. Gessner concluded.

There were, however, some moments when light broke through the clouds. The most surprising, and in an odd way the most moving, letter I received came from Doug Lewis, executive director of an entity called the Election Center. This vendor-funded group had harshly criticized me and our report. In my mind, he had, until now, ranked just behind the ITAA's Harris Miller as an outspoken and dangerous critic. His letter revealed how reviled I was by the vendor community, but as unsettling as it was, his letter also restored, in some measure, my faith in people.

Avi:

I sent this message below to a small group of about 40 people.

I am already catching heat from some of our own folks who believe I am playing by "Marquis of Queensberry" rules when that is not the case from all quarters in this deal. I hope that at some point . . . the emotional aspects of this matter will subside. And, I am not without my share of emotional response in this so I am not casting stones here.

I want you to know from me that I will not be a party to anything that impugns integrity. We can all fight hard about our beliefs in how best to serve the voters and the process without stooping to trying to destroy personal reputations.

I misspelled your name and it was one of the reasons that I could not find your email address to send this message to you directly before now. . . . I asked David Jefferson to assist me with that but his auto responder says that he is out of town.

Here is part of the message Doug Lewis sent:

By the way folks:

For the record, while I disagree with the way Avi handled the "study" and while I think he and others have not used balanced and fair judgment on some of their charges, I do not for a second believe that Avi Ruben [*sic*] could be "purchased" in this deal. I believe that each of the folks who have engaged us in this fullisade [*sic*] about voting systems are honest in their beliefs. And I think it does little good to impugn the integrity of people we disagree with on issues. I do not mind vigorous debate and I know that folks on both sides of this issue can get heated in discussing it . . . me included.

I sent Doug a sincere and heartfelt thank-you note in which I said that the VoteHere fiasco was the hardest thing I'd endured in my professional life. We ended up speaking on the phone for an hour and a half. Neither of us made much impact on the other's way of thinking, but we established a cordial relationship, something that perhaps I alone in the computer security community can claim to share with Doug Lewis.

9

Election officials in Carteret County are scrambling after a
machine malfunction destroyed 13 percent of the
ballots. . . . "The bottom line that we have heard from the
manufacturer is that these votes are not missing. They're
lost," [the county commissioner] said. "It's very
disheartening. It really is."
—*WRAL News, Raleigh-Durham, North Carolina,
November 8, 2004*

I had been at Johns Hopkins for only about eight months
when this whole episode began. Certain parts of the university population were familiar and comfortable for me—our
institute, the computer science department, the media relations
office—but I knew very little about the overall administration
of the school. Coming to Hopkins had been something of a
gamble. When I left AT&T Labs, other universities had offered
me tenure, but Hopkins had been more cautious, promising only
that I would come up for tenure in my first year. Ann and I were
confident enough in the situation to have sold our home in New
Jersey and moved with our three children to a comfortable
house in a quiet suburb of Baltimore, where we were all settling
in quickly and happily, though I had no actual job security. Now,
with the VoteHere "scandal" swirling all around me, I couldn't

stop thinking about how tenuous it all suddenly felt. I was still in Santa Barbara when I saw the e-mail from Marc Donohue, associate dean of research, a man I'd never met. When I realized I had battles to fight closer to home, the panic rose inside me. Perhaps I overreacted, but the thought of uprooting the family again was too much.

Marc intimidates some people. An academic superstar, he had become chair of the Hopkins chemical engineering department at age thirty-three while still an associate professor, and he had continued to rise through the university hierarchy. He is sharp-witted and perceptive and doesn't like to waste time. His e-mail was short and to the point and had been copied to Andrew Douglas, the interim dean of the School of Engineering, who was critical to my tenure promotion.

Avi:

I was stunned by your posting on the Media Relations web site. Why were these relationships not disclosed? Below is an email exchange we had last year in which I made your responsibilities clear.

He referred to an e-mail exchange in which, just after my arrival at Hopkins, I had asked my department chair if there was a procedure for clearing my advisory board relationships with the university. The chair had sent me on to Marc, who sent me a copy of the Hopkins policies regarding external consulting and advising. The policies required me to disclose all advisory board agreements. As upsetting as Marc's message had initially been, I now started to breathe just a little easier. Suddenly, I was happy about the orderly, methodical, always-be-prepared elements of my personality that my family had been teasing me about for years. Not only had I read the policies and sent a note to my department chair disclosing them, but I was able to find that note quickly in my e-mail archives. I sent it immediately to Donohue, with copies to the dean of engineering and Darren Lacey.

But that original e-mail, as much as it showed I had been aboveboard with the university, didn't completely ease my nerves or my conscience. I called Darren Lacey to ask what to do about Marc Donohue and to try to gauge how much trouble I was really in. Darren was supportive, as always, but very frank with me. He explained that Marc's job required him to be extra sensitive to conflict-of-interest matters and anything else that made Hopkins look bad, and right now that meant me. Some of the bad press about me was starting to treat the university as guilty by association, and I needed to get on the same page with Marc as soon as possible. Following Darren's advice, I set a meeting with Marc for the day I returned from Crypto.

I had heard the expression "dark night of the soul" but never really experienced anything like that until the night before my meeting with Donohue. I lay awake, tormented with anxiety about my family, my home, my career. And if I didn't have enough to worry about, Darren had told me that the university lawyers were considering opening a formal investigation into the VoteHere matter. He assured me that could only help me, by getting the whole thing out in the open. I imagine that was supposed to comfort me, but the effect, of course, was quite the opposite. In the middle of the night, Ann woke up and did her best to talk me down. I knew that my sin was one of omission, that my worst crimes were naïveté and inattentiveness, that in the intensity of the moment I hadn't stopped to think through all the angles, that I hadn't done anything terribly wrong. But what I didn't know was whether these sins were enough to do me in. It was the low point of my working life.

I had no idea what to expect when I walked into Marc Dono-hue's office the next day. Marc fixed me with his penetrating gaze and, without saying anything, managed to convey the impression that he could effortlessly tear me apart with words. Before he got the chance, I asked if I could start by just telling him the full story. "Please do" was all he said. I started at the beginning, telling him how Bev Harris had found the Diebold code on the Web, how David Dill had called me, and how we did the analysis. I even went into some of the details of the security problems. I was relieved to see that the basic issue of insecure voting machines genuinely disturbed Marc. I went on, explaining that I was on nine advisory boards and that it had never even crossed my mind that my VoteHere relationship was relevant. They were not even a competitor of Diebold's, and it was ludicrous to connect our analysis in any way to my position with VoteHere. For dramatic effect, I concluded by saying that even if I had been the largest shareholder in VoteHere, it wouldn't have changed the facts we had uncovered in our analysis. I probably should have left out that last part.

I did not know at the time that Marc was deeply immersed in handling a major lawsuit involving Johns Hopkins. He asked me to write up for him some thoughts about how such problems could be avoided in the future, not just for me but for anyone in the university, but I didn't hear from him again regarding Diebold or VoteHere. Several weeks later, he invited me to lunch at the Hopkins Club and asked me to fill him in on what was going on in the e-voting world. I've had nothing but pleasant dealings with him since.

FOR A WHILE, it felt like I'd never shake the VoteHere story. I remember sitting down to what I thought would be a quiet, peaceful breakfast at Crypto a couple of days after Marc Donohue's first e-mail, scanning the national headlines in my complimentary copy of *USA Today*. Right after "Congressman Could Be Charged in Fatality" and "Two Dead in Ohio Shooting," I read, "Voting Machine Researcher Linked to Rival." It was really just a news "brief" and was generally accurate and straightforward, but it called me out by name, and there was that word "rival" right up there in the headline, the one misleading word that turned it into something wicked.

I'd see mentions of VoteHere in different media, but after a while the coverage started to even out a little. About a week later the *Baltimore Sun* ran a piece that made the point that had been missing from too many stories. The article quoted Steve Fought, a staffer for Ohio congresswoman Marcy Kaptur, who said, "He should have made those interests known up front and early, but I don't think that takes away from the validity of the report."

The thing about the press is how quickly you can become yesterday's news, but on campus they weren't quite through with me. Several days after my meeting with Donohue, Darren Lacey called me in and confirmed that Johns Hopkins was indeed launching a formal investigation. Darren tried everything he could think of to convince me that this was really no big deal, but it didn't work. He told me just to tell the truth and everything would work out fine, but the very idea of it was freaking me out. Even with people like Darren expressing sympathy and support, the experience was humiliating.

As much of an ordeal as it was for me, perhaps it was fairly routine for the investigators, because I had to ask Darren a few weeks later what had happened. I was glad I asked. He told me that I had been completely cleared and that they had determined that Diebold and VoteHere were not competitors. They had spoken to a few other people involved, like the CEO of Vote-

Here. Darren added that I had behaved admirably, even going beyond the call of duty by resigning from the company's technical advisory board. So maybe I had gone a little overboard, but at least it demonstrated commitment to doing the right thing. Finally, the sky was brightening a little, but there was one last bit of business before things were right again at Hopkins.

William R. Brody, the president of Johns Hopkins University, is an imposing figure. An MD and PhD and a former professor of electrical engineering and radiology at Stanford, Brody had co-founded several medical device companies, contributed to the invention of magnetic resonance imaging (MRI), and joined the President's Foreign Intelligence Advisory Board before assuming the leadership of Hopkins. Each year President Brody hosts a lavish dinner for new faculty and their spouses at Nichols House, the stately Georgian home that serves as the presidential residence on campus. President Brody and his wife stood at the door and greeted the three hundred or so guests as they arrived. As Ann and I shook hands with the president, he read the name on my badge and said with a warm smile, "So, you're the big troublemaker." I guess that answered my question about whether he knew about the VoteHere flap.

The president addressed the assembled guests, welcoming us to the Johns Hopkins community, after which we helped ourselves to a sumptuous buffet and found a place to sit and eat. Later, when I went back to the buffet table to get some rolls, I ran into President Brody, who ended up walking back with me to the quiet study where I had left Ann to fend for herself with a group of strangers. Brody pulled up a chair and quickly became the focal center of the room. He charmed us all with his graciousness and intelligence, sharing personal stories about his early days as a researcher and describing for us the career path that had led to his becoming president of Hopkins. With everyone put at ease (well, at least I tried to pretend to be at ease, speaking with the university president), he changed tack and asked me about the electronic voting research. He listened carefully as I told him the whole saga, after which he expressed his belief in the importance of the work I was doing and even went so far as to say that he was glad someone like me was on the case. I thanked him with all the mature professionalism I could muster, even though inside I was bursting like a kid with both pride and relief. Later, as we left, President Brody bid Ann and me good-night, telling me to stay out of trouble, but adding with a wink, "Well, don't get into too much anyway."

10

It's not the people who vote that count.
It's the people who count the votes.
—*Joseph Stalin*

You'd think that signing up as an election judge would be easy, considering the state's aggressive effort to recruit volunteers to fill a well-publicized shortage. Perhaps it is easy if you don't have a reputation that precedes you, but I got the impression that the local election administrators weren't in too big a hurry to have me on the team. Mary Kiffmeyer, secretary of state for Minnesota and president of the National Association of Secretaries of State, had suggested it to me after my talk at the NIST symposium in Gaithersburg, Maryland. Mary's suggestion was simple but profound: I needed to focus less on pointing out problems and more on finding solutions. In practical terms, she thought I should become an election judge in the March 2004 primary—Super Tuesday—and learn about the process from the inside.

I filled out an application at a local grocery store and was told to wait for a call from the Baltimore County Board of Elections.

I waited. And waited. Eventually, I gave up and called the county office; I was connected to the head of elections, who sent me to a mandatory training session a couple of days later. The state of Maryland, of course, had signed on with Diebold, and so I trained for two hours on every aspect of voting with the Accu-vote TS machine, the very machine we had analyzed. I was taught how to teach people to vote electronically, certified as a qualified election judge, and told I'd get a call assigning me to a precinct.

Again, the call never came, so I dialed the board of elections in frustration and explained my situation. They assigned me to the Trinity Assembly of God in Timonium, about twenty minutes from my home. (I would have to cast my own vote by absentee ballot.)

On primary day, I reported to my precinct bright and early. There were two chief judges, one from each party, and seven other judges, and as we all introduced ourselves I immediately sensed a frostiness. Marie and Jim, the two chief justices, mentioned somewhat disdainfully that they'd read about me in the paper that morning. It turned out that the *Baltimore Sun* had run a story that morning about my working as an election judge in which I was quoted describing the other judges I had trained with as being in the "grandparent category." In fact, most of my colleagues on primary day were a generation or two older than me, and they all seemed ready to take me on. The *Sun* reporter had suckered me, pressing me for a comment on the age of the other judges, which I resisted. He finally had asked me if they were "in the grandparent or parent category," and I answered, "The former." I should have known better, but this was, after all, my friendly local paper.

Four of the judges were "book judges," one from each party

handling A–K and the same for L–Z. One judge handled provisional ballots, used by people who for some reason were not listed in the registration books. Provisional ballots are mandated by HAVA, although implementation has varied from state to state. The remaining two judges, "unit judges," assigned voters to particular machines. I was a book judge, working with Andy, who was in fact a grandfather of many and whom I grew very fond of as the day went on. Andy's wife, Anne, and Sandy were the other two book judges. Actually, there were two Sandys that day, plus Bill, the provisional judge, who was married to chief judge Marie. One of the Sandys, Joy, and I made up the younger contingent of judges. Joy was the most knowledgeable of the judges, having trained dozens of groups on both the Diebold machines and election procedures in general. Her experience was invaluable, and the chief judges deferred to her on any major issue that came up.

The job of the book judges was to find the index card bearing each registered voter's name and cross-check it with the roll booklet, a process that generally went smoothly. I wore a little electronic sleeve on a string around my neck; once a voter's registration was confirmed, I slid a smartcard into the sleeve and pressed a few buttons to designate whether the voter would receive a Democratic or Republican ballot, depending on how they were registered (for the primary). The system also provided options for magnification on the screen and even audio for the blind.

We set up the voting booths in the hour before the poll opened at 7:00. This involved unplugging all the machines and moving them because they were facing the wrong way, but the machines have a five-hour backup battery and were unaffected by this. As we were setting up I realized that there was no way I was going to be another anonymous election judge. My colleagues knew exactly who I was, and they knew about my public criticism of electronic voting, and of the Diebold machines in particular. More disconcerting, my suspicions that the election officials had known my reputation when I applied was confirmed when Diebold representatives arrived at our poll about 6:30. Even though my badge read simply "Avi," I heard the Diebold people refer to me as "Professor Rubin." One of them was Bob Urosovich, president of Diebold Election Systems.

Before the first voters arrived, we printed a "zero tape" of each machine—a list of all the candidates with a zero next to each name, representing the total number of votes cast so far, to show that there were no votes already stored in the machine. This didn't impress me much. I knew anyone could write a five-line program to print out a zero tally regardless of what was in the machine. It was a bit like a magician who quickly shoots his cuffs to show there's nothing up his sleeves before he performs a magic trick. When we opened the polls at 7:00, Jim, one of the chief judges, cast the first vote to a round of applause from the rest of us.

As the early-morning voters slowly trickled in, the unspoken tensions with my co-workers persisted, and then burst into the open when the media showed up. First was a camera crew from a local Fox News station who asked the chief judge for an interview with me. A call to a "super judge" at the main office confirmed that an interview was out of the question, even when the reporter insisted on speaking directly with the super judge. A hostile exchange with the chief judges ensued, which made me question my decision to work the polls. This was very far from what I had hoped for and anticipated from the experience, and I tried to explain that to the other judges as soon as the room was empty of voters. I told everyone that I took my service there very, very seriously. I had no intention of staging any kind of publicity stunt and would not speak to any reporters. A reporter and photographer from the *Baltimore Sun* didn't help my cause any by showing up a few minutes later. I kept my promise not to speak to the reporter, but the photographer was allowed to take pictures of me checking in voters and programming smartcards, causing yet more angry words. The other judges made no effort to hide their unhappiness with my presence, and I felt miserable.

I tried again to make a little speech about my desire to be just another objective judge, but things seemed to go from bad to worse when one machine spit out a voter's smartcard. We gave him a new card, which worked, but the incident concerned me, and I asked Marie to count the ballots and check them against the count in the machine after the voter left. The count was fine; the smartcard really had failed, but afterward I overheard Jim complaining to Joy that I had only made a big deal about it because the *Baltimore Sun* reporter was there. Of course, nothing could have been further from the truth, but nonetheless, the chief judges made a new rule that not only could I not speak to reporters, but for the rest of the day, in order to make sure I'd have no contact with the press, another judge would escort me if I left my post to go to the bathroom or even to get a drink of water.

Fortunately, the business of running the poll kept us all occupied for the next several hours. Every hour or so we'd check our counts, comparing the number of voter authorization cards (different from the smartcards) kept in an envelope taped to the machine to the number of votes counted by the machine. We also compared the totals on the machines to the totals in the registration rosters we used to check people in. For something that was billed as a paperless electronic election, we sure spent a lot of time counting pieces of paper throughout the day. I tried to make peace during the breaks and gingerly explained the security problems of electronic voting machines to Marie and Joy. They listened carefully and caught on quickly. They admitted that they had been quite unhappy about my being there and had been ready for a fight, but now thought I maybe "wasn't such a bad guy after all."

All of the tallies were stored on digital memory cards in the voting machines. When the polls closed, we loaded the data from each card onto one machine that we called the zero machine. Once all the tallies were loaded from the individual memory cards onto the zero machine, we were supposed to send them via modem directly from the machine to the board of elections, but we couldn't get the phone line to work properly. The machine did print out the final tallies, however. One copy went onto the outside door, where talliers and poll watchers were waiting. The other went into a pouch with the memory cards, each wrapped in a printed tally of the machine it came from. The two chief judges drove the pouch to the board of elections office.

What amazed me most throughout the day was that the voters, with very few exceptions, really *loved* the electronic machines. They positively raved about them, frequently commenting on how easy they were to use. Perhaps I wasn't expecting people to have much of anything to say about the physical act of voting, but I certainly wasn't prepared for so many to volunteer such praise. Of course, nobody mentioned anything about security or verifiability, or even seemed curious about how their votes were recorded. The issues that had been consuming me for months couldn't have been further from their minds, and I couldn't bring them to anyone's attention in my role as an election judge. Even when one woman complained to Joy that she wanted a paper ballot to verify, I kept my mouth shut. Joy assured the woman that these machines represented the state of the art and there was nothing to worry about, while casting a sly wink in my direction.

The lightest moment of the day was also the most curious. From in front of one of the machines, a voter deadpanned, "What do I do if it says it's rebooting?" Everybody froze. Chief judge Marie seemed to literally turn white, and Joy's jaw dropped. My heart started to beat faster. Then, with a comedian's timing, the man laughed and chirped, "Just kidding." A couple of seconds of silence passed before the room erupted with roaring laughter. The reaction to the joke was very telling. The relief that everyone felt when we realized that nothing actually had happened revealed that, for a moment at least, people were willing to believe that something did happen. And yet I have no doubt that prior to the incident, each of the other judges would have claimed that a reboot was impossible.

As the day passed I felt much less uneasiness with the other judges. Some of them even began to have some good-natured fun at my expense. In the afternoon, a voter complained that she had received a Republican ballot, although she was registered as a Democrat. I had mistakenly miscoded her smartcard, and both of the chief judges were required to void her ballot. I was the only one to make such a mistake all day, of course, and the more senior judges weren't about to let me forget it, pointing out my youthful carelessness and incompetence and making sure we all knew that the old folks could manage an election just fine on their own, thank you very much.

On my way home after the polls closed, I called my office voice mail and heard messages and requests for interviews from ABC News, the *Baltimore Sun*, the *Washington Post, Wired News*, CNN, several radio stations, and even the *New York Times*. I assumed they all believed my experience as a poll worker would have given me important new insights, but at that moment my biggest concern was that too many people around the country would share the enthusiasm of my own election co-workers, who believed that Super Tuesday had been a clear triumph as far as the voting process went. As more people became excited about e-voting, the more quickly and widely it would be adopted, increasing the risk when someone finally decided to exploit the very real weaknesses in the system.

My experience as a poll worker on that primary day, seven months after the release of our original report on the Diebold machines, was rich, rewarding, edifying, and humbling. I wrote my thoughts down while they were still fresh in my mind and posted them on my Web page. Summaries of that write-up began appearing the next day in a number of news outlets, including *Slashdot*, which is followed religiously by the technical community. By the end of the day, my Web logs showed forty thousand hits. The *Baltimore Sun* invited me to prepare a condensed version, which it published as an op-ed column. Later I learned that one of the reasons I was invited to testify at the first public hearing of the U.S. Election Assistance Commission was my experience as an election judge. The commissioners, it seems, had read my story.

Since that time, the debate over electronic voting machines versus voter-verifiable paper ballots has intensified on the national stage. In June 2004, I saw Mary Kiffmeyer again, and she graciously complimented me on my service as an election

worker and expressed the hope that others would follow my example. When I thanked her for suggesting that I volunteer, she
didn't even remember that she had ever done so. Ms. Kiffmeyer,
like many of the secretaries of state with whom I've worked or
spoken, always impressed me as thoughtful, open-minded, and
dedicated to the safeguarding of our elections. I would come to
long wistfully for such fair and noble public officials in the days
to come.

11

U.S. voters calling in to a toll-free number had reported more than 1,100 separate incidents of problems with electronic voting machines and other voting technologies by late Tuesday during the nationwide election. In more than 30 reported cases, when voters reviewed their choices before finalizing them, an electronic voting machine indicated they had voted for a different candidate.

—The Industry Standard, *November 3, 2004*

n the months following the release of our Diebold report in the summer of 2003, I began to feel like I had turned my whole life over to e-voting. The press became my constant companions. I was a newcomer to the issue compared to people like Doug Jones and Rebecca Mercuri—or David Dill, who had launched a national grassroots movement in support of voter-verifiable paper ballots—but the media had adopted me as the unofficial spokesperson on e-voting security. On a slow day I'd get three or four calls, and some days two or three times that. I'm not the kind of guy who's comfortable with a lot of loose ends, and I prided myself on returning calls and answering e-mails promptly, but now I just couldn't keep up. Getting an assistant, as some suggested, really wasn't practical, but Gerry Masson finally assigned the institute's receptionist to help me out.

It was as if I had taken on a second full-time job as an e-voting expert, and some of my Hopkins colleagues had to share that burden. For example, my office is in a hospital building, and the school required that someone from the media relations office accompany any camera crews who came to interview me there, to protect patient privacy. Poor Phil Sneiderman had to drive out from his office several times a week—sometimes several times a *day*—to escort them and their equipment. I was on *The Today Show* a couple of times and on NBC's and CBS's national evening news shows, and I even made an appearance as the "Moment of Zen" on *The Daily Show* with Jon Stewart. NPR made me a frequent guest, featuring me on *All Things Considered* and *Morning Edition*. And then there were the local stations and newspapers. One of the more interesting interviews was with the Academy Award–nominated documentary filmmaker William Gazecki for a new film in progress called "Invisible Ballots."

I found myself quoted in magazines ranging from *Time* and *Newsweek* to *Vanity Fair, Sports Illustrated,* and even *Playboy,* of all things. *Baltimore* magazine, which I was used to seeing in the supermarket checkout line next to the gossip tabloids, named me one of ten "Baltimoreans of the Year." There's nothing like trying to pay for groceries when the person next to you in line shouts, "Hey, that's you!" while pointing out your picture in a magazine.

I had decidedly mixed feelings about the press. On the one hand, the attention was gratifying and a little flattering and made me feel a part of something big and important. On the other hand, it was simply overwhelming and at times painfully tedious and repetitive. Many times I wished I could just turn it off for a while, but inevitably I'd be drawn back in, compelled to respond to some new piece of misinformation fed to a journalist by a vendor or election official or the ITAA. If I tried to limit the interviews, I'd find my point of view underrepresented in the stories. Finally, I resigned myself to handling as many interviews as possible and giving each one my full attention, but it wore me down.

Granted, the technical aspects of the subject are complex, but the need to educate journalists could grow frustrating, particularly for the majority who had no technical background or had never bothered to read our report. I was further exasperated by reporters who got their information from published accounts from other reporters, regardless of the accuracy. Often, I would politely suggest that reporters read the study and then call back if they had questions, but they tended to be working on deadline and would plead with me to just summarize the main points. One reporter told me that a state election official had told him that our report was full of flaws and inaccuracies, but when the reporter asked if the official had actually read the report, he was told, "No, but everybody knows what's in there." This kind of thing reminded me of Dan Quayle's infamous condemnation of Salman Rushdie's *The Satanic Verses* and made me want to just throw up my hands.

The press was also just as guilty as anyone else of trying to politicize the e-voting debate. One day I did a telephone interview with Al Franken for his self-described liberal radio show, *The O'Franken Factor*. Franken made no effort to hide his political leanings, of course, and kept trying to get me to talk about Diebold's relationship with the Republican Party. (The CEO of Diebold was an outspoken supporter of Bush and a heavy contributor to the Republican Party.) For my part, I tried to steer the conversation back to technical issues, but Franken did get a laugh out of me when he asked if I knew what he meant by the term "ying-yang." He was referring to a leaked internal memo from Diebold in which an employee had recommended that if states demanded a paper printout of ballots, the company should charge them "out the ying-yang." Fairly soon after that I did a nationally televised live interview on Fox News, Franken's perennial nemesis in the media. The fact that the e-voting debate could command the attention of two such openly biased and politically opposed media outlets was ultimately a testament to the truly nonpartisan nature of the issue.

As my public profile grew, I became a lightning rod for anybody with anything even remotely connected to electronic voting on their mind, from legitimately interested individuals to nuts of every stripe. Losing political candidates called to see if I could help them blame the machines for their defeats. Vendors, of course, came out of the woodwork, bursting with ingenious secure solutions and poised to revolutionize voting around the world. Some were more persistent than others, and a number of them would get indignant with me if I didn't respond. One vendor cornered me at a congressional hearing after I had testified and demanded to know why I hadn't gotten back to him; I didn't even recognize his name. After the VoteHere experience, I wanted to stay as far away from vendors as possible, even those like Avante or Populex, which appeared to have good products that provided for voter-verifiable paper ballots.* I needed to maintain my impartiality. I deflected any questions from the press about specific companies or products, limiting my answers to comments about specific technologies.

---

* I have no direct relationship with or interest in either of these two companies.

One forward-looking company was TrueVote. Athan Gibbs Sr., the company's CEO, was tragically killed in a car accident in Tennessee a week before he was due to give testimony about his technology in Ohio. Voting (especially electronic voting) is catnip to conspiracy theorists, and in what might have been the most bizarre conversation of my entire experience with e-voting, I got a call from someone who warned me that Gibbs's accident was no accident at all and I should watch my back. I laughed, thinking about how the caller might have reacted to that white Diebold van that had given Adam and me such a start in California. I saw one article that described people who denied any connection between Gibbs's death and his advocacy of paper-based e-voting as "coincidence theorists." That would be me.

My need to remain impartial also affected my relations with the countless activist groups that sought me out. I spoke with the national office and several regional chapters of the American Civil Liberties Union (ACLU) and was contacted by several grassroots organizations that had sprouted up in support of paper ballots. I consistently declined invitations to speak before any of these groups, even when I had the chance to share the dais with prominent activists and celebrities. DeForest Soaries of the Election Assistance Commission later told me that this posture strengthened my credibility. I once asked Soaries why he hadn't invited David Dill to testify at the EAC hearing on e-voting, and Soaries said plainly that Dill struck him as having too much of an activist agenda. I had heard that Dill's advocacy didn't sit well with many people in Washington. I felt that was terribly unfair, and told Soaries that Dill would have been just as useful on such a panel as I was, if not more so.

Several high-profile plaintiffs in suits against their states asked me to serve as an expert witness. Some offered to pay me, but I did not feel that I could take money for any of my voting-related activities. I couldn't help everyone who called, but I did sign several affidavits, including one in the case of Jeffrey Liss, who had brought suit in Maryland. When Liss voted on the Diebold machine, the Senate race did not appear on his ballot, causing an *undervote*. An undervote occurs when someone votes in one race but not in all the others in a given election. Liss submitted a provisional ballot, but it was denied. Further investigation revealed that there had been more undervotes in the Senate race on that particular machine than the expected norm. As of this writing, Liss's case was still pending.

At Hopkins, the alumni magazine and the engineering magazine ran long stories about me. My alma mater, the University of Michigan, ran an interview with me about e-voting in one of its magazines. I couldn't help remembering the words of wisdom that my PhD adviser, Peter Honeyman, had passed on to me. He told me to always think of myself as a computer scientist and to make sure I stayed general. "Don't let yourself be pegged as a security guy. Don't forget that the field of computer science is much broader than that." Well, now it was worse. I wasn't even just a security guy. I had assumed an alter ego: e-voting guy.

I couldn't escape it, even in my off-hours. Everywhere I went, it seemed like e-voting was the only thing anyone wanted to talk about with me. This one saw me on television, this one read about me in the newspaper, this one had a few things to get off his chest about e-voting and the future of democracy. The neighbors, the women in my wife's mah-jongg group, the other parents at school, the people at our synagogue—everybody had something to say. Even the contractor working on our house got into the act. "Hey, you're that e-voting guy from television!" he said, before giving me chapter and verse on the total corruption of our government. He went so far as to tell me that he thought I should run for the Senate.

ON SUNDAY, AUGUST 8, 2004, the *San Jose Mercury News* ran an editorial that I wrote at the request of its editors. The same day I appeared in a *New York Times* editorial, in the *Chicago Tribune*, in the *San Antonio Express*, and on the *CBS Sunday Morning* show. The editorial served as a neat summary of my arguments against electronic voting, focusing on reliability rather than on security. Diebold had adopted an irritating new PR tactic, which was to say that our study was "flawed" because it concentrated on the risk of people hacking into voting machines via the Internet and their machines were not networked. We had never said they were, and rather than get into that argument again, I used the editorial to make a point about the fragility of both electronic data and the large-scale computer systems on which we increasingly depend. I spoke of how often and easily computer malfunctions occur and the impact of such problems, citing the August 2003 blackout in the Northeast and a recent grounding of flights by two major airlines. I showed how we had as much to fear from fraud and malicious intent as we did from unanticipated malfunction. I concluded by making the argument that given these frightening possibilities, paperless voting that allows for neither voter verification nor meaningful recounts poses an unacceptable risk. I had been all over the media for months, arguing this point or that, and although I had addressed the larger picture in front of computer scientists and governmental officials, I was glad to finally have the chance to make my case directly to the public, in one clear and focused statement.

The attention and responsibility, the long hours and the travel, were taking their toll at home too. We were a young family, just settling into a new community when my colleagues and I released the Diebold report. Our daughter Elana was four, and our twins, Benny and Tamara, were only one. Ann had stopped working when the kids were born, but three little children can be overwhelming under the best of circumstances, and now I was around even less than before. It wasn't uncommon for me to call home at the last minute, saying I'd be home late because I had to go downtown to a television studio for an interview. The mornings were no better—some radio stations would call at 7:00 A.M., or even earlier, for interviews. More than once they acted as an unwelcome wake-up service for the family. We were able to get au pairs and babysitters, but it wasn't the life we'd envisioned. Elana was old enough to really feel her daddy's absences and started complaining whenever I had a trip coming up. "Oh, man, you travel too much," she'd complain. Who could blame her? Ann was supportive and believed in my work, but over time the novelty of it all wore off, and she had more trouble keeping the little daily disappointments from building up.

The same inadequacies and resentments I was feeling at home were mirrored professionally. For starters, an academic whose work receives a lot of press has to be prepared for some amount of grief from his peers. There are some purists who believe that if the general population is interested in something, it must not be "real" science, and plenty of them have no problem letting you know how they feel. On one occasion, at a research retreat sponsored by DARPA, the Defense Advanced Research Projects Agency, a professor I respected a great deal turned on me in a very public way in front of my peers. In the middle of a technical discussion, he silenced the room with one sarcastic crack: "Well, I'm sorry that I don't publish my research in the *New York Times*. I just write code." The remark came out of nowhere and wasn't even relevant to the discussion, but it was clear to me that this professor had been saving it for a while, waiting for a chance to slip it in. When he left the room, other conference members told me to shrug it off and said that they admired the work I was doing, but none of that reassurance eased the embarrassment or relieved the doubt that his remark caused.

These barbs weren't reserved just for me. My student and colleague Adam Stubblefield took some heat as well. Adam presented our paper at the IEEE security and privacy conference, in front of hundreds of attendees. When the floor opened up for questions after Adam's presentation, the first question came from a famous professor from a prestigious university. In front of the entire conference, he asked Adam, "How is this 'research'?" The question would have been totally inappropriate for any speaker, much less a graduate student, and it seemed a clear attempt to embarrass Adam and, by extension, me. If the professor had a problem, he should have brought it to the conference program committee, which, in selecting the paper had obviously concluded that it belonged. Personally, I don't believe a high profile in the press is any measure of the value or quality of research, but that opinion is not shared by everyone in the competitive world of academic politics, some of whom never let us forget it.

As if I didn't already know the high cost of my involvement in e-voting, the point was driven home when I received my teaching evaluations for the spring 2004 semester. My relationship with my students had always been a point of pride for me. I took my teaching as seriously as my research and devoted a huge amount of effort and attention to my students, which was re-flected in the consistently high marks on my evaluations. Many of my students that spring were very complimentary, but a handful complained that I'd missed lectures because of my e-voting work. Several got pretty nasty, saying that I was full of myself and had let all the press and commotion interfere with my teaching responsibilities. The comments stung more than I wanted to admit.

Not quite a full year into the e-voting mess, I was struggling, running around trying to do the right thing by too many people and in the end not serving any of them well enough. I wasn't spending nearly enough time with my family. Some of my stu-dents felt neglected and were bitter about it. My research was on hold, and I was spending every waking moment it seemed talk-ing to reporters, racing off to e-voting workshops, meeting with politicians and election officials, and giving lectures and writing articles on voting. I had given over my life to an obsession with e-voting and election security. I kept reassuring Ann, telling her that it was just one very, very unusual year and that life would get back to normal after the election in November. I prayed that it was true, or at least that she would believe it more than I did.

12

An electronic voting machine in hotly contested Ohio added
3,893 votes to President Bush's tally in a suburban
Columbus precinct, even though there are
just 800 voters there.
—New York Times, *November 6, 2004*

O n August 6, 2003, I stepped out of my office for a couple
of hours; when I got back, I was surprised to find that
there were nine voice-mail messages waiting for me.
Clearly, something was up. My e-mail box was also full of messages from reporters, all wanting my comment on the latest development. Robert L. Ehrlich, the governor of Maryland, had
ordered an independent review of the Diebold voting system
that the state had purchased. He had assigned that task to Science Applications International Corporation (SAIC), a company
already under contract to the state.

At first, this seemed like great news, but quickly my mind
started spinning with the possible implications of what I might
say to the press about it. My gut reaction was to offer strong support of SAIC and to say that I was sure its report would be consistent with ours. I knew people at SAIC and thought they were
top-notch. In fact, SAIC had purchased my former employer,

Bell Communications Research (Bellcore); before the turnover I had met several of the SAIC technical staff and was impressed. I had no doubt that Diebold machines were no good, and I was confident that a well-respected company like SAIC would never compromise itself by endorsing them. And yet I worried that if for some reason SAIC went easy on Diebold in its report, it would have the effect of discrediting our report.

The state of Maryland was a major client of SAIC's, generating a lot of revenue for the company. Various Maryland election officials, including Linda Lamone, the director of elections for the state, had publicly attested to the total security of the Diebold voting machines and had never missed an opportunity to try to discredit us and our report. I was fairly sure that this crowd would exert whatever pressure they could on SAIC to write a positive report, but I had no way of knowing how SAIC would respond to such pressure. Of course, I knew I was too much of a novice about politics to trust my own judgment. Perhaps Ehrlich, as a new Republican governor, had some other agenda. After all, Linda Lamone was a holdover from the outgoing Democratic administration, and for all I knew, Ehrlich ordered the study hoping to show that purchasing the machines had been foolish in the first place.

Ultimately, I told every reporter I spoke to that I knew SAIC, that I believed the company was excellent at what it did, and that I supported the governor's move. I added that I was confident that SAIC would give Diebold failing marks, since it was sure to discover the same security problems that we had. It was something of a gamble, but I thought that somehow having such comments on the public record might make it more difficult for SAIC to bow to any pressure it might encounter.

The SAIC report would be available in four weeks, the governor said, and since the press had to cover something, it became four weeks of dueling public speculation. The state officials would express confidence that SAIC would vindicate their commitment to Diebold, and I would say, with equal certainty, that SAIC would vindicate our report. Gilles Burger, the chairman of the state board of elections, said:

> I welcome Governor Ehrlich's decision to order an independent review of Diebold's electronic voting system. We at the state board have confidence in the Diebold system and our tailored implementation methodology. We hold the utmost value in voter integrity and security and take credible claims of vulnerability seriously. We are also a learning organization. We are wholly committed to taking all appropriate steps to safeguard the voters' right to an accurate election process. This review is an important step toward that goal.

The ambiguity of the statement disturbed me. Burger wanted people to believe that the state was open and receptive to criticism and commentary and genuinely committed to fair and secure elections. At the same time, he was acting almost as if an endorsement of Diebold was a foregone conclusion.

As the anticipated release date of September 6 approached, I grew more nervous. A *Wired News* story claimed that the report had been written and even quoted someone who had read it, but it wasn't clear whether the state of Maryland was planning to release the report in its entirety or only in selected bits and pieces. Once again, I was buried in phone calls and e-mails, but by that time there just wasn't anything left for me to say. I repeated yet again my certainty that SAIC could only find that the machines were insecure.

A week passed, and no report. I imagine that there were, at best, only a handful of people in the state of Maryland who felt the tension of that waiting period as acutely as I did. A second week passed, and then the state announced that the report would be released at the end of one more week. Darren Lacey pointed out that people often release at the end of the week if they're concerned that a story is negative or unflattering, but who knew?

Finally, the week of September 15, 2003, arrived, and I started counting down the days. On Friday, September 19, the residents of Maryland got a surprise, but it had nothing to do with e-voting. Hurricane Isabel slammed into the state's coast, creating havoc and devastation. In our area, over a dozen people were killed, and millions lost power. For the time being, Governor Ehrlich and the rest of the state government had more critical priorities than the SAIC report, and frankly, so did I. Our house was without power and water for days, and with three very small children at home, e-voting was the last thing on my mind. As if the press hadn't already been making me nuts, however, a few reporters actually called and asked me to comment on the hurricane's hitting our shore on the very day that the SAIC report was to be released.

Maryland and its people got back on their feet, and the state announced that the report would be released on September 24. Adam, Yoshi, and I went to work early that morning with our nerves frayed. I knew that our study had been accurate and fair and would be difficult to challenge, but I couldn't shake the premonition that SAIC was going to find fault with our work and declare the Diebold machines secure. It seemed clear that the whole purpose of commissioning the SAIC study was to put the Diebold controversy to rest and that doing so would inevitably involve discrediting our report. Everyone had a theory about it. David Dill predicted that the SAIC report would be a total whitewash. SAIC would find a few minor problems that Diebold could easily fix, and that would be the end of it. Bev Harris dug up a connection between SAIC and VoteHere that apparently had huge and terrifying implications, which I confess I never quite understood. Lynn Landes managed to link my relationship with VoteHere and SAIC's relationship to VoteHere, a sure sign of conspiracy. Thank God she never discovered I had once worked for Bellcore (which was purchased by SAIC)—an amazing oversight considering that she unearthed the far more obscure fact of my advisory position with VoteHere.

Kim Zetter of *Wired News*, the reporter who had rightly scolded me in an e-mail after the VoteHere fiasco, called just before the news conference was to begin. If there was any ill will, she gave no sign of it. Kim wanted to be the first to get my reaction to the SAIC report, and we set up a three-way call with the two of us and one of Kim's colleagues who was at the conference with a cell phone. The reporter sat in the front row and held her cell phone in the air like a microphone so that I could hear everything live.

The news conference opened with the announcement of a Web address where the SAIC report would shortly be available. I immediately tried to access it, but it wasn't there yet, and I applied myself furiously to hitting the reload button. Meanwhile, I could hear Gilles Burger begin to speak, and my heart sank. Citing the importance of voter confidence, he said that the SAIC study would put to rest any doubts about the security of the wonderful machines Maryland had purchased from Diebold. Others spoke, all reiterating the same theme. The machines were fine. End of story. Kim was asking me if I could believe what I was hearing, but I was too stunned and depressed to respond.

The next time I looked at my computer screen, though, the report was there, entitled "Risk Assessment Report: Diebold Accuvote-TS Voting System and Process." I quickly scanned the executive summary, which referred to our study as the "Rubin report." The whole report felt vaguely like the result of a negotiation, as if the precise wording of each phrase had been argued over, perhaps by Maryland officials and Diebold people, or representatives of SAIC. I felt more encouraged when I got to the third paragraph of the summary:

> In the course of this Risk Assessment, we reviewed the statements that were made by Aviel D. Rubin, professor at Johns Hopkins University, in his report dated July 23, 2003. In general, SAIC made many of the same observations, when considering only the source code. While many of the statements made by Mr. Rubin were technically correct, it is clear that Mr. Rubin did not have a complete understanding of the State of Maryland's implementation of the AccuVote-TS voting system, and the election process controls or environment. It must be noted that Mr. Rubin states this fact several times in his report and he further identifies the assumptions that he used to reach his conclusions. The State of Maryland procedural controls and general voting environment reduce or eliminate many of the vulnerabilities identified in the Rubin report. However, these controls, while sufficient to help mitigate the weaknesses identified in the July 23 report, do not in many cases meet the standard of best practice or the State of Maryland Security Policy.

This was what I was looking for. "In general, SAIC made many of the same observations, when considering only the source code," meant that our understanding of the source code had been correct, and this conclusion blasted a hole in Diebold's characterization of our study as "flawed." SAIC's observation that I had clearly and repeatedly stated both my assumptions and my lack of expertise in election procedures represented the kind of professional acknowledgment that academics seek and that the Diebold spin doctors had long neglected. The level of professionalism and seriousness revealed by the report so far bolstered my confidence that SAIC's conclusions would match ours.

I was still listening over the phone to the lovefest in Annapolis when I got to the final paragraph in the executive summary. I knew we had been vindicated.

> The system, as implemented in policy, procedure, and technology, is at high risk of compromise. . . . Any system implemented using the present set of policies and procedures would require . . . mitigations.

There would be no reasonable way to spin that. The point here was obvious. Had we not published our analysis, the state would never have commissioned the SAIC study and most likely Maryland would have deployed a voting system that was "at high risk of compromise." What was not obvious was why the overriding message at the press conference seemed to be exactly the opposite. Any reporters in that room who took those public statements on faith and didn't read the report for themselves would assume that the "Rubin report" had been off base and that Maryland's machines were secure. Most would not only assume it—they would write it. The prepared remarks wrapped up, and a question-and-answer session followed. The *Wired News* reporter on the other end of my phone connection asked if Kim or I had any questions, which was pretty exciting, since I'd never been in a position to ask questions at a press conference before. I fed the reporter the following:

"Listening to this press conference, it sounds like the Diebold machines get A-plus marks for security. And yet, I'm looking at the printed report that you handed out, and the last paragraph states that the system, as implemented in policy, procedure, and technology, is at high risk of compromise. How do you explain the disconnect between what is in the written report and what you are saying?" She did a great job with the question. I think it was Burger who answered with some vague comments about there always being room for improvement but basically everything was fine. At the very least, the question would have sent any responsible reporters in the room to check out the executive summary in the report, which is all I could have hoped for.

Before I hung up the phone with Kim, I scanned the rest of the SAIC report. I was stunned to see whole sections, including some that were clearly security-sensitive, completely missing, replaced only with the totalitarian-sounding "Redacted." Most of the security issues that we had found were also cited in the SAIC report, but it was as if anything else they found had been excised from the public version of the report. About two-thirds of the report had been redacted. I wasn't surprised that new problems had come to light. After all, we had looked only at the source code, and only for a few days. SAIC had had more time, four weeks, and more resources, not to mention the cooperation of Diebold and access to the machines' complete system and to the documentation.

Despite the spin that Maryland officials tried to put on it, SAIC had found plenty of vulnerabilities in the Diebold system, and even the redacted version of its report blasted many of these.* Considering that it had left intact passages that strongly condemned the Diebold system, I couldn't imagine how bad the redacted passages must have been. I had to believe that

---

* A link to the text of the SAIC report can be found in the resources section at the end of this book.

Maryland had sat on the report for almost a month because it was negotiating the wording of the text of the report with SAIC; later I learned that was exactly what had happened. To its credit, SAIC kept the primary message intact, while clearly making every effort to accommodate and satisfy its client. This alone, however, was enough to worry me greatly. I could maybe understand reworking the language of a report to please a commercial client—but to do that when the client was the people of a state and the subject was the security and reliability of the voting process? That made no sense. I wondered who needed protecting in this situation, and how that could be a higher priority than the public's interest in the unvarnished truth.

The SAIC report contained an "Appendix B" that provided detailed commentary on the assertions we had made in our initial analysis. SAIC agreed with many of our findings and stated that other problems we had identified could be handled by proper procedures. David Dill weighed in on Appendix B, saying, "Appendix B, which contains a point-by-point analysis of the claims of the Johns Hopkins/Rice report, is filled with irrelevant responses and misconstruals of the original threats in that study." He also pointed out that the SAIC report had failed to make the most useful and most obvious recommendation available—that these insecure touch-screen DREs should *not* be used in elections.

After reading the report through several times, I spent the rest of the day handling calls and e-mails from the media. A few callers were clever enough to ask if I had been on the other end of the cell phone in the hand of the reporter in the first row asking the tough questions, and I acknowledged that it had been me. The reporters told me that Maryland had justified the heavy redacting of the report by saying that it didn't want to provide "a roadmap for the attackers." Computer security experts have heard this "security by obscurity" argument time and again and know that it holds no water. If a system is truly secure, there is no roadmap for an attacker, and therefore nothing to hide. I had to wonder what the state felt it needed to keep under wraps. A number of people tried in vain to get a copy of the full report. Even the Freedom of Information Act proved unhelpful, and to this day the redacted portions of the report remain hidden from the public.

At the end of that long and draining day, my obsession with e-voting was forced to take a backseat to my obsession with soccer. I had tickets that night to the Women's World Cup games at RFK Stadium, and not even an interview with NPR's Pam Fessler was going to interfere with that. I did a quick interview by phone, and it was aired the next morning, just as Kim Zetter's story was hitting the wire.

In her article "Maryland: E-Voting Passes Muster," Zetter summarized the response to the SAIC report: "Despite a summary in the report that states the Diebold system used in several state elections is 'at high risk of compromise,' the election officials and representatives of the company that wrote the report said they now have confidence in the Diebold system, and that the state will proceed with its $55.6 million contract to purchase the machines." She quoted Gilles Burger, who called the report "the most robust information-system risk assessment ever conducted in the nation for election systems." Zetter played up my point of view, which was that the SAIC report had validated our work and that there was cause for concern, since the state of Maryland, "instead of responding with a sense of urgency, seems to be looking for ways to move ahead with Diebold despite this report." Additionally, I questioned the wisdom of returning the Diebold machines to the very same independent authorities that had tested—and passed—them in the first place.

Burger's comments revealed some very misguided thinking. To begin with, how could he have been proud of the fact that this was "the most robust information-system risk assessment ever conducted in the nation for election systems"? We were talking about the integrity of the democratic process, and this risk assessment wouldn't have been conducted at all if it hadn't been for our initial report. Moreover, SAIC had spent only four weeks on it. How was it that nobody had thought to do such a robust risk assessment—or *any* risk assessment—before this? Worse yet, the state officials were actually boasting about the effort, despite the incompetence it so plainly revealed. Furthermore, their comments illustrated a totally misplaced concern about voter *confidence* rather than about the actual security of the system. The notion that a sense of confidence was more important than whether the confidence was in fact justifiable spoke volumes about the triumph of image and perception over substance.

Diebold supported Maryland's campaign to prove that the emperor had clothes by issuing a press release claiming that the study had reaffirmed the security of its Accuvote TS. (One Internet organization awarded the company its "Black Is White" award for this outrageous example of public relations spin.)

For Immediate Release

Diebold Election Systems Moves Forward with Maryland Voting Machine Installation Governor and State of Maryland Issue Independent Review of Diebold Machines: Study Yields Positive Results

McKinney, Texas—Diebold Election Systems today commended Maryland Gov. Robert L. Ehrlich, Jr., and the state for undertaking the most exhaustive study to date into the security of an electronic voting system. By commissioning the highly-respected Science Applications International Corporation (SAIC) to conduct an independent study of all aspects of the Diebold system operating within the state's specific elections procedures, voters in the State of Maryland can now rest assured that they will participate in highly secure and accurate elections.

"We are pleased to be moving forward," said Thomas W. Swidarski, president of Diebold Election Systems. "The thorough system assessment conducted by SAIC verifies that the Diebold voting station provides an unprecedented level of election security."

SAIC's analysis, released today, was based on Maryland's recently adopted Information Technology Security Policy and Standards. Upon reviewing SAIC's recommendations, and the new Maryland standards, state officials announced that Diebold Election Systems' touch-screen voting systems meet these standards, which include enhanced encryption and programming flexibility.

As the country moves to modernize its elections systems to ensure access and fairness to all voters, we can expect further enhancements to the various systems in the marketplace. But, as the Maryland study shows, the technical foundation has been laid to provide the most efficient, secure and accurate elections possible. "Maryland has established a new standard of excellence for the electronic voting process," said Thomas W. Swidarski, president of Diebold Election Systems. "Diebold Election Systems looks forward to supporting the state as it strives to be a leader in election reform in this country."

It seemed that Diebold hadn't read the same study that the rest of us had. The SAIC report stated explicitly that Diebold

did not meet the Maryland standards. The heading in section
2.1.1 of the report read, "AccuVote-TS voting system is not com-
pliant with State of Maryland Information Security Policy &
Standards." The first paragraph under that heading clearly
stated:

> All Information Technology (IT) systems must be compliant
> with the State of Maryland Information Security Policy and
> Standards. The AccuVote-TS voting system does not meet all of
> these requirements.

Diebold's press release completely ignored this. The company
was pretending that the results of the SAIC study were utterly
positive. Diebold would demonstrate its contempt for truth
many times over the next year—whenever it threatened to tar-
nish the company's image, not to mention its bottom line.

Many other media outlets joined *Wired News* in covering the
SAIC report. The lead in the *Washington Post* story was, "An independent review released yesterday found 328 security weaknesses, 26 of them critical, in the computerized voting system
Maryland has just purchased, flaws that could leave elections
open to tampering or allow software glitches to go undetected."
Strangely, this information was followed by a quote from Governor Ehrlich: "Because of this report, Maryland voters will have
one of the safest election environments in the nation." It was
like some Orwellian nightmare, except it was real. Under the
headline "Voting System Found to Have Election Risks: Independent Study Says MD's Touch-Screen Device Is Vulnerable to
Tampering," the *Baltimore Sun* ran this quote from Gilles
Burger: "We believe we are prepared to roll out the revised
Diebold machines." The *Sun* had allowed me to weigh in: "If
you commission SAIC to study and write a report, and they

come back and say that the system is insecure, it would seem to make sense to suspend the plans to use the system until SAIC writes a report saying that it is safe to use them. It defies logic that Maryland has these plans to proceed given what SAIC says about the Diebold machines." The story continued, "Diebold officials said yesterday that the results confirmed that the electronic systems were safe to use," and went on to quote Diebold marketing director Mark Radke in a deft example of newspeak: "After the completion of the SAIC analysis, it's obvious that the security of our system is very, very sound, and voters should feel comfortable using our terminals. The current version of the product is very solid and accurate."

WITH ALL THE publicity swirling around the e-voting issue, the public grew increasingly uneasy. Sensing the need to address these concerns in a public forum, the Maryland House Ways and Means Committee scheduled a hearing on e-voting security for November 13 in Annapolis. The only two people scheduled to testify were me and Linda Lamone, the state's chief election administrator. They told me I would have half an hour to speak, followed by questions from the state House representatives. I had no intention of making any missteps and began my preparation by meeting with Johns Hopkins government relations people. They wanted to think the hearings through from all angles so that I could be sensitive to any hidden agendas or to anyone trying to make some political hay out of the situation. They worried, for example, that some members of the House, where the Democrats still held a majority, might be trying to embarrass the new governor publicly over his inappropriate response to the SAIC report. Hopkins even sent one of their staffers along with me to Annapolis for the testimony.

At the hearing, the icy stares from Linda Lamone and the

other assembled election officials made it clear that I wasn't exactly a welcome presence. The large press contingent watched with detached amusement as I set up my projector and prepared to make my statement. I didn't see many friendly faces, but some people at least made an effort at cordiality. David Heller, who worked for Lamone, introduced himself and greeted me warmly. Looking around, I could see that they had set up a Diebold Accuvote TS machine, and I overheard someone saying that Linda Lamone's testimony would feature a demo.

I began my testimony by describing the flaws we had found in our first analysis of the Diebold source code. Although I tried very hard to use language understandable to a nontechnical audience, it's hard to say how successful I was. I used the simplest and clearest examples I could think of. I described the smartcard attack we had devised, the one that would allow someone to vote more than once. I told the committee members that they would at some point see a demonstration by the state election officials in which a smartcard would be inserted into the machine and a vote cast. Next, the officials would insert the smartcard into another machine, demonstrating that it would not work, that voting twice would be impossible, and that thus there could only be one vote per person. I went on to say that I had no doubt that this demo would work exactly as planned, but that they needed to understand that it was in fact meaningless. It did not account for the real threat, which was that a voter could have another homemade card in his or her pocket and would not have to use the officially provided smartcard to cast multiple votes. I concluded my testimony by imploring the committee members to make the full contents of the SAIC report available for the public to read. I quoted directly from the report as part of my effort to convince everyone in the room of the gravity of the situation. I emphasized the need for transparency in the election process and pointed out that making the full report available would be an important first step in that direction. At the end, I shifted gears and turned to some possible solutions to the problems I had raised. I explained why voter-verified paper ballots would help bypass the security problems in the machines and why those paper ballots would help reduce the chances of rigging an election.

Most of the members who spoke up during the lively question-and-answer session that followed seemed to grasp the seriousness of the system's vulnerability and asked the kind of clarifying questions that helped sharpen some of the points. Not all of them, however, were so receptive. LeRoy E. Myers Jr., a Republican, got a bit combative. He began by excusing himself, with sarcastic politeness, for not being as smart as me, but insisted that he would trust these terrific electronic voting machines over paper any day. He wanted everyone to know that he simply did not believe me when I said that the machines could be rigged. I really had no clue how to respond to such head-in-the-sand intransigence, but rather than try to argue with him point for point, I simply restated my expert opinion that any electronic machine can be programmed to do whatever its developer wants. I emphasized that the Diebold code in particular was so amateurish that it would be easy to hide malicious code in any of the bugs in the system, and that the Accuvote TS didn't even have the basic protection one would expect to find in a home computer system.

When Linda Lamone took my place at the witness table, she didn't even make eye contact with me. Her testimony focused on the challenges of running credible elections and on the wondrous improvements brought about by the Diebold system. She dismissed the idea of using paper, saying it would be impossible to administer and prohibitively expensive. What she didn't say was that once you had already spent a bundle on a faulty system, the fix would only add to the bill. But my feeling was that if the proper analyses had been done in the first place, the state wouldn't have been in that position and could have saved itself some money. Lamone chose not to bother with the demo.

In the Q&A session, the members got right to the point, asking her to respond to my claim that malicious code could be hidden in the machines. She referred the question to one of her staffers, who in turn said he wasn't qualified to answer. The questioner pushed Lamone, asking if anyone in her large entourage might be able to answer the question, and she eventually called on Frank Schugar of SAIC, who had been the project manager for SAIC's risk assessment of the Accuvote TS. A rustle and murmur went through the room as people sensed an important interchange about to take place. It was like watching a great pinch hitter coming off the bench, and I have to say, Schugar knocked it out of the park. He started by praising me and my qualifications, even saying that they exceeded his own, and telling the committee of his great respect for me as a scientist. Linda Lamone was visibly squirming as he continued. He said that my points were valid, and he agreed that it was easy to hide malicious code in software. Although he declined to say that it was impossible to detect malicious code, he allowed that it was extremely difficult, that the chances of someone hiding code without being detected were 99.9 percent.

Afterward, the scene in the corridor outside the hearing room was straight out of a Hollywood movie. I was at one end, and Linda Lamone was at the other, each of us surrounded by a clamorous crowd of reporters shouting questions, jabbing microphones at us, or scribbling furiously in their notepads. At one point, as though on cue, the two gaggles of reporters simply switched places and started firing the same questions all over again. I agreed to step aside for a one-on-one taped conversation with Fraser Smith from Baltimore's NPR affiliate, and his first question made my jaw drop. "Linda Lamone just stated on the record that by questioning the security of the voting machines, you are undermining democracy. How do you respond to that?"

I wanted to answer that it was one of the dumbest statements I had ever heard but only managed to stammer out, "She actually said that?" It went against everything I had been taught to believe. I had been raised to question what I did not understand. I had been trained in the scientific method, to gather evidence and evaluate it objectively. I believed that democracy allows— no, depends on—the open exchange of ideas, that thoughtful dissent from authority is the truest expression of the democratic ideal. But here was a government official—one in charge of voting no less—saying that if I were a real patriot, I'd keep my mouth shut. She seemed to me to be acting more like an old Soviet-bloc bureaucrat than like a person entrusted with safeguarding our free elections. Her implicit call for blind faith in the government begged the question of a citizen's *obligation* to call something into question, to undermine the public's confidence when necessary and appropriate.

Lamone's remark was featured in the story when it aired, prompting many angry listeners to contact me, expressing outrage over her comments and stating their support of our efforts. The blow to Lamone's credibility was immediate, and I believe that her insistent reiteration of the comment throughout the next year ultimately sealed her political fate. In September 2004, the Maryland Board of Elections suspended Linda Lamone as administrator, although she appealed the suspension and was reinstated by a judge who declared that the action would cause too much disruption in the process so close to an election. The press reported that Lamone's suspension was purely political in nature, stemming from the fact that Republicans now were running the statehouse and intended to put their own people into important positions.

When the reporters were done, I got a chance to speak with Frank Schugar, who approached me with a compliment on our work on the Diebold analysis. In addition to being smart and likable, he confirmed my high opinion of SAIC's professionalism and expertise. Schugar made it clear that the state had acted alone in making the redactions, but declined to give me a copy of the complete report and did not breach any confidences. After our conversation, I was more convinced than ever that the state had tried to discount the report's negative findings regarding the Diebold machines and that SAIC had probably helped somewhat. Still, in the end, although the report clearly damned the Diebold machines, plenty of stories in the press repeated what the various spinmeisters wanted them to rather than taking the real truth out of the report itself.

The Annapolis hearing received almost as much press as the initial release of the SAIC report. The *Baltimore Sun* printed a lengthy summary that included Schugar's complimentary comments about me and ended, "Del. Jean Cryor, a Montgomery County Republican, said she came to the briefing thinking Rubin would be a 'smart aleck, though he was far more credible than I [had] thought. I was disappointed the [election] administration didn't come forward with stronger and more focused responses to what his complaints had been since day one.' "

Soon enough I found myself appearing live on NPR with Governor Ehrlich. After the usual pleasantries—I thanked him for ordering the SAIC review and recognizing the importance of analyzing the security of election systems, and he offered his administration's gratitude for the good work our research team had done—I pressed the case for making the complete SAIC report available to the public, arguing that if there were no security problems cited in the redacted portions, there would be no problem making them public. The longer the state kept it under wraps, the more it would appear that the state was hiding something. Ehrlich dodged the point entirely, making only some general statements about safeguarding voting rights and democracy and the need for using the best possible technology. I chose not to push the point any further, partly out of respect for his position and partly so as not to spend all our airtime beating a dead horse. A number of my computer science colleagues criticized me for that decision.

The state of Maryland's continued defensiveness about the Diebold machines was illogical and inexplicable to me. Officials responded to every criticism of the machines as if it were a criticism of the officials who had chosen them. We had given them more than enough ammunition with which to make the whole thing Diebold's problem, not the state's, and even to get out of the contract if desired. But nobody blinked, nobody budged. Some activists went so far as to speculate vaguely about shady financial ties between Diebold and some state election officials. Not only was there no evidence to support those suggestions, but after my VoteHere experience, there was no way I was going anywhere near that. Besides, those innuendos only distracted from the real issue. The Diebold machines simply did not meet the basic requirements for a safe and secure election, but rather than demand a quality product from her vendor and do right by the state of Maryland, Linda Lamone preferred to spend her energy convincing the world that my colleagues and I were a bunch of incompetent rabble-rousers.

13

The right of voting for representatives is the primary
right by which other rights are protected.
—*Thomas Paine*, Rights of Man, *1791*

M aryland wasn't the only state in the union struggling
with electronic voting. Even before the release of the
SAIC report, the state of Ohio had suspended its purchase of Diebold voting machines, citing security concerns.
Washington Technology, a tech publication for computer systems people in government, reported, "The state of Ohio is delaying its $136 million purchase of new voting equipment and
services until it can complete further security reviews and audits
of electronic voting devices, Ohio Secretary of State J. Kenneth
Blackwell announced today." The media was watching Ohio
closely—not only did the state plan to adopt electronic voting,
but Diebold was headquartered there. I had heard from two
Ohio politicians, state senator Teresa Fedor and U.S. congresswoman Marcy Kaptur, both concerned about the relationship
between state officials and the company.

The four leading national vendors—Diebold, ES&S, Hart

InterCivic, and Sequoia—were competing for e-voting contracts in Ohio, and Secretary Blackwell had commissioned two studies of the various machines. I read both reports, from InfoSENTRY and Compuware Corporation, when they were released in early December and found both of them a little lightweight, especially in comparison to the SAIC report. Compuware's report, the more lengthy and useful of the two, identified security risks and other flaws in all the machines. Of the fifteen security risks it identified in the Diebold machine, Compuware labeled five "high-risk."

Compuware presented most of its findings in the form of a huge table with columns labeled "Requirement," "Test Scenario," and "Test Results." Under the first head would be the basic security requirement, such as, "The system shall prevent modification of the voter's vote after the ballot is cast." The next column described Compuware's test methodology for that requirement, and the last contained its findings. I found the table generally superficial and at times misleading. Here's an example:

Requirement	The system shall ensure that a voter's exact voting record cannot be traced back to the voter.
Test Scenario	Try to access the information needed to reconstruct a voter's exact voting record.
Test Results	Individual vote records are not reported from the AccuVote-TS or tally software. The voting records are not kept in any specific order and the voter is kept

anonymous. The system will provide for
provisional voting by creating a sequence
to list provisional voter records.

The lack of detail in the test scenario rendered the results
meaningless, as far as I could tell. How had Compuware's testers
tried to access the information, and how many different ways
did they try? Had every possibility been considered? Recall that
our study had found fault with the use of an LCG (linear congruential generator), which should not be used for cryptography,
as the mechanism for keeping the votes in random order; there
was no indication that anybody who understood cryptography
had participated in the Compuware analysis. The report was full
of such inconsequential test scenarios, all with predictable results. Imagine if the same methodology had been applied to a
test of the old Ford Pinto's tendency to explode when rear-
ended. Compuware's safety analysis might look like this:

Requirement	Car should not blow up when hit from behind.
Test Scenario	Hit car from behind.
Test Results	Car did not blow up.

Unless we know that they have tested all manner of rear-end
collisions, at different speeds and angles, such a report tells us
exactly nothing about the real safety of the car. The testers
could have hit the car with a grocery cart.

Compuware missed other, more basic problems. At one point,
the analysis stated that the vote tallies on the Accuvote were

secure because Diebold had encrypted them using DES, the encryption technology that had been broken five years earlier.
That Compuware seemed oblivious to the fact that DES had
been replaced by AES, arguably the best-known development in
cryptography over the last decade, boggled my mind. Even
such a flawed analysis, however, managed to identify fifteen security flaws in the Diebold machines. The InfoSENTRY study
had been largely incomprehensible—Doug Jones called it
"bizarre"—and yet Diebold's tireless PR machine again found a
way to spin the reports as good news, issuing yet another glow-
ing, and brilliantly misleading, press release.

The real good news was that these two half-baked studies
would not be the last word on the subject. On January 26, 2004,
a reporter called me and asked what I thought of the "Red
Team" analysis of the Diebold machines. That got my attention.
In a Red Team exercise, skilled attackers are hired to try to pen-
etrate a system as a test of its security. As opposed to the theoretical analysis our group did, a Red Team uses any and all
available means to break the system. Red Teams can demonstrate beyond doubt that theoretical attacks are in fact feasible.
It is important to note that even when a Red Team attack fails to
break a system, one still cannot conclude absolutely that the system is secure. Where one Red Team fails, another might still
succeed.

I asked the reporter if she was saying that someone had hired
a Red Team to attack the Diebold voting machine, and she told
me that such a team had been hired by the state of Maryland,
which I found hard to believe. The state would be risking serious
embarrassment if the Red Team succeeded in compromising the
system. I wondered if the state was hoping to claim proudly that
it had staged an attack that had failed, but it also dawned on me

that state officials probably didn't understand that even a failure by the Red Team wouldn't confirm that the system was secure. At the same time, I knew that any decent Red Team would crack the system wide open. I couldn't get much else out of the reporter, who quickly realized that she was telling me things I wasn't supposed to know, but she did suggest that I could perhaps learn more from Bill Arbaugh, a computer science professor at the University of Maryland in College Park.

Bill Arbaugh and I knew each other well enough that we had once even contemplated starting a business together. Bill is a specialist in computer security and had worked at the National Security Agency (NSA) before graduate school. His doctoral thesis was the foundation for what became Microsoft's "Trusted Computing Initiative." Bill is one of the best, and if he was really part of any team analyzing the Diebold machines for Maryland, the state was in for trouble. I fired off a note to Bill, asking if a report was about to be released and if I could get my hands on an early copy. Bill got right back to me, wondering how I knew anything about it. He also told me he couldn't tell me anything for a few days. He copied his message to Mike Wertheimer, whom he called the project director for the report. Wertheimer had been the NSA's senior technical director—as high as it gets for a techie.

At the same time, I started getting calls from other reporters asking if I knew anything about a study by RABA Technologies. I could only respond that I'd heard something was up, but had no information at all. I was as curious as they were. RABA described itself on its website as a consulting company, composed largely of former NSA employees. Clearly, someone was leaking information to the press.

When Bill Arbaugh finally called, he confirmed that RABA

had performed a Red Team exercise and that there was a report. As he described it, the state of Maryland had brought in RABA to do the analysis with a charter to discredit me and my report. However, as soon as the RABA team scratched the system's surface, they started finding flaws. Lots of flaws. They were as stunned as we had been by the dismal quality of the system. RABA had confirmed that our theoretical smartcard attack was feasible. But there was a catch. Despite all the corroboration, Bill told me that I would not like the report. Apparently, the report contained harsh critical comments about me, and he felt the need not only to warn me but to apologize. He had argued against including those statements in the report, but Mike Wertheimer, the project leader, had overruled him. I was stunned. Mike Wertheimer and I didn't even know each other, and I couldn't imagine what he could possibly have against me, especially if our studies backed each other up. My excitement about reading the report was suddenly tinged with dread.

The twenty-five-page RABA report was released in its entirety. Though the executive summary made no mention of me, it didn't hesitate to cite serious security problems:

The State of Maryland election system (comprising technical, operational, and procedural components), as configured at the time of this report, contains considerable security risks that can cause moderate to severe disruption in an election. However, each of these vulnerabilities has a mitigating recommendation that can be implemented in time for the March 2004 primary. With all these near-term recommendations in place, we feel, for this primary, that the system will accurately render the election and is worthy of voter trust. However, between the March and November elections we strongly feel that additional actions must be taken to mitigate increasing risks incumbent on a system that will receive broad scrutiny. Ultimately we feel there will be a need for paper receipts, at least in a limited fashion.

This seemed perfectly reasonable, and again validated the importance of our study. The RABA report went on to say that its highest priority was to discuss both our report and the SAIC report. When I turned to the section titled "The Hopkins Report," Bill's warning suddenly made sense.

> A considerable amount of press has been given to the "Hopkins report." The subsequent revelation of a conflict of interest involving one of its authors with a Diebold competitor has only served to detract from the substance of the results. Moreover, many of the statements made by the authors appear to function more as attention gathering "sound bites" than actual statements of fact. Every attempt was made to sort through this posturing and evaluate the specific software vulnerabilities the authors uncovered.

There it was. VoteHere. How long would that haunt me? It made me angry to see them repeating the old nonsense about VoteHere being a Diebold competitor. In any event, it had no bearing at all on RABA's findings. I could only assume that either Wertheimer had some problem with me or that he had been pressured by Maryland officials to call our report into question. I needed to get beyond that gratuitous swipe, though. It didn't ultimately diminish RABA's scathing critique of the Diebold system.

> The single most relevant finding in this section is that the general lack of security awareness, as reflected in the Diebold code, is a valid and troubling revelation. In addition, it is not

evident that widely accepted standards of software development . . . were followed. . . . We generally agree with the conclusions of the Hopkins Report on purely technical matters.

The RABA report backed us up on the voter access smartcards
and the supervisor cards used by administrators, stating, "The
passwords used to protect both types of smartcards . . . appear in
the source code that the Hopkins team evaluated. Initial guess
on the [red] team's part provided instant access to the cards' contents." The RABA team had been able to duplicate smartcards
and produce bogus smartcards, just as our report had predicted.
RABA added, "The use of hardcoded passwords is surprising
both as an inferior design principle and in light of them being
published openly in the Hopkins report. It must be assumed
these passwords are well known." The study went on to confirm
our assertion that the supervisor cards, as well as the smartcards,
could be duplicated. These cards control the functions of the
voting machines and could be used to cancel votes or even termi-
nate the election.

RABA also focused on the fact that the bay used to lock the
memory cards containing the vote tallies in the voting machine
was protected by a simple key that was identical in every individual machine. Red Team members were able to duplicate the
keys at a local hardware store, but in truth they didn't need to,
since they had been able to pick the lock so easily. They showed
that once the lock was picked, they could easily change or erase
votes on the memory card. It almost went without saying that if
those cards were lost or stolen, all of the votes placed on that
machine that day would be lost. There was no other place—no
CD or other drive—where the votes were stored. RABA filled
two pages with serious attacks against the integrity of the code.

Its Red Team had taken all the attacks that we had theorized and actually carried them out. Further, they had analyzed the system in its entirety, whereas we had examined only the source code. RABA had found even more serious problems in the back-end processing server, which accumulates vote tallies from various precincts. The report was devastating: "The team also verified that the current version of the . . . software still contains many of the vulnerabilities widely published on the Internet. It was disappointing to see that no obvious attention was paid to addressing these weaknesses." When I read that the Red Team was able to completely annihilate the server and totally control all of the election data, I understood that the Diebold voting machines were much, much worse than I had realized.

At the time, I thought I was witnessing the beginning of the end of Diebold. I couldn't imagine that anyone would want to go anywhere near those machines now that this information was public. *Wired News* hit the nail on the head the next day with a story that read, in part, "Computer security experts hired to hack electronic voting machines manufactured by Diebold Election Systems found that flaws in the machines could result in malicious insiders or outsiders stealing an election. . . . The report stated that the Diebold machines did accurately count the votes but could be compromised."

Diebold's response was predictable. I agreed with the subhead on its press release, but the rest was shameless fabrication, stating that the RABA findings were consistent with those of SAIC and that both had validated the machines. I heard through the grapevine that when Mike Wertheimer read Diebold's release, he blew his top. RABA's exercise had proven that the machines were insecure in every conceivable way. Anyone could easily change or delete votes without being detected. With minimal effort, hackers could break into the central tallying server where the votes from different precincts were accumulated and do virtually anything they wanted. And yet. And yet. There was Diebold, once again, smilingly telling the world that black was white and white was black. It was dispiriting to watch the work of so many honest, committed, and hardworking scientists so handily dismissed by the corporate propaganda machine.

Several weeks later, Mike Wertheimer sent me a long, conciliatory e-mail, acknowledging the misbehavior of Diebold and the Maryland officials. He asked me to consider him a friend. Reading between the lines, it was clear that he regretted the personal comments about me in the RABA report. I have met Mike several times since then, and indeed I do consider him a friend. There's no denying that parts of the RABA report were painful to read, but that was a small price to pay in light of what it accomplished. I believed then, as I do now, that RABA's work demonstrated a "clear and present danger" to American democracy.

THE WIDESPREAD PUBLICITY and intense scrutiny focused on the Diebold Accuvote TS machine used in Maryland eventually led to a lawsuit that pitted one Linda against another. Linda Schade, an activist who founded an organization called TrueVoteMD, sued the Maryland Board of Elections and Linda Lamone, seeking a temporary injunction against the state's use of Diebold DREs in the November election. In its suit, TrueVoteMD demanded that voters be given the option to vote on paper ballots. I was absolutely overwhelmed with work at the time, but the group's lawyers, along with Cindy Cohn, called on me to testify about the problems we had found with the Diebold machines. I had testified before Congress and the Election Assistance

Commission and had been involved in more than my share of public debates. I had even been trained as an expert witness for patent litigation cases, but none of those ever made it to trial. I had never been through hostile, or even aggressive, cross-examination on the witness stand, and I was more than a little apprehensive.

A couple of days before the hearing, the plaintiff's lawyers and I went over the questions they intended to ask. I recommended against some of the questions and suggested a few of my own. It wasn't even clear if the complaint I had read was the final version, and the feeling of flying blind made me even more nervous. Not for the first time, I turned to my wife, Ann, a lawyer with litigation experience, who spent two hours the night before the trial putting me through a kind of mock trial. The practice, and Ann's expert grilling, proved invaluable. She told me how to handle myself on the stand and how to watch for lawyers' tricks and traps. One small advantage I would have over many other expert witnesses was that I was working pro bono. Lawyers always try to discredit experts by making sure the jury sees them as hired guns, but I had passed on a potentially lucrative consulting job in order to make myself available.

The next day I dug out my suit one more time and drove to Annapolis. I took the stand shortly after I arrived, and despite the nerves and my conscious focus on keeping my wits about me, a part of my mind was able to step back and take in the scene. I was surprised by how young the plaintiff's attorneys seemed. Although they were clearly bright and energetic, I got the impression that they were perhaps overmatched against the two seasoned pros at the other table, the assistant attorney general for the state and a lawyer representing the National Federation of the Blind (NFB). The interests of disabled Americans, particularly the blind, had a significant place in the e-voting debate. Some activists in the blind community very publicly supported DREs, which added another level of complexity, and sometimes confusion, to the controversy.

The tactics of the slick defense team involved objecting to what seemed like every other question or comment. It would have been comical if not for the fact that the judge allowed most of their objections. I could see the plantiff's young attorney questioning me on direct examination get flustered several times, and from time to time I tried to help him out, politely re-phrasing his question in the way I thought he intended to ask it before giving my answer.

The attorney first walked me through my résumé, education, publications, and awards to qualify me as an expert. The defense raised no objection to my status as an expert, but asked to make an objection that would weigh on all of my testimony. Both sets of lawyers approached the bench for a private conference. Al-though loudspeakers filled the courtroom with static to mask the private discussion with the judge, I could hear every word from the witness chair. The defense lawyers were challenging the idea that the code we had analyzed was the actual code in the Diebold machines, as I knew they would. The plaintiff's lawyer prevailed, but this would become a critical issue during cross-examination.

Next, I was asked to define several fundamental terms, such as "source code" and "encryption." I gave what I thought was a clear and lengthy explanation, but when the judge said, "I don't understand. What is source code? Like some kind of booklet?" I knew I was in for a long day. I explained that it could be printed out like a booklet, but that he would do better to think of it as more like an MS Word file. I went through the basic process, describing how files on the machine contain instructions for running the computer, how the code is annotated with comments by the developers, and how the code is then compiled into binary form consisting of ones and zeros, which the computer interprets. Even as I was speaking I was growing more anxious. My gut told me that the judge just wasn't getting it, and I began to despair over the possibility of a judge who couldn't grasp the meaning of source code ever understanding the subtle differences between patching source code and patching binaries, or managing to see that the wrong binaries could be installed on a machine after the source code had passed muster.

When I answered no to the question of whether recounts were possible with the Diebold DREs, the judge interrupted again. "Wait a minute," he said. "A recount was done in 2002 on these very machines." Patiently, and I hope respectfully, I reiterated that a *meaningful* recount was not possible with DREs. What they had done in 2002 was to print ballots that were actually just a paper record of the information stored electronically in the machine. Such data are identical to the data already under scrutiny and aren't likely to help resolve any controversy. I made the universal point that an independent audit trail cannot be based on the same data it seeks to audit, but I didn't get the sense that I was getting through. As frustrating as it was that vital decisions were being made throughout the legal system and the government by technically illiterate people, this actually went deeper. This wasn't even a technical issue as much as it was a point of basic logic, and still it seemed lost on this judge, the man who was going to rule on the security of the Diebold voting machines.

As we wrapped up, the plaintiff's lawyer took steps to do away with the VoteHere issue before the defense tried to discredit me with it. He had me confirm each point in my press release—that I hadn't profited in any way from the relationship, that Vote-Here was not a competitor of Diebold's, and that none of my collaborators had any relationship with the company. The issue never came up again.

Left to my own devices during the lunch recess, I walked out of the courthouse—right into a mob of reporters and camera crews. At first, I didn't even realize that they were all there to cover the e-voting case, but I was glad to see that so many news outlets thought the case important enough to cover aggressively. I ended up speaking on camera with reporters from most of the major networks and some from several cable channels I didn't recognize. Generally, I got the same questions about the problems with e-voting and repeated the same answers to a variety of journalists, but one of them took it a little deeper. He asked me why it had taken so long for this issue to land in court and whether I thought it would go all the way to the Supreme Court. I believed that it could indeed go that high. The need for equipment that could count votes in a reliable and auditable way was not merely a local concern but a national one, and fundamental to the democratic process. The issue would remain alive as long as state officials insisted on buying and defending insecure voting machines. When I was able to extricate myself from the microphones and notepads, I strolled through downtown Annapolis until I found a quiet little Chinese restaurant, where I sat alone in a booth, collecting my thoughts over a plate of banana chicken and rice.

After lunch, we concluded the direct examination, covering the details of our report, my experience as an election judge, and the general security problems with electronic voting. I had given about an hour and a half's worth of testimony, punctuated by the incessant objections of the defense. Those tactics seemed to have worked, since the plaintiff's argument never seemed to gather any real momentum or force. It felt to me like we didn't make as strong a case as we could have.

As the attorney for the National Federation of the Blind rose to cross-examine me, I felt a slight adrenaline rush, in anticipation of a confrontation, but again, the feeling was mixed with a certain curiosity and fascination with the process. There was nothing tentative about this lawyer as he confidently and easily took control of the courtroom. His first series of questions, simple factual ones to which he could get a predictable yes or no response, clearly seemed designed to lead up to some dramatic "a-ha!" moment. I tried to make it difficult for him, qualifying my answers or offering more elaborately detailed answers, but he would ask the judge to have my comments stricken from the record or to instruct me to only answer the questions. The judge did as he was asked. I knew where this was all heading, and there was nothing I could do to stop it.

"Do you know for a fact that the code you analyzed is running in the Diebold machines that the state will use in November?"

"No."

"Do you know, as a matter of fact, that the machines that will be used in November perform encryption using broken encryption?"

"No."

"Do you know, as a matter of fact, that Diebold has not fixed the flaws you identified in the machines?"

"It is my opinion that some of the problems we found were inherent to the system and could not be fixed without a total rewrite of the system, and such a rewrite would take longer than Diebold and the state have had." I was reprimanded at this point and told to answer the question only with "Yes," "No," or "I don't know." The lawyer kept at it. He asked if I had built a scientific mathematical model of security in which to analyze the risk of the Diebold machines. I replied that the security threats were so obvious that such a model was unnecessary and that besides, there were too many variables that could not be easily measured. How could I come up with a scientific measurement of the likelihood that a rogue programmer would rig the machines?

As I testified, it dawned on me that giving only yes or no answers was inconsistent with the oath I had taken to tell the truth, the whole truth, and nothing but the truth. Answering yes or no to a deliberately misleading question might confirm some minute fact but would not reveal the "whole truth," at least not as I understood the concept. I was sorely tempted to answer the next such question by declaring that a yes or no answer would violate my oath, but knew that would be unprofessional and could make me look like a smart aleck. A litigator friend later confirmed for me that I was part of a noble tradition: countless witnesses before me had been frustrated to the point of distraction by this kind of questioning, and I wasn't the first one to think of trying the "oath tactic." He explained that if the yes-or-no questions were designed to mislead, part of the purpose of redirect was to clarify the misleading questions and answers and hopefully make the other side look foolish in the process.

The lawyer next tried a different tactic, firing questions at me in quick succession.

"So, Dr. Rubin, are you saying that electronic voting machines are all insecure?"

"I believe that paperless electronic voting machines that are available today are susceptible to fraud."

"So, you would say that they are not secure?"

"That is correct."

"Would it be correct to say that you don't believe that any machine can be secured?"

"That is incorrect."

"So, electronic voting machines *could* be secure?"

"Paperless voting machines available today are not secure enough."

"But didn't you just say that they could be secured?"

"You said 'machines,' not 'voting machines.' "

He hesitated, then gave a little embarrassed smile. "How terrible for a lawyer who is supposed to be precise with language to be so careless. You are absolutely correct. My mistake. It must have been enjoyable for you to catch my mistake." For some time after the hearing, I thought about this exchange, wondering if he had really slipped up or had deliberately tried to trick me. If I had answered that I didn't think any machine could be secured, would he have started asking me about airplanes and toasters? I'll never know, of course, but I sure was glad I had been listening so closely.

He moved on and next asked me if I had applied for a $10 million grant to study voting machines. I had anticipated this question, since the defense knew that several of us had applied to the National Science Foundation for a grant to set up a center to study issues around electronic voting. I had come up with a response while driving down to Annapolis that morning.

"No," I said.

The lawyer looked startled. "No?" he asked incredulously. I could see that he smelled blood. I answered that a collaborative group involving eight universities had applied to establish an NSF center to study the science underlying voting issues. I said that I was participating and that I had requested funding from the center to pay for two graduate students and some equipment, as well as a couple of months of my salary in the fourth and fifth years of the grant. He asked me if I received money from the government to analyze systems, and again I surprised him by answering no. I explained that my government grants were to design protocols and build new technology. If we received the NSF grant, we would study precisely the kind of scientific mathematical analysis that he had asked about earlier, not perform evaluations of specific machines on the market. I knew he wanted to link my criticism of the Diebold machines to my desire to obtain grants. Sensing that he wasn't going to get anywhere with that line of questioning, he soon abandoned it and, to my great relief, told the judge he had no more questions.

It had been a long and rough session, but what I didn't know (and neither, it seemed, did the plaintiff's attorneys) was that I was only half done. The other defense lawyer, the assistant attorney general for the state of Maryland, was ready to take his whacks at me, and this guy made his colleague seem positively gentle. He barraged me with aggressive, rapid-fire questions, cutting me off or asking the judge to silence me whenever I tried to answer with more than a word or two. He grilled me about the Maryland statutes, about which I knew precious little, about the Federal Election Commission standards, and about the Help America Vote Act. His questions were purposefully obscure and specific, so that I could only answer, repeatedly, "I don't know." That's not something you want your alleged "expert" saying over and over again from the witness chair. The plaintiff's attorney kept trying to object but was overruled by the judge as often as the defense's objections had been upheld, which was very disconcerting. The assistant AG projected a section of the Maryland statute on a TV monitor so that I could comment on it. The plaintiff's lawyer objected—of course, to no avail. Now I was in the totally inappropriate and uncomfortable position of having to comment on a statute of law, although I was not a lawyer, and having to argue it with a courtroom pro. But something unexpected happened. I noticed a detail in the statute that would let the air out of the argument the defense was trying to make. The statute displayed on the screen stated that a voting machine had to be able to produce a paper record of the votes cast on that machine. Could the Diebold DREs do this? I argued that although the Diebold machines could in fact produce a paper representation of the data they contained, if the votes had not been recorded correctly in the first place because of a security breach—if the data being printed were incorrect— then the machines could not comply with the statute. The lawyer paused for a moment, read the statute again, and reconsidered his position. Then he quickly changed the subject, and I chalked up a small victory.

It didn't all go this well. Although I don't believe he scored many big points during the remainder of my testimony, he did manage to maneuver me a few more times into answering, "I don't know," sometimes to questions that seemed irrelevant or that simply led nowhere. Perhaps he was just tormenting me, or perhaps he figured that any time I spent saying, "I don't know," was time I couldn't spend criticizing electronic voting machines.

Mike Wertheimer of RABA followed me on the witness stand, and he pulled no punches. Mike said that the state had not installed security patches on its voting machines, patches that were required by the Microsoft operating system. He explained that when the state had tried to install the patches, the system no longer worked. Although I'm sure the irony was lost on many of those present in the courtroom, it turned out that if the voting machine was to work properly, it had to be insecure. I thought Wertheimer's testimony was a high point.

After Wertheimer, the defense called to the stand Michael Shamos, a computer science professor from Carnegie Mellon. Shamos based much of his position on assumptions that I could not accept, chiefly that the lack of fraud in previous electronic elections made the concerns about it unrealistic. Not to beat a dead horse, but I believe in assessing vulnerability, not past performance. Potential, not experience. In addition to his credentials as a computer scientist, Shamos is also an attorney, and I'm guessing he's a good one. He could always argue me into a corner, getting me to agree with point after point and then tying them together into a conclusion that was absolutely wrong. Michael and I disagreed, but I respected his intelligence.

On the stand, Shamos was in his element. He characterized my team as applying a "standard of perfection" in our analysis and said that RABA had applied a "military" standard to the security of voting systems. It seemed that Shamos's own idea of perfection was simply to eliminate the administrator PIN of 1111 and the hardwired key in the software. Of course, Diebold could have implemented most, if not all, of the recommended improvements, and still their system would have fallen far short of perfect. And if I understood what he meant by "military," RABA's standard hadn't come close. What I really wanted to know was why either of those standards—military or perfection—would be considered too high for a voting system. Wasn't that what such a system should strive for?

Shamos's comments had the feel of prepared "talking points," an impression that was confirmed several weeks later when I heard Jim Adler, the CEO of VoteHere, testify at the

EAC's Technical Guidelines Development Committee (TGDC) hearing. Adler used the very same words Shamos had used, saying that our report and the RABA exercise had applied perfection and military standards, which he considered overkill for elections. I had to consider the stunning possibility that they had orchestrated a strategy for discrediting our studies, even though each man had separately told me that he agreed with the "Hopkins/Rice" report. Adler had complimented me on that work repeatedly when I was in the middle of my VoteHere crisis, and Shamos had told me on several occasions that he believed Diebold had bungled its opportunity to build a DRE. Shamos believed that DREs could be made adequately secure, but he also believed that Diebold had fallen far short of the mark. Criticizing my team and RABA for applying too high a standard was absolutely disingenuous, since even using Shamos's or Adler's standards, however they characterized them, Diebold had failed.

All the jokes and nasty cracks about lawyers are by now so common that they are clichés, but I still found this first intimate experience of court terribly depressing. Justice did not seem to be the objective. The lawyers who examined me had not come into that courtroom in search of the whole truth. For these people, the courtroom was an arena, with victory their only goal. Whoever played the game best took home the prize. Smarter, more experienced lawyers walked all over their more junior opponents and anyone else who stood in their way. Whether they were right or wrong was beside the point. I listened to them knowingly quote me out of context. I saw them distort and misconstrue statements and events and turn half-truths into evidence. I watched as they cleverly pulled out random bits of minutiae from the mass of evidence or from legal precedent and assemble them into the "proof" that supported an incorrect hypothesis. Intellectually, I understand that in an adversarial system each side must be argued and defended to the fullest, using all available means, but in my heart I can't quite understand treating truth as something fluid and subjective in order to win a case, especially one in which our democracy was hanging in the balance. As a close lawyer friend of mine likes to say, paraphrasing Churchill on democracy, "Ours is the worst legal system in the world, except for all the other ones."

Perhaps I'm naive, an idealist. But I am also a scientist, trained to consider all contradictory arguments, giving them equal weight, and to withhold conclusions until the evidence is irrefutable. Anyone who did what I did for a living and failed to adhere to those principles would very quickly find themselves selling computers at the mall.

What suddenly became very clear to me in the wake of that hearing was that a court of law, a trial pitting two sides against each other, was perhaps the single worst venue in which to debate this issue—or for that matter any issue of science, or any issue concerning the public interest. These issues should not be subjected to semantic debate and selective fact-finding. They are issues in which all sides should be working toward the same goal—finding objective truth through comprehensive analysis. Reasonable people can disagree on how to act in light of that finding, but that's a policy debate subject to the democratic process, not a prize to be fought over and won. In our case, *Schade vs. Lamone*, or the Battle of the Lindas, the state of Maryland could win its case and then, as its prize, be saddled with a dangerously insecure voting system.

I WALKED OUT of the courthouse and wandered the streets of Annapolis. As fate would have it, I soon found myself standing

in front of a Ben & Jerry's shop, watching some kids come bop-
ping through the door with ice cream all over their faces, chat-
tering happily to their parents. I thought about how long it had
been since I had been able to spend that kind of lazy, carefree
time with my kids. I also had to laugh a little bit. Ben Cohen,
one of the Ben & Jerry's co-founders, was known to be very active politically, and one of his chosen causes was e-voting. In
fact, he was one of the celebrity activists with whom I'd been invited to share the dais at some conference, but I had reluctantly
declined in order to maintain my scientific impartiality. The
young woman behind the counter took one look at me and asked
if I'd had a hard day. I told her about the hours I'd just spent being cross-examined in court and announced that this ice cream
was my reward.

She scooped out the ice cream and asked for three dollars. But
then she hesitated and said, "You know what? Just take it." I insisted on paying, but she refused to take my money. She hoped
the ice cream would cheer me up a little, and I told her, in all
sincerity, that she had just made my day. I'm sure Ben Cohen
would smile his approval on this random act of kindness. And
then another thought occurred to me: what if Lynn Landes
found out? Aha! Hidden payment from the activist movement!
"E-Voting Researcher Caught in Ice-Cream Scandal!"

A week later, to no one's surprise, the judge ruled in favor of
the state. He found that the plaintiff had failed to prove that the
threat to the voting machines was real. The judge denied
TrueVoteMD's request to require a paper ballot option for Maryland voters, finding that there had been successful recounts in
2002 using the Diebold machines. Apparently, my argument
that meaningful recounts were impossible with those machines
had fallen on deaf ears, as had my explanation of the difference

between an independent audit and a meaningless exercise involving a printed representation of already tainted data. Linda Schade's attorney filed an appeal the next day. The appellate court heard the case only two weeks later and promptly upheld the lower court's ruling.

14

The Broward County Elections Department has egg on its
face today after a computer glitch misreported a key
amendment race. . . . Amendment 4, which would allow
Miami-Dade and Broward counties to hold a future election
to decide if slot machines should be allowed at racetracks,
was thought to be tied. But now that a computer glitch for
machines counting absentee ballots has been exposed, it
turns out the amendment passed.
—*Channel 4 News, Jacksonville, November 4, 2004*

The Diebold analysis had by now come to represent a point
of demarcation in my life—there was the time "before
Diebold" and now the time "after Diebold." It was easy to
lose sight of the fact that the Hopkins/Rice study of the
Diebold source code had not been the beginning of my involvement with e-voting, although it certainly sometimes seemed
that way, given how my life had changed. My testimony on the
subject before the National Science Foundation in 2000 and the
subsequent article I published about it had brought me into
the circle of computer scientists concerned with the issue. By
the time I first heard about the Diebold code, the e-voting debate was thriving in many different forms, and I knew many of
the players. Sometimes I was one of them.

In May 2003, a couple of months before the fateful phone call from David Dill, I received a unique invitation. It seemed that the FVAP of the USDoD was forming an SPRG for its SERVE project. Language like that could only come from the federal government. Translated, the Federal Voting Assistance Program of the United States Department of Defense was asking me to join the Security Peer Review Group for an initiative it called the Secure Electronic Registration and Voting Experiment. Wary of "invitations" to volunteer my time, I tried to find out what I could and started with an e-mail to David Dill.

David was able to tell me about some of the others whom the FVAP had invited to join the SPRG, and they included some of the top people in the field. In addition to David Jefferson, the great champion of secure voting, there was Barbara Simons, a highly respected computer scientist, former president of our top professional association, the Association for Computing Machinery, and an activist against paperless voting, and David Wagner, a brilliant young professor specializing in computer security and cryptography at Berkeley whom I had known since he was a graduate student. I had met David Jefferson and Barbara on that first NSF panel; ordered by President Clinton to study the feasibility of Internet voting, the panel had featured a blue-ribbon collection of federal officials and academics from many disciplines. The panel's final report, which was distributed widely on the Internet, concluded emphatically that secure voting over the Internet on Windows machines was not yet technologically feasible. It went on to suggest the more realistic short-term objective of *poll-site voting*, a system that would allow any U.S. citizen who was away from home to go to any voting precinct and vote on a machine that would call up the correct ballot for his or her home precinct, with all the local choices. We were a ways off from building such a system securely, but the panel believed that remote poll-site voting was more likely to be securable than Internet voting.

I have learned a great deal from David Jefferson about how to handle myself in these arenas. I value his rare mix of expertise, passion, and diplomacy and felt lucky that he was able to fill me in on SERVE. The system was designed, at a cost of $22 million, to allow overseas voters to register to vote and to cast absentee ballots over the Internet using standard Windows computers. The Uniformed and Overseas Citizens Absentee Voting Act (UOCAVA) mandated that all members of the uniformed armed forces and their dependents, whether in the United States or abroad, as well as civilian Americans living overseas, be enabled to cast votes. Unreliable mail systems from remote locations have always made voting a challenge for these people. In fact, 30 percent of such votes had been lost in the previous election. SERVE was a well-intentioned attempt to rectify that terrible situation. It was to be used in seven states in the 2004 primaries and in the general election.

David Jefferson had participated in a small "proof of concept" study, "Voting Over the Internet" (VOI), the predecessor to SERVE, in which eighty-four binding votes had been cast in the 2000 election from twenty-one states and eleven countries—at a cost of millions. David had been disappointed that mere traces of his detailed criticisms had made it into the FVAP report, on which the authors' names did not appear. He felt further hamstrung by the nondisclosure agreement, which had prevented him from discussing his knowledge of the system with anyone outside the peer review group. Nonetheless, David urged us to come on board. In response to my concern that perhaps the FVAP only wanted a seal of approval from some prominent computer security experts, he pointed out that the fact that he had been reappointed despite his pointed criticisms four years earlier seemed to demonstrate the FVAP's sincere desire for honest review. I was skeptical, but our little group proposed that the FVAP dispense with the nondisclosure agreement and allow us to issue our own independent report on the system, which we could release to the public. After some touchy negotiations, the FVAP agreed to our terms, deciding to limit our access to certain highly sensitive material. A week after I joined and began poring over the documents, the FVAP issued a press release, announcing its plan for a large-scale Internet registration and voting demonstration for the 2004 election. The release pointed to the success of the much smaller VOI study as the foundation for this new effort.

Right away an alarm went off in my head. Success on a small scale does not guarantee success once the scale of a project is enlarged. Like those mutual fund ads always say, past performance is no guarantee of future results, especially when it comes to security. In this case, it was reasonable to ask why anyone would bother to attack the VOI system with only eighty-four votes at stake. As the system took in more voters, it would, of course, become a more tempting target. If SERVE was deployed without any glitches, I worried that would be used as evidence that Internet voting was secure, even if this system actually was not. The FVAP's press release showed no hesitation about relying on this kind of faulty logic.

Given that 100,000 votes were to be cast in the election, I would hardly have called SERVE an "experiment." There were more than enough UOCAVA votes in Florida alone to have decided the outcome of the 2000 presidential election. It also worried me that in the three years since the NSF study, Internet security had deteriorated greatly. Defensive measures could not keep pace with the rising number of known and exploitable bugs just in Windows and Internet Explorer. It struck me as unlikely that Accenture, the company that the FVAP had hired to build SERVE, had figured out a way to secure the Internet that none of us on that panel had been able to anticipate.

From the beginning, it was clear that the SPRG would be lively, perhaps even contentious, since there were a number of people in the group whose perspectives diverged significantly from ours. Whereas the DoD people listened attentively to our occasionally harsh feedback, Accenture's project manager would get very defensive and need to be calmed down by Carol Paquette, the very able team leader. By contrast, Carl Almond, the technical lead from Avanade, a subcontractor of Accenture's, was the kind of colleague I'd value on any team. His humor and fairness were welcome, and his substantial technical skill made me sure that he knew what an impossible assignment he had taken on. Over time, though, I came to understand that this was exactly what drove Carl. He relished the challenge of a problem that the experts described as unsolvable.

With Carl Almond at the helm, the design team had done as good a job as anyone could have, given the inherent constraints. I was pleasantly surprised by the first meeting, which I was only able to attend by phone. It was congenial and productive, and both the FVAP and Accenture seemed unafraid to share openly the details of the system. Those details, unfortunately, horrified me. The first thing I saw was that SERVE included what's known as a remote ActiveX control. ActiveX is a term for a Windows program that is digitally signed and downloaded over the Internet to run on a user's computer. Digital signing is a cryptographic process designed to ensure that such a program hasn't been altered or modified in transit. I was well versed in the serious security problems with ActiveX, having written about them in a technical book. Most notably, there is no way to determine the trustworthiness of the person who digitally signs an ActiveX control. Even with e-mail, you can choose not to open a message from someone you've never heard of, but you don't have that control over an anonymous ActiveX control automatically downloaded from the Internet. Microsoft determines whom it will trust to digitally sign an ActiveX program, but people have demonstrated that they can become ActiveX signers by fooling Microsoft into issuing them the needed credentials. An untrustworthy signer can turn an ActiveX control into a highly dangerous Trojan horse. And even though the ActiveX control used in SERVE would presumably be trustworthy, voters would be required to enable ActiveX in order to vote, thus exposing themselves to many unrelated dangers, including attacks on the system itself. ActiveX is an ideal platform for attackers, since it allows for the potential compromise of any Windows computer on which active scripting is not disabled, and no security expert worth his or her salt would ever condone a system that relies on it.

It further alarmed me that with Internet voting the very infrastructure needed for voting could be disrupted or wiped out on the day of the election. The Internet has several known points of vulnerability. In the past, targeted attacks known as *denial of service* attacks had made the network completely unavailable. A more extreme version called *distributed denial of service* attacks, in which many compromised computers on the Internet are programmed to attack the same target at the same time, had become commonplace. Such an attack against SERVE could disenfranchise thousands of voters.

Neither of these, however, worried me as much as *phishing*. This is what we call the kind of Internet sabotage in which attackers set up bogus Web pages that mimic existing legitimate pages. Overseas voters would be lured to phony SERVE pages that looked just like the real thing via e-mail or Web links, perhaps just a simple reminder to vote with a link. Once voters had arrived at the phony site, even the most brilliant security system back on the real SERVE site would be meaningless. Whoever set up the fake site could just take the voters' passwords, log on to the real site, and vote however they chose. SERVE contained no countermeasures or protection against this sort of attack. As far as I knew, none existed.

Our report on the Diebold code came out in between the first and second meetings of the SPRG. That controversy was in full swing by the time I drove down to Reston, Virginia, for the second gathering. In addition to all the previous members, this meeting was also attended by Glenn Durfee, a very sharp cryptography expert from the Palo Alto Research Center, and Michael Shamos from Carnegie Mellon, who had been so maddening at the Maryland hearing. Shamos and Ted Selker of MIT got a lot of mileage out of the fact that they were the only two computer scientists in the country from highly regarded institutions who supported electronic voting and opposed paper ballots. It seemed that every time I testified or participated in one of these things, I found myself coming up against one or both of them.

Shamos was up to his usual tricks. In this context, he was making the case that the threat of a new virus targeting SERVE was unlikely because we had never seen such a virus before. I argued that of course we had never seen it before; this would be the first large-scale use of Internet voting in a U.S. presidential election. This would be my first chance to meet him in person, and even though he infuriated me, I confess I was secretly excited about it. It turned out that Michael and I shared a secret passion—shooting pool. I thought I was pretty serious about the game, having turned my living room over to a tournament-sized table and once even hiring a professional to give me a lesson, but Shamos was in another league. He had written books on the subject and had made a name for himself in the world of billiards. We were able to find a pool hall one night at the SPRG meeting and were both happy for the opportunity to move beyond our debate for a while and enjoy the simple pleasures of some eight-ball. He wiped the table with me, of course. I didn't mind being bested in a game of pool; we had more serious contests in front of us.

SERVE had also changed between the first meeting, when we had reviewed only the design, and the second, when the nearly completed system was ready for analysis. That there would be little chance of implementing any significant changes that we might recommend raised once again the concern that the FVAP was only looking for a rubber stamp. They seemed to be moving full steam ahead with SERVE, promoting the system through press releases and other activity.

Verisign, the world's largest vendor of public key technology, handled the cryptographic key management in SERVE and had a representative at all of our meetings. In cryptography, keys—which are not physical objects but rather special sequences of zeros and ones used to scramble or authenticate data—are set up in a kind of hierarchical pyramid. At the lower levels, large numbers of people are issued keys, which are in turn managed by a smaller number of keys at the higher levels, and so on, all funneling into one "master" key called the *root private key*. If the root private key was somehow exposed, the cascading impact would undermine the security of the entire Internet.

We took a field trip to inspect Verisign's heavily guarded underground design facility—it was like visiting the secret NORAD missile command center or the villain's secret headquarters in a James Bond movie. The root private key, stored deep within the facility, was kept in a safe, with multiple locks, which was protected in turn by a cage that required two different people with two different keys for access. In addition, the private key was stored within a device that could generate keys and sign other keys, but did not afford access to the private keys themselves. Root keys need not be accessed often, and the security of every system that utilizes a Verisign key depends on the company's ability to protect the root private key. We also learned that Verisign hosted the SERVE Web servers, and were told about their impressive bandwidth capacity. Unfortunately, the FVAP group didn't seem to grasp that fat data pipes do not equal a secure system.

The FVAP had been very open, sharing every relevant piece of the SERVE design, and in the same spirit our little cadre of e-voting critics had remained completely open-minded, evaluating the system objectively and without prejudice. And yet, most of us felt that we had seen all we needed to see and now needed to wrestle with the business of writing a report. We speculated about what might have caused the FVAP to bring in such a group of known Internet-voting critics. Perhaps they hoped that negative marks from the security experts would give them a face-saving excuse to put an end to the project, which was still far behind schedule and clearly flawed. Or maybe they wanted it killed before a security breach marred the next election. For my part, I gave the FVAP the benefit of the doubt, having observed their candor and commitment through the entire difficult review. I believed that they were sincere and only wanted the most incisive and expert criticism so that they could build the best possible system.

After the second day of review, several of us determined that if we failed to act, SERVE would almost certainly be adopted and implemented. We knew by then that a strongly worded report from us would have a far-reaching impact (yet still we managed to underestimate that). We set at it immediately, working late into the night and continuing over the next couple of weeks, firing drafts back and forth to each other over e-mail. Glenn Durfee had to decline our offer to join the report because of restrictions from his employer, and David Jefferson's employer, Lawrence Livermore National Labs, created some major stress for us. LLNL received a great deal of funding from the Defense Department, which it did not want to risk alienating by having one of its people co-author a report that criticized Defense so strongly. The issue ended up on the desk of the lab director, who determined that if the report was issued with David's name on it, the Pentagon should receive a fair warning. David finally got permission to participate.

We agreed that fairness also required us to give Carol Paquette an advance copy. We assumed Carol would share the report with her FVAP and Accenture teams, to ensure that we were accurate regarding the details of the system, and we asked her to get back to us within two weeks. At the same time, we asked David Dill and Doug Jones to review the report. We had hoped to manage the release of the report to the media carefully, as had happened with the Diebold report, and so tried to keep the number of eyes on it to an absolute minimum to avoid leaks. To that end, I convinced the others to work again with John Schwartz of the *New York Times*.

When all the comments were in hand, we finalized the report and wrote an executive summary—essentially a list of our basic findings. The summary encapsulated the fundamental problems with Internet voting, and to some degree with electronic voting in general. It pointed out, for starters, that SERVE shared all the problems of DREs, including vulnerability to insider (programmer) attacks and lack of voter verifiability. In addition, SERVE introduced a new dimension of security concerns simply because it required the Internet to function and the Internet is inherently insecure. We made it clear that it was beyond anyone's power to predict the probability of such attacks but that they could be very widespread. Moreover, as much as we supported the DoD's need and desire to facilitate voting for members of the military, we did not believe SERVE could be fixed through simple design changes; nor could we propose a viable alternative Internet-based system.

In the end, all our best-laid plans for the media release of the report fell apart. The day before our allegedly exclusive release in the *Times*, while the Berkeley media people were still hoping to give the story first to NPR, it was leaked to the press. Several tense hours of urgent phone calls followed as we tried to get a handle on the situation. Later we learned that Accenture had leaked an uncorrected version of the report, hoping that whatever minor errors still existed could be used to undermine the report's credibility. We all ended up fielding numerous calls from reporters, and on January 22 the story broke in various outlets, barely upstaged by John Kerry's victory in the Iowa primary. The *Washington Post*'s front-page coverage began as follows:

Pentagon's Online Voting Program Deemed Too Risky
Dan Keating

A Pentagon program for Internet voting in this year's presidential election is so insecure that it could undercut the integrity of American democracy and should be stopped immediately, according to computer-security specialists who were asked to review the $22 million pilot plan intended for about 100,000 overseas voters. The critical report released yesterday is intended to halt the momentum building for national Internet voting as the least expensive and most convenient way to upgrade election technology that was exposed as unreliable in 2000.

In Pam Fessler's story on NPR's *Morning Edition*, representatives of the FVAP and Accenture defended SERVE, cleverly referring to our report as a "minority report," invoking the Spielberg film that was playing at the time. They made the point that the SPRG consisted of ten people, that four of us had issued this rogue report, and that the other six didn't necessarily agree. When John Schwartz had asked us why Accenture referred to our paper as a "minority report," we were able to deduce this strategy and prepare a response to counter it. We explained that the four of us on the report were the only computer scientists on the SPRG to attend both meetings and that the only other security expert in the group, Glenn Durfee, had agreed with our conclusions but was constrained from joining us as a co-author. John Schwartz listened attentively and communicated those facts with his usual care and clarity.

The media blitz that followed rivaled what I had experienced with the Diebold report, but at least there were three others to share the load. In each interview, I hammered home the point that since the FVAP had agreed to let the only security experts in the SPRG write a public report as a condition of our joining the group, they knew what they were in for. One week later, on January 30, 2004, Deputy Secretary of Defense Paul Wolfowitz sent a memo to the undersecretary that stated: "In view of the inability to ensure the legitimacy of votes that would be cast in the SERVE Internet Voting Project, thereby bringing into doubt the integrity of the election results, I hereby direct you to take immediate steps to ensure that no voters use the system to register to vote via the Internet."

And thus died the threat of a compromised election due to SERVE. For a while, the DoD toyed with the idea of continuing with SERVE as an experiment, in parallel with real, traditional ballots, but eventually it canceled the project completely.

I had gotten a little used to feeling like a voice in the wilderness, struggling to be heard against the roaring momentum of electronic voting. It felt good to know that, at least in this case, our expertise had mattered, our criticisms had been taken seriously, and something good had come of our efforts. That sense of triumph, however, was diminished by the sympathy I felt for the FVAP members who had worked so hard on the doomed system, with nothing but the best of intentions.

Two months before the 2004 election, the states of Missouri and North Dakota announced a system for absentee overseas ballots that made the security of SERVE look ironclad in comparison. The plan was to allow voters to request ballots by e-mail, fill them in, scan them, and then e-mail them back to the Pentagon. A third-party contractor would then print out the ballots and fax them to the appropriate election officials. As far as I could tell, there were no design documents for this process, and no security peer review group. The system required voters to give up the secrecy of their ballots and put control of the votes in the hands of an independent contractor. The attacks we had envisioned against SERVE would have at least involved some technical sophistication. Corrupting a system based on fax and e-mail would be child's play.

15

Trust but verify.
—*Ronald Reagan*

I traveled to Washington early in May 2004 for the first public hearing of the Election Assistance Commission. A friend of mine who lived there and was out of town at the time insisted on my staying in his apartment, in a building called the Lansberg. On the morning of the hearing, I rose early, dressed in my "testimony suit," and went out and rang for the elevator. When the elevator doors opened, a natty-looking gentleman rushed out past me, clearly heading for someplace important. Guessing that he thought he was in the lobby, I told him he was on the third floor. He thanked me and reclaimed his place in the elevator.

I'm not entirely sure why the moment stood out so much in my mind. He was a rather distinguished-looking African American man, with a small, squarish patch of bright white in a neatly coiffed head of black hair. His elegant clothes, confident posture, and gaze that was at once kindly and very direct combined to give him an aura of gravitas. And yet at the same time, he seemed quite friendly. As this was Washington, I entertained myself for a moment by imagining him as a visiting dignitary, maybe an ambassador, or a high government official. We exchanged a few mild pleasantries and bid each other a good day when we parted ways at the lobby.

I had to laugh when the EAC hearing was called to order and the same distinguished gentleman with the piercing eyes looked down at me from the podium. It's funny how the impressions I formed in that brief moment on the elevator proved to be true as I got to know Dr. DeForest "Buster" Soaries. The Election Assistance Commission hearing was something of a defining moment for the national e-voting debate—and for my involvement with it.

Perhaps the battle lines had been drawn before, but the hearing brought a new level of focus and national attention. For me, it was the first time I would be confronting such acrimonious opposition in such a high-level forum. As if I weren't nervous enough, the scene in the hearing room made me weak in the knees. The room was packed nearly to overflowing with senior representatives from the e-voting machine vendors, secretaries of state, and representatives from the National Federation of the Blind and the American Association of People with Disabilities. The press was out in force, highlighted by a phalanx of photographers, some crouched on the floor right in front of the witness table, their shutters clicking and their cameras whirring. I had the immediate sensation of being the lone computer scientist, with all the forces in support of electronic voting arrayed before me. I had worked hard in my career to get comfortable sparring with brilliant scientists in academic meetings, but the world of politics and policy, with the media anxious for some fireworks, was new and thoroughly intimidating to me.

The commission was appointed by President George W. Bush, and confirmed by the Senate, with a mandate to establish standards and guidance for voting equipment and to dole out several billions of dollars to the states to use in reforming the election process. Soaries, a Republican, chaired the committee and served with three other commissioners, Paul DiGregorio, another Republican, and two Democrats, Gracia Hillman and Ray Martinez. Dr. Soaries had spent his life as a minister and an educator and had a long history of community involvement. Although not a professional politician, he had served the public as secretary of state for New Jersey and had learned a great deal about the voting process and the current controversy. He imbued the proceedings with the kind of plainspoken thoughtfulness and grace one might expect from someone with his background.

Soaries opened the proceedings by reminding us all about the Florida troubles of 2000 and laying out the current situation. In addition to myself and my old nemeses Brit Williams and Stephen Burger, our technology panel was rounded out by Ted Selker from MIT. Soaries introduced us as a "dream team" of computer scientists, emphasizing that we were to our chosen profession as Michael Jordan was to his. The compliments would have embarrassed except that, to me, our panel resembled a ragtag Bad News Bears. Not only were there so many other more eminent scientists who could have spoken, but this particular team was frighteningly lopsided in opposition to paper ballots, a fact that angered many activists at the time and threatened to present the commission with an imbalanced picture of electronic voting.

Dierdre Mulligan, a brilliant law professor at Berkeley, had reviewed my testimony and recommended that rather than focusing on the importance of paper ballots as opposed to DREs, I make some points about the computer security community, which had been largely overlooked in the ongoing debate and whose occasional contributions and recommendations had been repeatedly rejected by e-voting proponents. Dierdre's counsel proved very wise. Some other panel members had expected me to discuss paper ballots directly, and when I didn't even mention the word "paper," their comments, intended to put me in my place, came off as a little hollow, even petty. Each panelist submitted written testimony but was also allowed to speak for seven minutes. I used my comments to supplement my written testimony; Mark Radke from Diebold did little more than repeat what he had already submitted, drawing several admonishments from chairman Soaries.

In my statement, after laying out my credentials and my experience with e-voting, I lamented the disregard demonstrated by vendors and election officials for the authoritative critiques provided by the computer security community. I focused on conceptual points, such as the difference between security and functionality in computer systems, and bemoaned a development process for computer-voting technology that was not at all transparent and almost guaranteed problems down the road, particularly if the input of experts was not sought out and incorporated.*

When I was through, Stephen Burger of IEEE testified regarding the standards process for voting machines and emphasized that there had been great contributions from a great many people to establish our current voting systems.

The clear implication was that Diebold and other manufacturers had acted only out of altruism and civic-mindedness and

---

* A link to the text of this statement can be found in the resources section at the end of the book.

that those of us who failed to honor their work were heartless whiners. Even as Burger argued for retaining the value already created by these great Americans, he acknowledged that voting technology had room for improvement. He added that he believed that all the easy problems had been solved and that the remaining ones involved complex interrelationships, and hence compromises, between competing requirements, such as security, reliability, usability, affordability, and access for the disabled. He suggested that these competing requirements could be addressed through "innovation," recommended the adoption of a "consensus" process, and urged that all stakeholders be allowed to guide the process. I'm sure that I wasn't the only observer who wanted to chime in with the point that there is in fact only one stakeholder in this process—the voting public—and that the business interests of vendors should carry absolutely no weight in the discussion.

The stakeholder question was not the only obvious problem with Burger's testimony. The easy problems had *not* all been solved, not by a long shot. For example, the Diebold encryption problems—using a broken, outdated cipher in an incorrect way, with a fixed, hardwired key—could have been addressed. Ensuring the integrity of the voting process should not involve complex compromises, but it should require trade-offs of one property for another. An accessible, affordable voting machine that is insecure is as useless as a secure and reliable one with a confusing and unworkable interface.

The next speaker, MIT's Ted Selker, got off to a questionable start by looking straight at me and saying that some people were "spouting off" about technology when what we really needed was testing. He then launched into a tirade about voter registration, citing the large number of votes lost due to registration problems in the 2000 election. This is one of Selker's favorite subjects, but he was totally off topic. The next stop in his wandering testimony was the issue of standards, which he felt should be performance-based. Performance-based testing makes perfect sense with regard to functionality, but it is not how you prescribe security. Next, Selker stated that parallel testing could detect the kinds of fraud that I had been talking about, but that's simply not true.

Here's how parallel testing works: To see if voting machines are rigged, officials remove randomly selected machines from randomly selected precincts on election day and test them under realistic conditions. Early in the morning on election day, testers from the board of elections arrive unexpectedly at polling sites and take the random machines to a lab, called a *phantom precinct*. There, testers cast votes on the machines, just as would happen in an actual precinct. At the end of the day, they compare the electronic results as recorded by the machines to the actual votes cast on those machines. In theory, the testers would be able to discover that the machines were rigged if the totals did not match. California uses video cameras pointed at the touch screen to produce a video record of the test voters' actions. When the calculated totals fail to match the expected totals, and before the testers conclude that malicious code is present, the video should reveal whether the test voters made any mistakes. Testers discovered four such discrepancies in the California primary of 2004, all resolved by appeals to the videotape.

The point of parallel testing is to fool any malicious code that was written to perform properly in a test but to cheat in an actual election. Testers have to assume that anyone trying to rig the machines will have studied election procedures carefully and can write software that can tell the difference between actual election conditions and lab tests. The challenge is to mimic those conditions exactly so that the software will not recognize it is engaged in a test rather than the real thing. The test must occur in real time, taking as long as the actual election, with an expected number of votes entered at realistic time intervals and the machine's clock set to the appropriate time and date. The votes must be entered via the touch screen, not through an electronic file or any other means. The party names and candidates must be real (that is, not "Party 1" or "Candidate A"), and testers must even take pains to cast votes for parties and candidates that mirror the expected results at the precincts from which the machine came. Even the most experienced election workers can't think of every possible nuance or subtle variation, especially if they don't think like a programmer.

There are other practical problems with this kind of testing. First, it's hard to imagine that testers will be able to examine more than a tiny fraction—less than 1 percent—of the machines in a given state. A probabilistic attack that cheats only a small percentage of the time, or only on a small number of machines, can easily go undetected by parallel testing. Furthermore, parallel testing probably won't uncover a "knock" attack: malicious activity triggered by some action by the voter, such as touching the screen in an unusual way or in unusual places several times. When I brought up the threat of knock-based attacks with Pamela Woodside, the CIO of the state of Maryland, she assured me that they had tried touching the machine in unusual ways to make sure that no such threats existed. I could only shake my head in dismay, wondering if she actually believed she could anticipate every possible quirky knock that a programmer might build into an attack or if she was just giving me the knee-jerk response that there was no way for anyone to rig the machines. Suppose the knock required touching the upper left corner of the screen once, touching two of the candidates' names at the same time while tapping another part of the screen three times, and then touching the bottom of the screen twice. Had they tried that one?

After making his exaggerated claims about parallel testing, Selker continued his EAC testimony by stating that he couldn't see any reason to have a clock in the machines. Without a clock, a programmer could not write malicious code to trigger at a specific date or time, like on the morning of election day. That made sense to me, as did his next, more fundamental question: "How do we vet the qualifications of the people that we need to get us through this process? We need to develop experts that can be trusted and that can help the EAC." Selker finally arrived at his real area of expertise: usability. He criticized the inadequate training of poll workers and reminded the group that both Democrats and Republicans had signed off on the infamous "butterfly ballots" in West Palm Beach in 2000. He wondered why nobody was running tests to see if ballots worked well from the usability perspective. Selker was on solid ground when it came to user interfaces, and I agreed with him on all those points.

Brit Williams got the pleasure of the final say. As he started, I realized how valuable Dierdre's advice had been. He had prepared his remarks with the expectation that I would speak for seven minutes about voter-verifiable paper ballots, and he seemed uncomfortable now that those remarks rang hollow. Williams acknowledged that our voting systems leave room for improvement, but echoing Stephen Burger, he urged that accuracy and security must compete with availability, affordability, and maintainability as legitimate requirements. I could not agree that all these factors carry equal weight. Without accuracy and security, the other elements are simply irrelevant.

Williams argued, not unreasonably, that the nation must consider any change to voting technology in the context of its impact on the entire system and that we must resist the temptation
to settle for quick and easy fixes to complex problems. But from
that commonsense premise, his conclusions got shakier.
Williams claimed that the problems caused by any hasty and ill-
conceived plan—such as adding a paper receipt to an existing
voting machine—would greatly outweigh any advantages it
might offer. Not for the first time sitting next to Brit Williams,
and not for the last, I wanted to jump up and shout, "Hey! Wait
a minute!" What about the hasty and ill-conceived plan of
adopting paperless DREs on a wide scale? Was nobody concerned about the problems of that idea outweighing its benefits?
Williams didn't believe there was any imminent danger, and
yet, as David Jefferson likes to say, this is a matter of national security we are talking about.

His prepared remarks then addressed me specifically, stating
that my recommendations could not be implemented in the
short term, which he defined as the next four to six years. Of
course, I hadn't actually made any recommendations yet, except
to involve the computer security community further and to add
transparency to the process. Moreover, one state, Nevada, had already managed to add a paper audit trail to its election process
in just a few months, using Sequoia's reel-to-reel system.
Williams insisted that changes were not possible for the November 2004 election, only seven months away, adding, "We're going
to have to dance with them what brung us."

The rest of Brit Williams's testimony was familiar. He trotted
out his favorite airplane metaphor, reminding the commission
that no system is 100 percent secure and that he and others
would still happily board his flight home, knowing that the
plane might not get there. The comparison between voting and

air travel is completely specious, since there is absolutely no connection between air travel and the possibility of a developer hiding code in a voting machine that could change the outcome of an election, or with Diebold's buggy code, or with the fact that DREs provide no audit or evidence trail.

But since so many people seem to think the analogy is relevant, we might as well examine it more closely. To begin with, planes have manual override: a pilot can take control of an airplane if there's a problem with the computer systems. Would Williams fly home in a pilotless plane driven only by software? Second, there is a long record of successful terrorist incidents involving airplanes, with catastrophic results. Although one can reasonably assume that a successful attack on the voting process wouldn't directly result in the loss of life, it could ultimately be no less terrifying. Third, I've spoken to people who write the code to run airplanes, and even though they employ very stringent development and testing processes, none of them have total confidence that the software will always work. I'd certainly feel better about voting systems if the code were written under the same exacting scrutiny as the code for airplanes, but that wouldn't solve the problem of the audit trail. Aviation systems require redundancy; voting systems require verification. Aviation systems are designed to be reliable, but not necessarily secure. If a pilot wants to crash a plane, the system might trigger some kind of alarm, but it will not be able to stop him. If a voting machine only issues a warning about tampering with results but does not prevent it, it would not qualify as secure.

What if we accepted the airplane analogy as legitimate and took it to its logical end? Imagine that somebody invents a magic technology that prevents malicious code from causing a crash, but that new technology adds five dollars to the price of every ticket. Would we adopt the technology? I can only believe that the FAA would make it the law. Voter-verifiable paper trails are the equivalent of such a technology, and there's nothing magical about them. They simply ensure that buggy or malicious code is not able to corrupt the results of an election without detection. It's almost embarrassing even to be engaging in the debate about planes or elevators and acceptable risk and about balancing requirements. These misleading comparisons are the tactics of desperation. They are not scientific, they are not even logical, and they do not advance our search for the truth. The weak and useless analogies that keep coming up in the e-voting debate make me feel like my head is about to explode.

Williams then made a few recommendations based on his experiences in Georgia, chief among them that the EAC establish a nationwide secure library of voting system software, modeled after the library for law enforcement software at NIST. Recall that there are two basic kinds of software: source code (programs in the format in which programmers produce them) and binary code (the sequences of ones and zeroes created when source code is run through a compiler). Source code can be read and analyzed by humans, if they have the proper training, but cannot be run on a computer. An excerpt from Diebold source code looks like this:

```
/*      Find the page that the cursor's data is on.
        If the candIdx is < 0 then find the page the
        race header starts on otherwise find the page
        the race's candidate is on.
*/
int CBallotWnd: :FindPageForCursor (const CBallotCursor& cursor) const
{
```

```
        CRect rect;
        CRaceCell* pRace =
(CRaceCell*) (CBallotCell*)m_BallotCellList.GetAt (cursor.m_RacePos);
        if (cursor.m_CandIdx == NO_CANDIDATE) {
                rect = pRace->GetRect ();
        } else {
                CCandCell* pCand =
(CCandCell*) pRace-
>GetCandidate (cursor.m_CandIdx);
                rect = pCand->GetRect ();
        }
        return rect.left / m_PageWidth;
}
```

Binary code looks like this (for illustration, the zeros and ones are compacted into an equivalent *hexadecimal representation*, which is the form in which scientists typically view binary data and a shorthand in which each digit represents a binary sequence):

0356100	23c8	96e8	1982	b70a	5541	3f86	33df	b114
0356120	e9ca	3cd7	9330	aae7	f124	588a	cdfc	e0cb
0356140	2152	aa15	4038	da7e	be9f	e153	35a6	e420
0356160	6d67	c7cc	31c1	1ebf	a1e2	b78c	b9e4	a37d
0356200	7b98	24b9	5dde	e501	6b29	3b56	32a8	78c9

Computers can interpret ones and zeros and translate them into action. In the library that Williams envisioned, a cryptographic *hash*, also called a *fingerprint*, would be computed on the binary after the software is compiled. The hash would be stored in a secure location, and whenever a machine is rolled out, its software would be rehashed and the hash compared to a stored value, just as fingerprints might be compared. If they match, the software is authentic. If they don't match, officials are alerted to a problem and can deal with it through predetermined procedures. If the binary is changed, the computer's behavior is likely to change as well. Williams proposed using a function that would check if a voting machine's binary has changed from what was authorized.

The suggestion is constructive, but not entirely dependable in practice. First, it is very common to compile the same program in different environments and produce binaries that are different. The compilation process often requires software libraries and depends on compiler settings, as well as on operating systems to some degree. A binary produced by compiling on a Windows 2000 machine will certainly differ from a binary produced by compiling the same program in Windows XP. Even with no tampering with the code, the hash function that Williams proposed for checking binaries would often not match.

There are other practical obstacles. Most large software packages rely on standard protocols and packagers. The code in Diebold's voting machines is no exception, and in fact it runs on top of Windows, so it depends on a huge amount of code from Microsoft. These standard protocols change from time to time in order to improve performance or correct security weaknesses, so Microsoft frequently issues system patches. The updates require that applications, in this case the software running the voting machine, be recompiled. Once that happens, the new binary no longer matches the one in the library. A static library cannot keep pace with the natural and appropriate evolution of software. To make Williams's scenario successful, manufacturers would need to either forgo security improvements that would counter newly discovered vulnerabilities or change their system, regularly recomputing hashes for storage in the software library and having to seek recertification each time.

Beyond its impracticality, the idea of a software library fails to address the most serious threat posed by paperless electronic voting—the insider threat. If a programmer decides to insert malicious code into a voting machine, having the code registered in a library would only serve to ensure that it becomes standard on all future machines. Brit Williams also recommended increasing poll worker training. In Georgia, he said, each county office has a state-certified person with at least sixty-four hours of training. I have no issue with increased poll worker training, but sixty-four hours of training in procedures won't help an election official deal with a software bug in a voting machine on election day.

As the first speaker of the day, I had dutifully kept to my allotted seven minutes, which I regretted as I listened to Williams go on for twenty minutes or more. Fortunately, I was able to make up for it in the question-and-answer session, in which I was able to give my point of view a fair hearing against the three panelists on the other side. Commissioner Ray Martinez directed the first question at me.

"I've followed the debate between computer scientists and election officials. Both are talking at and over each other. You served as a poll worker. What are your general impressions about the experience of working as a poll worker? You took off the hat of a computer scientist and put one on of an election administrator for a full day. What's changed in your view in terms of vulnerabilities, and what has reinforced your views?"

I explained that I had become a poll worker in response to the criticism that computer scientists need to learn more about elections. I had seen that people clearly liked the e-voting machines and that we should try to preserve the successful elements of their design, such as the ease of use. I told Martinez that I had felt like a hypocrite supervising voting on machines that I knew to be insecure, but that the process had helped me focus on vulnerabilities. Some seemed worse than I expected, while I now worried less about others. I had valued the real-world experience greatly, since I was now able to speak about the vulnerabilities with a lot more authority.

I went into some detail about the smartcard problem. In my precinct, with nine poll workers, five machines, and 199 votes cast, we would have been able to spot anyone voting more than once. But I identified a new vulnerability working the polls that day. After the polls closed, all of the memory cards were placed one by one into one of the voting machines, which read the votes off of them. The code that performs that tabulation represented a serious point of vulnerability: someone could rig the system to rewrite the totals on the cards as they were supposedly being read in. The process introduced so many new variables that parallel testing wouldn't be likely to detect the problem, especially since the testing would be less rigorous for this part of the process than for others.

I added that the cryptography in the modem communications was implemented improperly. I later learned that the modem only communicated results to be used for early release to the media and that the magnetic cards contained the authoritative totals. This situation actually made the threat posed by an attack on the memory cards more alarming.

Martinez then asked, "So, is it possible for election administrators to become a computer scientist for a day?"

I chuckled and said, "I don't think so."

"That's what I figured," Martinez continued. The question

may have sounded flip, but it had a serious point. Computer scientists can make important contributions to the process by learning about how elections run, but there's no realistic way for election officials to develop a technical understanding of their own computer systems. Despite their total lack of familiarity with cryptography, program verification, and formal risk analysis, however, election officials don't hesitate to give their opinions on the security and reliability of their voting systems, and the press takes their pronouncements as seriously as anything the computer experts say.

Martinez next asked me to talk about the potential attacks we had described in our Diebold report. I walked the commissioners through the report, using the plainest and simplest language I could and taking care to distinguish between generic attacks on paperless DREs and those specific to Diebold. My biggest concern was that anyone with access to the development environment of the code that runs these machines could produce any chosen outcome.

Referring to the quality scale I had made up, with 1 being "very good" and 10 "terrible," Martinez posed this question: if, in the interest of our democracy, Diebold and I decided to go into business together, what could we do to move the machines up on that scale? "From your perspective, is a voter-verifiable paper ballot the only way to fully secure our elections?" Noting that nothing could be 100 percent secure, he asked whether paper was really necessary. With the million-dollar question finally out on the table, the hearing room went silent. I had avoided discussing paper up to that point, but now I had to step up to the plate. I said that there was a short-term and a long-term answer to the question. In the short term, VVPB was absolutely necessary. It is the only reliable and realistic check against inherent security problems in the machines. The tangible, verified record that voters can leave at the polling place makes meaningful recounts possible. I said that in the long term—the long, long, *long* term—we should explore cryptographic options, but the most efficient and economical solution was to get VVPB into the process right away. I added that I was much less worried about a poll worker dealing with a printer problem during an election than with a software bug.

Commissioner Paul DiGregorio, who followed Martinez, asked Stephen Burger about the vendors' lack of compliance with the 2002 FEC standards. What could be done, he wondered, to bring them in line by the 2004 election? Burger sidestepped the question, saying only that vendors should be part of the process of establishing standards because they alone know what they can and cannot implement quickly. DiGregorio slipped in a compliment to me on my election service, saying that he had read my write-up of that experience and that he wanted to encourage the public to get involved and participate in the running of elections.

The next questioner, vice chair Gracia Hillman, wanted to know why voter verification was such a critical issue for electronic voting considering that nobody had complained about the lack of a voter-verified paper trail during the ninety years we had been using lever machines. Owing to time constraints, she asked that we all submit our responses in writing after the hearing. I wrote that the lack of voter verifiability was just as much a problem for lever machines as for DREs, but that fully electronic DREs have at least two additional disadvantages. First, tampering in the physical mechanism of a lever machine would be tangibly visible, whereas tampering on a DRE would be contained in data stored on magnetic media. Also, the programming of a lever machine is relatively simple, on top of which it is open to the public and recorded on videotape. The code that runs electronic voting machines is proprietary, and even if it were available for public inspection, the tampering could remain undetected, even by experts. Such is the nature of software. The second difference between the two technologies is the difference between retail and wholesale fraud. To rig an election with lever machines, you'd have to tamper with each individual machine, but someone could tamper just one time with the code that goes into many, if not all, of the DRE machines produced by a vendor, especially if that person has access to the development environment. Finally, I didn't believe we could use the fact that lever machines aren't voter-verifiable as an excuse to build electronic machines with the same deficiency. Two wrongs don't make a right.

Hillman asked Brit Williams to share his observations about the role the independent testing authority plays in certifying voting machines. Williams answered that the ITA provides a uniform starting point and that when the ITA evaluates a system against an objective standard, he knows that means the system is reliable and maintainable and that the engineering is of high quality. It means to him that the functionality is correct, the security has been evaluated, and there is no fraudulent code. Williams added that the ITA does not evaluate usability or affordability. He was certainly wrong about the security, and he did not mention that if the ITA had evaluated the security or the quality of the code before it certified the Diebold Accuvote TS, it was either completely incompetent or, worse, in on the fraud. When Hillman asked if the ITA process is transparent, Williams said that the process is not secret or proprietary, but that because vendors pay the ITA for the evaluation, the *rela-*

tionship is proprietary. He failed to mention that because of that proprietary relationship, the reports are kept secret and the public never sees what the ITA wrote about the machines.

As part of his summation, chairman Soaries asked a question that straightened everybody up in their seats. The 1990 FEC standards made reference to a standard for paper verification, Soaries said, but no such reference existed in the 2002 standards. He wanted to know if this was a conscious deletion or a simple oversight, and if the former, why was it taken out? I was stunned, as were most of those present. How had we all missed this? How had the press missed it? There was a dramatic pause as everyone let this revelation sink in. Williams hesitated a moment before saying that he didn't believe the omission had been a conscious decision. He couldn't recall any discussions at those meetings about removing paper verification, and so he now assumed it must have been an oversight. Burger said that he didn't get involved in the process until the paper verification standard had already been removed and couldn't recall any discussion about it since getting involved. The implication was staggering. The leaders of the standardization process for electronic voting machines were saying that the removal of the standard for paper verification between the 1990 and 2002 documents was the result of a simple oversight. And these were the people to whom the nation had entrusted its election process.

Before our panel finished, Soaries asked if there were any studies to determine whether voters would actually look at the paper if VVPB were used, but none of us knew of any. He closed by stating a fact that we all knew, or should have: the horses had left the stables, and we'd have to figure out how to build the corral around them. Our panel was followed by three other panels. The vendors used their time to reiterate that their systems were totally secure and that there was no need for paper, although they left the door open, saying that future-generation machines would have a paper component, since it seemed to be what the public wanted. The one exception was the CEO of Avante, which had already produced a machine with a paper trail; he reinforced the idea that paper keeps voting machines honest. The panel for election officials also offered no surprises. Everyone stuck to the script, including the final panel, the activists.

The press was all over the EAC hearing but, of course, were not invited to Dr. Soaries's noble and memorable effort to bring Brit Williams and me together for peace talks. For a day or two it seemed like I couldn't turn on the television without seeing myself testifying. The following week I happened to be leafing through *Newsweek* when my name jumped out at me. There was my line, "On the spectrum of terrible to very good, we are sitting at terrible," right there on the "Perspectives" page next to pronouncements from Britney Spears and Osama bin Laden. Not the kind of crowd in which I usually find myself.

16

More than 4,500 votes have been lost in one North Carolina
county because officials believed a computer that stored
ballots electronically could hold more data than it did.
Scattered other problems may change
results in races around the state.
—USA Today, *November 4, 2004*

Congressman Rush Holt, a Democrat, represents the
Twelfth District of New Jersey, which cuts a swath across
the middle of the state from the boardwalks of Asbury
Park to the rolling horse country on the Pennsylvania border.
He is a scientist by training, having earned a PhD in physics and
later serving as the assistant director of the Princeton Plasma
Physics Laboratory, but his entry into politics was perhaps inevitable. His father was the youngest person ever elected to the
U.S. Senate, at the age of twenty-nine, and his mother was the
only woman to serve as secretary of state for West Virginia. Holt
once demonstrated his broad base of knowledge by becoming a
five-time winner on *Jeopardy*, an accomplishment that, as a
friend of mine joked, might have played into his selection for
the House Intelligence Committee.

Rush Holt called me one day while I was having lunch with a
colleague from Hopkins and asked if I could brief him on the

results of the SAIC study—he was preparing a speech on the subject. The congressman's personal interest in voting technology was understandable: he had won two consecutive elections by virtue of recounts. In 1998 Holt was at first declared the loser to Republican Mike Pappas, but he recognized that his loss in at least one county where he had clearly led the polling seemed suspicious. An investigation revealed that a county election official had inadvertently reversed the Pappas and Holt tallies; when the problem was corrected, Holt became the overall victor. Two years later, the final tally had him leading by only fifty votes, and his opponent, Dick Zimmer, demanded a recount. Holt's lead increased with each passing day of the recount, until Zimmer conceded. Rush Holt wasn't about to endorse a voting system that did not allow for reliable recounts. (In 2002 he won reelection by defeating none other than New Jersey secretary of state DeForest Soaries, who went on to become the chairman of the U.S. Election Assistance Commission.)

Holt had made voting technology one of his central priorities even before the release of our Diebold study. His alarm over electronic voting machines that produced no meaningful paper record led him to introduce the Voter Confidence and Increased Accessibility Act (HR 2239) in May 2003. The bill, designed as an amendment to the Help America Vote Act, mandated that every voting machine be equipped to produce a voter-verifiable paper record for each vote. It also called for a form of spot-checking: one-half of 1 percent of all precincts, selected at random, would perform a manual recount and compare the paper record to the electronic tally. The paper trail was to be in place before the November 2004 election, which was still a year and a half away.

As my work brought me deeper into the cause of verifiable

voting, it was inevitable that I would cross paths with Rush Holt. He and I had participated in conference calls together in the period after our Diebold analysis, and I had finally met him at the Election Assistance Commission hearing.

You would think that HR 2239 would be a no-brainer for all elected officials, regardless of party affiliation. Their legitimacy, the inherent trust of their constituents, depends first and foremost on the legitimacy of the process that brings them to office. Yet Rush Holt's bill had trouble gaining traction, largely because in the polarized environment of Washington, e-voting came to be seen as a partisan issue. A Democrat had introduced this bill, and initially only Democrats came forward to support it. Republican politicians treated opposition to e-voting as a Democratic issue. It didn't help that much of the early attention drawn to the issue by Bev Harris focused on allegations about ties between the DRE manufacturers and the Republican Party. Diebold CEO Wally O'Dell threw fuel on the fire by stating in a fund-raising letter that he was committed to delivering the state of Ohio to the president. That letter of July 2003, the same month we released our Diebold report, had sparked a media storm, and O'Dell never quite lived it down.

In addition to Holt's bill in the House, several efforts were ongoing in the Senate, all but one sponsored by Democrats. In December 2003, Florida's Bob Graham introduced a Senate companion to HR 2239 that contained many of the same provisions. In April 2004, Graham joined forces with Barbara Boxer of California and Hillary Rodham Clinton of New York, merging his bill with one they had proposed. The resulting bill quadrupled the required random recounts from 0.5 percent to 2 percent, but it contained a loophole that allowed states to waive the VVPB requirement if it was "technologically impossible" to comply. A month later, in May, Senator John Ensign of Nevada became the first Republican in either house to put forth a bill related to e-voting. Called the Voting Integrity and Verification Act, his bill required that all electronic voting machines purchased in the future include voter-verified paper ballots and stipulated that those ballots would take precedence over electronic tallies in the case of a discrepancy. It was the only e-voting bill in the Senate with bipartisan support.

In this climate, it became increasingly difficult for people like me, the allegedly objective technical experts, to maintain the appearance of political neutrality. Clearly, I was sought out more often by Democrats, who, intentionally or not, made me feel like they were enlisting my support rather than seeking my objective analysis. The way things had fallen out, our findings usually lined up with their interests, and one could understand why Republicans might perceive us as aligned.

At the same time, I was in fact being drawn more visibly into an activist role. If you were to do even the laziest research on the e-voting issue, you'd come across my name, and given that the anti-e-voting movement was looking for authoritative voices to help carry its message, I was pursued relentlessly. And to be perfectly honest, I got to the point where I didn't always want to say no.

At best, I'm a reluctant activist. I spent nine years at the University of Michigan in Ann Arbor, less than a generation ago known as much for its storied contributions to the 1960s protest movement as for its regular appearances at the Rose Bowl and the NCAA finals. When I was there in the late 1980s and early 1990s, you didn't hear much about those heady days, but the activist spirit still showed up. Large demonstrations were common on campus. They were usually accompanied by a counterdemonstration, and at least one time I can remember, a counter-counterdemonstration. I'm no head-in-the-sand reactionary, but I confess to wondering occasionally if all those people singing songs and carrying signs didn't have something else to do, or someplace else they needed to be, especially considering how much it cost just to be there. Even when I supported the principle, such as when students formed human chains around buildings to protest the university's failure to observe Martin Luther King Day, I shied away from the event, preferring to find a quiet place to study. I spent so much time holed up with my books and computers that when I did find a spare moment, I'd choose to decompress by playing sports or hanging out with friends rather than trying to change the world. So you can imagine how awkward and self-conscious I felt when in my new role as a crusader for verifiable and recountable voting I found myself on the political stage.

Electronic voting seemed like a juggernaut to me. With each passing week it seemed to gain more—and more powerful—supporters. So, if I was in Washington or someplace where a rally was happening nearby and they wanted me to speak, I was now more likely to agree.

In fact, I met Rush Holt for the first time at just such a rally, outside the EAC hearing. True Majority, a group founded by Ben Cohen of Ben & Jerry's Ice Cream fame, had asked me to speak at a rally outside the hearing. On its website, True Majority identified itself as "a grassroots education and advocacy project of Priorities, Inc., a non-profit, non-partisan, tax-deductible 501(c)(3) corporation." The group had recruited activists across the country and launched a campaign called "The Computer Ate My Vote." For the first time in my life, I agreed to participate, joining Linda Schade of TrueVoteMD (the grassroots group that had brought suit against Linda Lamone in Maryland); Congressman Rush Holt of New Jersey; and Kevin Shelley, secretary of state of California.

When one of the organizers introduced me as the first speaker and I stepped to the microphone, I saw a phalanx of network television crews separating me from the hundred or so onlookers who had gathered. About twenty-five people stood behind me wearing yellow T-shirts bearing the slogan "The Computer Ate My Vote" and a large cartoon computer with huge teeth chomping on a paper ballot. There was even someone dressed like one of those mascots at sports stadiums, except that his costume was a giant cardboard computer with a ballot in its mouth. I scanned the crowd as I began speaking, and my eyes fell on Linda Lamone, standing behind the crowd with a cynical smirk on her face, coolly puffing on a cigarette.

I suppose I had a few things to learn about the theatrics of protest. My speech, a model of academic decorum, laid out a well-reasoned case, although I did try to sound more impassioned than I usually do. But when I heard Holt and Shelley speak, I felt downright sheepish. These seasoned pros understood they were onstage, and they gave electrifying performances. They knew how to play to the crowd, not to mention the cameras, and it worked. Their speeches featured prominently in the television coverage that evening.

I began to realize that I didn't actually have a problem being associated with an advocacy movement when the focus of the advocacy was fair and secure elections. I have always considered this to be both a nonpartisan and fundamentally patriotic goal. But the more outspoken I became on behalf of verifiable voting, the more often I found myself in company with Democrats and activists whose politics were generally to the left of center. If politics is perception, my increasing profile as an advocate was complicating the situation. I did what I could to counter this perception, jumping at any opportunity to meet with Republican politicians. I was thrilled, for instance, to be asked to discuss e-voting with senior staffers in Indiana Republican Richard Lugar's office sometime later and dropped a previously scheduled engagement in order to make myself available.

I got a taste of how these deep divisions between the parties played out in the real world when staffers from the House Committee on Government Reform invited me to meet with them. The Democrats on the committee invited me to Washington. The staffers listened attentively to my explanation of what we had found in the Diebold machines and why voter-verifiable paper ballots help protect against fraud in the machines. They asked me if I would be willing to testify to what I had told them at a congressional hearing (I was perfectly happy to do so), but added that all they could do was to suggest my name—not actually invite me—because it was a Republican-controlled committee. When the Republican staffers called a few days later to invite me to meet with them for the same purpose, I asked if they had gotten my name from their Democratic colleagues, but they said they had found me independently. After I had gone to Washington again and met with the Republicans, I mentioned that it would have been more convenient for me if the two groups, both working on the same issue for the same committee, had coordinated their efforts and saved me a trip. The Republican staffer gave a sort of rueful smile and explained that wasn't how things worked on Capitol Hill.

A subcommittee of the government reform committee scheduled a hearing for May 12, 2004, just a week or so after the EAC hearing, and asked me to testify. By that time, of course, it felt

like my life was "all e-voting, all the time," and I was already
booked to travel to California, where Adam Stubblefield was
presenting our Diebold analysis paper at the IEEE "Symposium
on Security and Privacy" in Berkeley. I grudgingly canceled that
trip and prepared my congressional testimony. Meanwhile,
staffers for the House Science Committee, having read that I
would be in Washington that day, asked me to brief them on
electronic voting the morning of the hearing. I did meet with
them on the morning of the twelfth, after which we grabbed
some lunch in the House cafeteria. As we took our seats I noticed
several of them exchanging nods of greeting with none other
than my old friend Brit Williams. I laughed to myself, thinking
that at least Washington would be getting the full spectrum of
opinion on this subject.

In the afternoon, one look at the hearing room told me I was
completely outnumbered. In addition to Brit Williams, I saw
Ted Selker and Jim Adler of VoteHere. As the room filled with
press and other onlookers, it seemed we were about to get under way, but a one-hour postponement was announced. Something was up, something unsavory or embarrassing. Maybe it
was the way all the staffers ducked our questions and avoided
making eye contact. When the hour had passed, the hearing
was canceled—after I had canceled an important trip to California, after Brit Williams had driven up from Georgia, after
Jim Adler had flown across the country. And no one ever told
us why.

Once home, I started e-mailing staffers from both parties, trying to find out what had happened. All they would tell me was
that the hearing was being rescheduled, but rumors circulated
that a fight had erupted between the two parties' representatives
on the committee about whether Rush Holt, who did not actu-

ally sit on the committee, would get to introduce a statement and ask questions. Although the staffers denied this, they did allow that the cancelation had been the result of a disagreement that could not be resolved in time. I was reminded of my toddlers fighting over a toy. In a power struggle, winning is the only goal. The subcommittee did reschedule the hearing, for July 20, which happened to be primary day in Georgia, preventing Brit Williams's attendance. Sanford Morganstein, the CEO of Populex, testified in his place. Populex manufactures voting machines capable of creating a paper trail. Michael Shamos replaced Ted Selker on the panel, which was a wash, but Morganstein represented a huge net gain for the panel. I had met him several times and had always found him lucid and persuasive on the importance of paper auditing in elections. Whereas Brit Williams's testimony always made me cringe, listening to Morganstein was delightful.

In the run-up to the new hearing date, the e-mail chatter intensified, revealing even more explicitly the split between the parties on e-voting. On one mailing list, I saw a solicitation for questions that Democratic committee members could ask Shamos and Adler. A great many people got their two cents in on this one. One activist organization sent me a list of "talking points," which put me in mind of Michael Shamos's testimony in Annapolis. The idea of even receiving such a list, much less adhering to it, made me resentful. For starters, my very involvement in the hearing rested on my status as an "expert." And beyond that, I couldn't imagine going into something like this with someone else's script to follow. In all of this chatter, there was an implicit assumption that the Democrats on the committee would push for paper ballots and the Republicans would oppose them.

At the rescheduled hearing of the House Subcommittee on Technology, Information Policy, Intergovernmental Relations, and the Census, the manipulating influences on both sides of the aisle were apparent from the beginning. After Adam Putnam, the shockingly young Republican representative from Florida, opened the hearing, the ranking member—the most senior member of the minority party—William Clay of Missouri, spoke about the importance of voter-verifiable paper trails and about the ease with which electronic machines can be rigged. Even though I'd heard all this a few dozen times before, Clay's rhetoric seemed eerily familiar. It took me a second before I realized that I'd seen the exact language in the e-mail exchanges of the preceding few days. He went on, making the point that elections are not about making the lives of the election officials easy, but about ensuring the security and integrity of the vote count. Michael Shamos, who was sitting next to me, made me laugh when he quietly asked me if I had written Clay's speech. I hadn't, of course, but I had a pretty good idea who had. This is how the system worked. The questions that Clay asked Shamos and Adler had appeared verbatim in the e-mails. So when chairman Putnam challenged me with a direct question, I knew it had been fed to him by folks in the e-voting camp, hoping to stump me in public.

"Dr. Rubin," he began, "after volunteering as a poll worker, you were quoted as saying that the experience showed you that one potential attack would be far more difficult to pull off than you and your colleagues had assumed. Is that an accurate quote, and do you still feel that a serious attack is likely?" Whoever had fed him this question—maybe Diebold, maybe someone like Selker—obviously didn't know that I'd fielded it many times before and had honed an answer that actually strengthened the case against DREs. I explained that my experience as a poll worker showed me that the machines were even more vulnerable than I had previously thought. I had written that at my voting precinct we probably would have detected people trying to cast multiple votes using homegrown smartcards, but other poll workers all over the country, I told the committee, had sent me e-mails saying that in their precincts such multiple voting would never have been detected.

Putnam pressed on. "Is it more or less difficult to perpetrate fraud using electronic devices over traditional paper ballots?"

This is the heart of the matter. "I believe it is more difficult to perpetrate fraud," I answered, "but the fraud would have much more far-reaching consequences if it were successful." I have learned that supporters of e-voting get hung up on the fact that it's so much harder to cheat the computerized systems than the old-fashioned paper ballots, but here they miss the point about wholesale fraud versus retail fraud. With the stakes so high, we have to assume that clever and resourceful people will attempt to subvert the process. It has happened too many times before, and will happen again. It isn't feasible to stuff ballot boxes across the entire country, or even in several adjacent polling stations. You just can't scale an attack against paper ballots. But when computers running exactly the same software are used in ever-larger geographical areas, a bug in the code, whether inadvertent or placed there intentionally, could corrupt the entire outcome of an election, especially when the margins of victory are as narrow as they have been in recent years.

Toward the end of the hearing, Putnam asked the entire panel of experts if we thought a voter-verifiable paper trail was feasible for the general election, given that it was only a few months away. We all agreed that it was not. Putnam then fixed his eye on me and asked what I thought should be done for November.

Obviously, there was no simple answer, or a realistic one, but I replied in all seriousness, "Test the machines like crazy, and hope the election is not close." I hadn't intended to be flip or disrespectful, but the whole gallery—full of activists, media, and other interested parties—erupted with loud laughter.

I felt the hearing had gone well. Despite the chairman's apparent bias in favor of electronic voting, ranking member Clay had stated the arguments against DREs and for paper trails for the record, supported by testimony from me and Sanford Morganstein. Representatives Rush Holt and Marcy Kaptur also participated and made sure critical questions were asked.

Unfortunately, other hearings got a little rocky. A couple of weeks earlier, the Committee on House Administration, with Republican Bob Ney from Ohio as chair and Connecticut's Democratic congressman John Larson as ranking member, held its own hearing on electronic voting security. This committee actually convened two panels, one with the usual cast of computer scientists, plus Yoshi, and the second consisting of state election officials all known for their fierce opposition to paper ballots, including Maryland's own Linda Lamone. Moments before the hearing began, Rush Holt approached me and said he had given ranking member Larson two questions to ask the panel. Then he told me what he thought the answers were, which rubbed me the wrong way, just as it had when people tried to outline talking points for me. How could anyone trust me to be an objective expert when someone was feeding me answers? I gave Holt the benefit of the doubt, however, believing he was only checking to see if I agreed.

Chairman Ney gave some hint of his own personal leanings

right from the start by blasting the *New York Times* for its "biased" editorials. The *Times* had been running a series of intelligent, deeply reasoned, and comprehensive editorials by Adam Cohen that I believed were all right on the money. Cohen had interviewed me for background material as part of what I knew to be exhaustive research for his articles. He had even traveled to primaries around the country to experience the election process firsthand. Ney went on to compliment me on my service as a poll worker, but his disdain for anyone who questioned voting technology was palpable, and he made sure to work in the implication that such criticism could keep voters away from the polls in the election.

Nonetheless, when my turn came, I had a chance to make a valuable statement. I began by telling the committee I had two things to say that they would probably find surprising. First, I stated that I was not fundamentally opposed to electronic voting. I elaborated, saying that a DRE with a paper trail was not a great design for a voting machine. There were plenty of ways to build voting machines, I said, that would make it difficult for the machine's designers, builders, and administrators to cheat, but the current generation of DREs didn't fulfill that mission. The advantage of a well-designed system, electronic or not, is that it does not require complex procedures to ensure security, takes control out of the hands of the manufacturers, and accounts for the needs of voters, including special needs. Such a system requires *transparency*, which can be partially achieved with open code; *independent audit*, where the audit is not controlled by system designers and is not performed using a record created by the data being audited; *peer review*; and *usability testing*. If I were to design a voting machine to meet these requirements, I said, it wouldn't be like the DREs available today.

My dream voting machine would have a user interface much like a DRE, but in reality it wouldn't be a voting machine at all. I call it a "ballot-marking machine." Voters would navigate through touch screens, just as with a DRE, and make their choices for candidates and for ballot resolutions. However, instead of clicking on Cast Vote at the end, they would select a Print Ballot option, and the machine would produce a filled-in paper ballot that the voter would be able to check for accuracy. The layout and typography of the ballots would be standardized, and the count would proceed completely independently from the ballot-marking process, in some cases even by hand. One possible variation would use optical scanners to count the ballots, provided that the manufacturer of the scanners had no ties of any kind to the manufacturer of the ballot-marking machine. Similarly, scanners outfitted with audio output could assist blind voters, who would feed their marked ballot into the machine and then be able to hear the choices announced in an earpiece for verification. The marked paper ballots could be retained by election officials and used for recounts, either in cases of actual dispute or as part of a random spot-checking system. Since the independence of the various manufacturers would be of paramount importance, I suggested that perhaps machines from a separate company could be used for recounts.

The ideal machine would have all the useful features of a DRE but would improve upon it in several key ways. It would allow for meaningful recounts of voter intent and would make it incredibly difficult for a vendor to rig an election. Most significantly, the system would provide citizens with the confidence that their votes were recorded and transmitted accurately and could not be altered after the fact.

The rest of the testimony went pretty much as it always did, except for a few new wrinkles thrown in by Michael Shamos. In a remarkable feat of misdirection, he referred to the great number of articles he had seen in the *New York Times* that reported on fraud in non-electronic elections. This didn't have anything to do with the insecurity of e-voting machines, but somehow he managed to imply that those machines were not the real problem. He did surprise me, however, by strongly criticizing the ITA process for testing and validating voting machines, a process that sorely deserved his skepticism.

I sat in the audience for the second panel and listened to the election officials condemn the use of paper in elections. In another meaningless stunt, Linda Lamone unrolled a thirteen-foot-long printed ribbon, claiming that it represented the typical paper record from a voting machine. She was making her point using a totally misleading worst-case example, as if she had accepted the idea that just because her Diebold machines represented a low in software quality, any paper technology the company selected would be equally bad.

Ney was eating it up and egged on Lamone and her colleagues with leading questions so that they could hammer home the virtues of DREs and the foolishness of paper. Soon after the hearing, however, he would tip his hand and open a window onto the deep partisan divide over e-voting. Prior to the hearing, Democratic presidential candidate Howard Dean had submitted a letter to the committee that carried the signatures of more than 127,000 concerned citizens. Dean had a strong interest in e-voting, and I had participated on a conference call with him at one point in which it was discussed. My personal experience of him as a grounded and reasonable politician didn't quite match the fiery persona that the press liked to present to the public. His letter bears this out:

To the Honorable Robert Ney and the Congress of the United
States:

We must act now to ensure that our voting systems produce accurate and verifiable results. Some states are planning to use
machines that will not allow voters to verify their choices. This
means that flaws in the machine or software will never be
caught—and no recount will be possible.

And the head of the largest e-voting machine company—
who is a major contributor to George Bush and has promised to
deliver Ohio to him—asks that we just trust him.

Today we call on you to require any electronic voting machine used in this election to produce a paper trail—one that
allows voters to verify their choices and officials to conduct recounts.

Signed,
Governor Howard Dean, M.D.

I couldn't see anything incendiary in the letter, but that didn't
stop Ney from turning it into an opportunity to play more partisan politics. A week after the hearing, he responded with a letter,
stating in part,

Dear Governor Dean,

I am in receipt of your letter dated June 22, 2004 and the ac-
companying petition you indicate has been signed by 127,469
persons. I note your website continues to solicit signatures for
the petition (along with contributions to your organization).

Left-wing groups like yours and America Coming Together
that are exploiting this issue to inflame your supporters and
raise money for yourselves are recklessly making claims that
are unsupported by the facts. You should realize that if your de-

mands to retrofit all electronic voting machines with printers before November 2004 were met, it would ensure an electoral meltdown that would make our last presidential election look orderly by comparison. In calling for nationwide deployment of a voting system that has never been used successfully in a single election in this country, you are doing a great disservice to the voting public you purport to defend.

. . .

Conspiracy theorists and others . . . are warning of unseen and unproven "dangers" posed by newer systems.

The issues surrounding the security of electronic voting are currently being reviewed by the Election Assistance Commission, in conjunction with the National Institute of Standards and Technology. . . . That is the appropriate way to handle this issue, not by making uninformed and premature legislative decisions based on misinformation and hysteria.

. . .

I hope that instead of persisting in making demands that would make our elections worse and less open to all, that you will work with me and the other Members of Congress, Democrat and Republican, who recognize that running clean and accurate elections should be a shared goal of everyone, regardless of party or ideology.

Sincerely,

Bob Ney

Not the kind of letter one writes in order to build bridges. The irony of the closing line almost smacked of sarcasm. In September, Representative Ney had a letter published in *Roll Call*, the "newspaper of Capitol Hill," denying that the Republican leadership had killed the Holt bill in the House. Ney wrote that he, Senate majority whip Mitch McConnell, Democratic representative Steny Hoyer, and Democratic senator Chris Dodd had written a letter criticizing the Holt bill and that this bipartisan letter was what ultimately killed the bill. He quoted Mike Shamos's testimony from the House administration committee hearing saying that paper ballots were less accurate than electronic voting machines. The letter in *Roll Call* closed with the statement that Congress should not "recklessly [impose] new costs and new requirements, just months before the 2004 presidential and Congressional elections, that have not been fully considered." At the time Ney and his colleagues sent that letter, HR 2239, Holt's bill, had 129 Democratic sponsors and only three Republican sponsors, hardly what anyone would call bipartisan. All 435 members of Congress have to get themselves elected, and I can't imagine a credible reason, beyond partisan politics, why support for more secure and auditable elections could be so one-sided. Rush Holt responded in *Roll Call* a couple of weeks later, writing, "The debate is not about 'voter receipts'; it's about whether voting can be audited. The real question is this: Are Members of Congress willing to do without the possibility of a recount in future elections, for themselves and other candidates across the country? That's the future that awaits us if we embrace electronic voting without paper back-ups; recounts would be meaningless."

Partisan politics were trumping common sense beyond the chambers of Congress, as I found out one night when I appeared as a guest to talk about e-voting security on C-SPAN's *Washington Journal*. The program features a call-in segment, during which one caller tried to "out" me.

"Are you a Democrat?" he asked.

"My personal political affiliation is unimportant. This is an issue that cuts across party lines. Both parties need to be concerned that our elections are auditable and that the election cannot be stolen due to the use of insecure voting machinery."

You could hear the gleeful triumph in the caller's voice. "I thought so!" he cried. "You Democrats are looking for an excuse before the election even happens so that you can whine once again and claim that the election was stolen." The host cut him off there.

In 2000, when I participated in an NSF panel on Internet voting, the atmosphere was respectful and collegial, even friendly. There was no sense of "us versus them." The election officials there expressed a sincere desire to understand security issues. After my talk, several officials from a number of different states joined me for lunch, and we had a lively and constructive talk about security and elections. We traded war stories, mine about Internet viruses and cyber-attacks and theirs about previous elections gone awry. People from all sides of the issue contributed to a balanced and comprehensive report that benefited from everyone's willingness to discuss and compromise.

Four years later, when the National Academy of Sciences (NAS) convened a panel on the issue, the spirit of cooperation had deteriorated into confrontation and bitterness. Panelists had assigned seats, and to my chagrin—albeit to the great amusement of most everyone else—I spent two days sitting one seat over from Linda Lamone. Eric Fischer sat between us, and though his actual title is Senior Specialist in Science and Technology at the Congressional Research Service of the Library of Congress, he was, for the purposes of this meeting, jokingly dubbed the "DMZ," or simply "Buffer Man," by several other attendees. Richard Thornburgh, the former U.S. attorney general and former governor of Pennsylvania, chaired the meeting, which was attended by a familiar lineup of computer scientists, as well as some political scientists and secretaries of state. The tension I had started to feel creeping into all of these gatherings was by now thick in the air and burst easily into the open. For example, the NAS workshop coincided with the day of coordinated protest rallies across the country called "The Computer Ate My Vote." Echoing Linda Lamone some months before, election officials had derided these rallies as events that undermined voter confidence and were likely to lead to lower voter turnout. I guess Thornburgh failed to see the irony in labeling the protest a disruption of the democratic process, but he voiced his agreement, as did others at the meeting. Ted Selker asked people to raise their hands if they had something to do with organizing the protests. Some people started scanning the room menacingly, like school kids waiting to see who was going to confess to stealing the teacher's apple. David Dill shot up his hand, declaring that he was proud to be part of the protests, and I swear I thought a fight might break out.

I felt a kind of emptiness after the NAS workshop and wondered how many more of these unpleasant meetings I could stomach. There was a sameness to them all. The facts didn't change, and neither did the main players. There was precious little new insight or information revealed from one to the next. As much as I enjoyed being a part of something big and having a voice in an important national discourse, I don't relish confrontation. I was starting to feel like I could do without the stress of all the personal antagonism that had seeped into the discussion. I had to remind myself that this was about the greater good and that I was in a position to make a real difference, but it was getting harder to stay focused and motivated.

The irrational partisanship over e-voting reached a high point—or maybe, more accurately, a low point—a month later in Florida. In late July 2004, against the wishes of Governor Jeb Bush, the Florida GOP paid to circulate a glossy full-color "memo" to party members. The party urged voters in Miami to use absentee ballots to make sure that their votes were counted. While Governor Bush was busily reassuring voters that touch-screen voting was reliable, the state leadership of his own party was singing a different tune. "The liberal Democrats have already begun their attacks and the new electronic voting machines do not have a paper ballot to verify your vote in case of recount. Make sure your vote counts. Order your absentee ballot today." This cynically political flyer contained two photographs of a smiling George Bush and in the end was condemned in the media by members of both parties.

The death of Rush Holt's bill could be laid at the feet of partisan politics. The polarized Congress couldn't overcome its paranoid culture, in which loyalty to party takes precedence over independent and objective reasoning, to secure our elections. The politicization of the e-voting issue resulted in the 2004 presidential election being carried out on untrustworthy technology in jurisdictions across the country. The United States invented constitutional democracy as we know it, yet that system had devolved to the point where it couldn't protect the only process that could ensure its survival.

17

Computer Scientists who question the security
of electronic voting machines are
undermining our democracy.
—*Linda H. Lamone, Administrator of Elections,
State of Maryland, November 3, 2003*

There is nothing easy about an election official's job. Under the best of circumstances, the task of facilitating the vote—staffing and equipping countless polling stations, establishing and monitoring proper procedures, collecting and protecting the vote data, and so on—is daunting, to say the least, and it's no wonder that these officials would seek ways to simplify the process with new technology. The job is also utterly thankless. Nobody notices the officials when everything goes well, but if there's a problem, they're likely to get crucified (not unlike security specialists, one might point out). I believe the work they do constitutes a remarkable and invaluable service to the nation.

I have, of course, butted heads with election officials as long as I've been involved with electronic voting, and I have come to believe that the actions of a select few have indisputably placed obstacles in the path to truly secure elections. I can understand where the DRE manufacturers are coming from, but not those people who have taken on the responsibility of enabling people to vote. That we share the same goal—to protect and secure our elections—makes it even more difficult to comprehend their blind, ironclad faith in e-voting and DREs.

Maryland's Linda Lamone, Georgia's Kathy Rogers and Cathy Cox, and California's Mischelle Townsend and Connie McCormick were among the state election officials who consistently blasted computer scientists for our criticism of their beloved touch screens. These people behaved as if they were the vendors whose products were being attacked, when in fact they were customers who had been sold inadequate products. I could easily imagine what motivated them. The DRE voting machines unquestionably made elections much easier to administer. They conveyed an element of progress as well. Officials who brought in these machines could feel proud about keeping pace with the "state of the art." This is especially significant in a culture that prides itself on its ceaseless quest for technological advancement and perceives anything digital as automatically superior to its antiquated predecessor. The new age is defined by an update of the old joke: Why did the digital chicken cross the road? Because it can.

In some cases, particularly in Georgia, officials had staked their reputations on the new machines. Cathy Cox, a lawyer by training and the first woman to hold the position of Georgia secretary of state, put her pride in the Diebold machines front and center. Her Web page featured a picture of her voting, on an Accuvote TS, on the question, "Which state was the first to adopt statewide electronic voting?" The screen displayed several states as options, and her finger was poised over the button marked "Georgia." Many people assume that Cox's leadership in automating the state's paperless election is one of the accomplishments she plans to trumpet in her rumored bid for governor in 2006. She had no affection for anyone who insinuated that the move had been a mistake and that her defense of the machines, once the security problems emerged, was a colossal blunder.

I had my first interaction with Cathy Cox the day the *New York Times* wrote up our Diebold analysis. That afternoon, Darren Lacey told me that Hopkins had received angry phone calls from the Georgia secretary of state's office. Apparently, we had inadvertently included a picture of Cox in our paper in a way that made it look like we were mocking her. Not wanting to use a picture of an Accuvote TS off the Diebold website, I had done a Google image search and found the photo on Georgia's website. I had no idea the woman in the picture was Cathy Cox. At the time, I didn't even know who Cathy Cox was. Darren explained that we were under no obligation to remove the picture, but that we might consider doing so as a courtesy. Indeed, we cropped the photo so that only the voting machine and Cox's hand were visible, and then re-posted the report.

Cathy Cox generally preferred to get her licks in when the public wasn't watching. Time after time, reporters would ask for my comment on something—usually derogatory and occasionally inaccurate—that Cox had said in an interview. One time, months after the VoteHere episode had been put to rest, she told a reporter to discount my critique because of that past relationship. There's no doubt that she knew this was a dead issue, and her naked attempt to sabotage my work revealed her complete lack of sincerity when it came to this debate.

Since Cathy Cox was down in Georgia, our paths never crossed. But I had real trouble closer to home with the chief elections administrator in my home state of Maryland, Linda

Lamone. Ms. Lamone has figured prominently in many of the key moments of my work in e-voting. I'm reluctant to paint her as a villain, although she has most certainly made it her business to vilify me. The first opportunity I had to meet with her, at the Maryland House Ways and Means Committee hearing in Annapolis, she would have nothing to do with me, not even any eye contact. Several weeks after that, at the NIST symposium in Gaithersburg, another computer scientist, Paul Herrnson from the University of Maryland, offered to introduce me to her. I told him that I didn't think that was such a good idea and that I was sure she would be uninterested, but he was gently insistent, cajoling me with a pep talk about how constructive it would be. I agreed, but when Paul called her over, things didn't go quite as he planned.

"Linda, there's somebody that I'd like you to meet."

As she walked over I saw her smile dissolve and her face harden as she realized who she was on her way to meet. She stopped, turned on her heel, and snapped loudly over her shoulder, "I don't want to meet *him*!"

"I told you she wouldn't want to meet me," I said, hopefully loud enough for her to hear.

Linda Lamone's open hostility was something I simply could not comprehend. When we released our study, I was sure that state election administrators would be eager to learn from it. Impartial scientists had uncovered flaws in a product the state had purchased. I wondered if they might ask us to work with them to mitigate the problems. I honestly believed we had performed an important service. None of us were looking for medals or pats on the back, but we were utterly baffled at the state's response. It was still a year and a half until the November 2004 election, but rather than spending that time seeking solutions, Lamone devoted her energy to defending the choice of the paperless Diebold machines and blaming us for undermining the public's confidence in the election. By my logic, the people of the state of Maryland had far more to worry about from Lamone and her insecure machines than they did from us. Raising the public's awareness about the dangers of the machines was a civic responsibility, not a crime against the state.

Lamone continued to find ways to avoid me as our paths inevitably continued to cross. A couple of months after the NIST symposium, I was invited to appear with her on an hourlong live call-in program on Baltimore's NPR radio station. I'm never good with confrontations, and the thought of sitting across from someone so hostile for an hour chilled me, but at the same time, I welcomed the chance to lay out the facts of my argument in a one-on-one setting. I wanted to get her to respond straight out to the facts about the Diebold machines. I prepared well and got myself psyched for the encounter, so you can imagine the letdown I felt when I arrived and learned that Lamone had canceled. The host explained that she had sent written comments instead, which he would read on the air and to which I would be allowed to respond. I actually felt a little bad for Linda; her failure to show up gave me a full hour to pontificate. When the host read her questions, it was like he was lobbing up fat pitches for me to hit, with nobody in the outfield. I had the last word on everything. The callers were uniformly sympathetic to my position, and some were openly angry with Lamone, who wasn't even there to defend herself.

The stunt that Lamone had pulled at Bob Ney's hearing—pulling out a ridiculously long register ribbon and claiming that it represented a paper ballot—was typical of the smoke and mirrors that she and her gang would use to argue their case. I'm sure they knew perfectly well that paper ballots wouldn't have to look like that. They wouldn't have to look any different from the paper absentee ballot already in use. In fact, a paper trail could be even smaller, since it would only need to list the voter's choices, not all the possible choices. This kind of tactic enraged me because it was a cynical attempt to manipulate people's understanding and emotions with false information. To this day I cannot fathom why any public servant would take the side of a vendor—a bad one, at that—over the interests of his or her constituency.

Sometimes Linda Lamone sent her minions to do her dirty work. A few weeks before the November 2004 election, I gave a talk in Maryland to InfraGard, an FBI-sponsored group of technologists at government agencies concerned with protecting critical infrastructure and combating terrorism. The members of this group have a very high level of technological sophistication, and the audience consisted of technical leaders from throughout the government, including the Departments of Energy and Homeland Security. Many of the members have security clearances. InfraGard had invited two members of the state board of elections to my talk, including Pamela Woodside, the chief information officer of the state, who in the context of elections reports directly to Linda Lamone. When I finished speaking about the problems we had discovered in the Diebold machines and the risks of DREs in general, I was amazed at the shallowness of the questions Woodside asked, given the position she held. When she even claimed that Maryland had instituted procedures that made its voting system the most secure in the country, there was muffled laughter in the room.

I approached Woodside afterward, and she told me that the state owed me a debt of gratitude for the work I had done and that none of the security measures would be in place if it hadn't been for our report. I was grateful, but marveled to myself at the lack of any public acknowledgment of our service, only Linda Lamone's statements about the disservice to democracy we had done. This two-faced attitude became starkly evident the next day when I read an account in *Government Computer News* of a talk Woodside gave after attending my lecture. The article said, in part, "The report's author, Avi Rubin, a Johns Hopkins professor and director of Hopkins' Information Security Institute, made some incorrect assumptions about the Diebold system, Woodside said. Rubin assumed the DRE computers would have an attached keyboard and be connected to the Internet, neither of which is the case, she said." Please. Woodside knew that I never said a word about a keyboard or the Internet. Either she was playing dirty or that was one hell of a misquote.

The ultimate expression of Lamone's and Maryland's stubborn ignorance and mindless support of Diebold's voting machines came in a pamphlet issued by the state board of elections called *Maryland's Better Way to Vote—Electronic Voting: Myth Vs. Fact.* I learned about it from a reporter who called and asked if he could fax it to me for comment. Apparently, the state had given it to reporters before posting it on the state website, hoping that its spin could dominate the early press stories, before computer scientists like me could have at it. The pamphlet featured six "myths" followed by the "facts" that purportedly laid the myths to rest, and it bordered on the outrageous—so much so that it would have been closer to the truth if the words "myth" and "fact" had been reversed throughout the document. Right from the start, the state seemed to have it backwards:

Myth 1: *"Electronic voting systems are inherently insecure and vulnerable to fraud."*

Facts:

- Maryland's new Direct Recording Electronic (DRE) voting system has been studied and analyzed more than any other voting system in the country.
- Not one of the security analyses conducted on Maryland's voting system showed evidence of fraud or manipulation or the ability to manipulate the voting system in a polling place . . .
- The changes made as a result of the analyses improve the security of the voting system and further diminish the likelihood of fraud.
- Additionally, as noted in a recent U.S. Congressional Research Report, "there are no proven cases of tampering with the Direct Recording Electronic (DRE) or other computer-assisted voting systems in public elections."

Whereas this "myth" strikes me as a true statement, the "facts" are misleading. The first bullet item is true, a sad commentary on the level of nationwide analysis of voting systems. The second bullet item probably should have mentioned that none of the security analyses have found proof of life on Mars, which they weren't looking for either. What they were looking for were vulnerabilities, and they found plenty. The point about there being no evidence of "the ability to manipulate the voting system in a polling place" has the added distinction of being wholly untrue. The smartcard proposed in our study and carried out by the RABA team illustrated *exactly* how to manipulate the system.

The third item is simply illogical. The security analyses found no evidence of fraud but prompted the state to take steps to further lessen that possibility. This "fact" reminds me of another joke: "Officer, I have never seen that man before, I never laid hands on him, and his lip was already swollen before I hit him." The final bullet seems almost desperate. It's like saying that in the 1700s more people died falling off horses than in car accidents or plane crashes.

The next five "myths" are no better. For example, myth 5 states, "Hackers could alter a voting system by introducing a 'Trojan Horse' or breaking into the election management system." Nowhere in our study, or in any public statement I ever made about Diebold, did I ever express this concern. I never heard David Dill, Barbara Simons, David Jefferson, or Dan Wallach worry about "hackers breaking in." The "facts" that dispel this "myth" include the statement that the machines are not connected to the Internet. They might as well have added a myth that "the voting machines may spontaneously detonate," followed by the fact that "there are no explosives in the machines that could cause this to happen."

Doug Jones from Iowa wrote an excellent point-by-point critique of Maryland's myths and facts, which he posted to his website. Since his analysis made it crystal clear that the brochure was an embarrassment to the state, he sent a copy to Nicole Trella, the contact person listed on it, and asked for feedback before he posted it. He received no response, but three weeks after his critique went up on the website, he received notice from his university that Linda Lamone had sent a letter to the president of the school requesting that the posting be removed so that Maryland could be "provided the opportunity to correct several incorrect and misleading statements contained in Dr. Jones' response." Doug never saw the letter from Lamone, only the letter from the university denying her request. When he wrote Nicole Trella again, forwarding portions of his initial request as proof that he had solicited their comments, she answered that she had never received his message and assumed it must have been blocked by her spam filter. Trella said she would provide comments, but Jones never heard from her again, nor from anyone else affiliated with the Maryland Board of Elections.

I SPOKE IN person with Linda Lamone for the first time on June 8, 2004, the result of DeForest Soaries's effort to bring together people from opposing factions in the e-voting debate. He rang me up on my cell phone for a friendly chat, during which he invited me to be his guest at an election officials' banquet where he would be speaking. I thought perhaps he wanted me to speak, but he replied, somewhat cryptically, that he just wanted to have me there as his guest.

I arrived a bit late, after the banquet was already in full swing, and it occurred to me as I walked into the room full of well-fed and cheerful election administrators that perhaps I was there as some kind of lamb for the slaughter. I wasn't exactly a favorite with this crowd. But I trusted Soaries, whom I greeted at the head table before being ushered to a table near the front of the room and seated with a group of senior officials and a pair of Diebold vice presidents. I felt a little like a Montague who had shown up at a Capulet feast.

After dessert, Soaries rose and delivered a charming and thoughtful speech. He's a captivating orator, having honed his skills preaching every Sunday at a Baptist church in New Jersey. He had the audience in the palm of his hand. About ten minutes into his speech, Soaries said that he had brought a special friend with him. He said that scientists pursue truth and that his friend embodied that ideal, even when it made him unpopular. He said that his friend was brave and sought only what was right. He then asked me to stand up and asked the audience to recognize me. The applause was surprisingly loud and long and seemed genuinely heartfelt. I was tempted to ask if they were applauding the fact that I had been brave enough to show up there. Soaries told the election officials that they should be grateful for my dedication and hard work. He even equated my public position to people who had spoken out against slavery a century and a half before. I was deeply embarrassed, to be sure, but I was also deeply moved by Soaries's magnanimous gesture. I believed his great praise would bolster my credibility with this skeptical group. Out of the corner of my eye, I could see Linda Lamone a few tables over, a scowl on her face.

Soaries had other intentions for his speech besides heaping praise on the likes of me. The EAC had in fact promoted the dinner and Soaries's speech as the occasion for critical announcements regarding the commission's strategy for securing electronic voting. He laid out the following five recommendations for the 2004 election, which, though I didn't believe they went far enough, constituted a good start:

1. The EAC should request that all voting software vendors allow election officials with whom they have contracted to analyze the proprietary source code of their software and to protect that process by using appropriate nondisclosure and confidentiality agreements. The EAC should assist in the analysis when needed.

2. The EAC should ask every election jurisdiction that uses electronic voting devices to identify and implement enhanced security measures in November. Options include paper verification, voice verification, cryptography, parallel monitoring,

chain of custody, testing practices, intergovernmental agreements for enhanced management, etc. The EAC will offer best practices and guidance on specific methods and will assist in the identification and execution of security methods when needed.

3. The EAC should invite every voting software vendor to submit their certified software to the National Software Reference Library (NSRL) at the National Institute of Standards and Technology (NIST). This would facilitate the tracking of software version usage. NSRL is designed to collect software from various sources and incorporate file profiles computed from this software into a Reference Data Set (RDS) of information. The RDS can be used by law enforcement, government, and industry organizations to review files on a computer by matching file profiles in the RDS. The NSRL was built to meet the needs of the law enforcement community for rigorously verified data that can meet the exacting requirement of the criminal justice system.

4. The EAC should solicit information about suspicious electronic voting system activity including software programming and should request aggressive investigative and prosecutorial responses from the U.S. Department of Justice Elections Crimes Branch in the Criminal Division.

5. The EAC should document incidents and record data concerning electronic voting equipment malfunctions in November. This information can be submitted to the EAC Technical Guidelines Development Committee that will be creating the new voluntary voting systems standards.

Soaries had electrified the crowd, and you could feel the affectionate regard for him in their ovation. That warmth seemed to pervade the whole room as the people at my table all told me how genuinely pleased they were to have met me, some even saying that the evening had reversed their opinion of me. Outside, Soaries gave me a big hug and then walked me over to Linda Lamone to introduce us. When I offered my hand, she took it, and I volunteered, "Nice to meet you—finally."

"Yes, finally," she said. Soaries tried to get the ball rolling with talk about my young children, but after we all agreed that I sure had my hands full, the conversation petered out pretty quickly. That was the sum total of our interaction. If anyone thought we might cast aside our differences and talk constructively about e-voting in an atmosphere of brotherhood and cooperation, they were sadly mistaken.

SOARIES HAD TRIED hard to play the peacemaker between me and Linda Lamone, but she wasn't the only Maryland official recklessly promoting the Diebold voting machine. Gilles Burger, the chairman of the state board of elections who at one time fired Linda Lamone (before she was reinstated by a judge), championed the machines in an op-ed piece in the *Baltimore Sun*. In the piece, Burger described the Diebold machines that Maryland had selected as the most accurate, reliable, and secure machines available. My research team had never studied, nor even commented on, the accuracy or reliability of the machines. As for their security, Burger offered no evidence for his claim. Not that it would have mattered—they might have been the most secure machines, but that did not mean they were actually secure. He praised the intensive testing procedures without mentioning that the "independent authorities" who tested the machine had been hired by Diebold, and he spoke grandly about the comprehensive risk analysis the state performed without coming clean about SAIC's findings of significant security problems. Burger's piece justified the machines' ongoing lack of voter verifiability by touting the redundant recording systems available on them, as if having multiple copies of corrupted data was an advantage. He concluded by boldly claiming that the state's two elections so far that had used the machines had been clean and successful. He didn't bother to explain how anyone could possibly have known that.

Florida, even with the eyes of the nation focused on its broken-down election system, had fared no better. After the near-disaster of 2000, the state turned to paperless DREs in many precincts in 2004. Among the vocal and prominent advocates for electronic machines were Theresa LaPore, the designer of the butterfly ballot, on which many people who believed they were voting for Al Gore inadvertently voted for Pat Buchanan, and Glenda Hood, the secretary of state. I once had an opportunity to debate Glenda Hood on national radio on NPR; she spouted the standard party line that they'd never experienced problems with electronic voting machines in Florida and that DREs were the best way to eliminate hanging chads.

Florida does have a computer-savvy election official, Paul Craft, the voting systems chief with the state division of elections. I had first met Craft in 1999 when he visited my group at AT&T Labs. An auditor by training, Paul knew how to program computers, and he spoke like a techie. Our paths crossed again in 2000 at the NSF panel on Internet voting. But three short years later, at the NIST symposium, he berated me in front of the entire conference for my criticism of the Diebold e-voting machines. He suggested that before I criticize election officials I should try to understand how elections actually work. We hadn't criticized election officials in our report, but clearly Paul had taken things personally.

IN CONTRAST TO Maryland, Georgia, and Florida, some states got it right, and leading the way was New Hampshire. William M. Gardner has served as secretary of state there since 1976, the longest tenure of any active secretary of state in the country. In Gardner's first year on the job, New Hampshire experienced the closest Senate election in U.S. history, giving rise to a culture of recounts. Assistant secretary of state Anthony Stevens says that in his state the recount requirement is the primary consideration in the design or selection of voting technology. Voting systems must, by definition, allow for easy and inexpensive recounts. In New Hampshire candidates whose margin of loss is under 1 percent can request a recount for $10. If the margin is 2 to 3 percent, the recount costs $40. In the year 2000 the state oversaw 32 recounts with 137 candidates. In 1994 the state adopted the first voter-verified paper ballot requirement in the nation.

In California, Kevin Shelley, who had been aware of the security concerns for some time, came out strongly in favor of a voter-verified paper trail of voters' intent. In response to the issues raised by David Dill in Santa Clara County, Shelley formed the California Ad Hoc Task Force on Touch-Screen Voting. The task force consisted of a uniquely balanced and diverse group of experts, from computer scientists like David Dill and David Jefferson to Mischelle Townsend, the Riverside County (Calif.) registrar of voters. The team also included a disabled rights activist, a representative of the state legislature, and the late Bob Naegele, a nationally respected expert in election standards. The task force issued a report calling for a voter-verified audit trail by 2006, although the members could not agree on the specific form it should take. Several months later Shelley went a step beyond the report's recommendations, issuing a directive that required an *accessible* voter-verified paper audit trail by 2006. Governor Arnold Schwarzenegger eventually signed a similar requirement into law, after the bill passed unanimously in both houses, putting the matter to rest in California.

Several other states, including Nevada, Missouri, and Oregon (where citizens vote by postal mail—another terribly insecure system), adopted paper-trail requirements for the 2004 election. However, forty-two states used some form of paperless electronic voting in that election. Nevada, Washington, California, Missouri, New Hampshire, and Ohio will all require voter-verified paper trails in 2006, but at this time it is unclear where the rest of the Union will come down on this issue. My great hope is that people will follow the path laid out by people like Buster Soaries, so that election officials and computer scientists can begin again to work in tandem toward a shared goal, letting all pride, partisanship, and territoriality fall by the wayside.

18

The Vanderburgh County Commissioners voted
unanimously to conduct an "independent audit" of the Nov.
2 election results, following complaints about possible
malfunctions of the county's touch-screen voting machines.
Reports of breakdowns of the machines and long voter
lines that forced some voters to wait up to three hours to
cast their ballots set the stage for the
decision at Monday's meeting.
—Evansville *[Indiana]* Courier & Press, *November 9, 2004*

I t goes without saying that awards and accolades weren't the
point of my work. While analyzing the data, writing the report, dealing with the press, and testifying in court and before
panels, committees, and boards, recognition and fame were the
furthest things from my mind. That's why nothing could have
prepared me for the call I got one day in March 2004 from Kat-
rina Bishop at the Electronic Frontiers Foundation.

"You have been selected," she began, "along with David Dill
and Kim Alexander, for the 2004 Electronic Frontiers Foundation Pioneer Award for spearheading and nurturing the popular
movement for integrity and transparency in modern elections."
For one of the few times in my life, I was speechless. "Hello?
Avi, are you there?"

Established in 1991, the EFF Pioneer Awards recognize "individuals who have made significant and influential contributions to the development of computer-mediated communications or to the empowerment of individuals in using computers and the Internet." The past winners constitute a who's who of luminaries in the world of computing and the Internet. Among them are Tim Berners-Lee, inventor of the World Wide Web; Linus Torvalds, creator of LINUX; Whitfield Diffie and Martin Hellman, inventors of public-key cryptography; Vinton Cerf, who led the development of TCP/IP, the fundamental Internet communications protocols; the highly regarded computer scientist Barbara Simons; Marc Rotenberg, executive director of EPIC; the computer security pioneer Peter Neumann; and my colleague at Penn, Matt Blaze. I don't offer this list in order to blow my own horn but to explain why I thought the call might be a prank. Pioneer Award winners are the people I have always revered, the people who have set the standards. Among them, I felt like an impostor.

I accepted the award in April 2004 at the "Computers, Freedom, and Privacy" conference in Berkeley, thrilled to be in the company of David and Kim, both of whom I consider among the great standard-bearers of the cause. My only regret was that the man at or near the top of my pantheon of heroes, David Jefferson, had been overlooked. I devoted much of my acceptance speech to thanking David, who had guided us all through the good and bad times of recent years even as he worked full-time at Lawrence Livermore Labs.

April was a good month. Shortly after receiving the EFF Pioneer Award, Johns Hopkins promoted me to full professor with tenure. It was Passover, and Gerry Masson called me at my parents' house in Nashville with the news. Later, as we were all lying around digesting the seder feast, my brother-in-law phoned from Texas to tell me to turn on *The Daily Show* with

Jon Stewart. We watched a segment in which they practically quoted from our Diebold report, and the "Moment of Zen" at the end of the show was a clip of me talking on the *CBS Evening News* about the hazards of Diebold's DREs. Ann couldn't get over the fact that I seemed more excited about being on *The Daily Show* than about getting tenure.

I had started the month as I always do—with an April fool's joke. Some of my colleagues saw it coming. After all, the year before I had schemed with my department chair to convince the rest of the computer science department that I was taking a leave of absence to be deployed to Iraq to secure the army's computer networks. I sent the following message to hundreds of people, and I did manage to get over on some of them:

From: Avi Rubin ‹rubin@jhu.edu›
Subject: Moving on
Date: April 1, 2004 7:31:25 AM EST

As many of you know, this past year my career took an unexpected turn, as I became embroiled in the issue of the security of electronic voting. While initially, I was very happy with my move from AT&T Labs to academia last year, I now think that this is not the place for me to carry out my new mission to protect democracy. So, as of May 1, 2004, I will be leaving Johns Hopkins and taking on a new position where I feel I will be best able to make a difference. You may be surprised to hear this, but after several weeks of intense and secret negotiations, I am going to join Diebold as their Chief Security Officer. I know that many of you may feel that I have "sold out" by doing this, but please hear me out. Yes, the salary is astronomical, and yes, I will no longer be able to say what I really think about the insecurity of their machines, but there's more to it than that. Think of the possibilities of my new position. I will have the ability to almost single-handedly pick our next President. However, paperless and fully electronic DREs are only the beginning. What about paperless ATMs? As Diebold CSO, I will be able to help them design ATMs that not only do not carry receipts, but that also do not dispense money. Instead, we can reuse the smartcards from the voting systems and dispense electronic cash. Without the need for paper money and paper receipts, the machines would never need to be serviced, thus saving both in convenience and money....

So, I hope that you will support me in my career change. I believe that it is time to try to really make a difference, and the best way to do that is to go where the action is.

Avi Rubin

Either I'm a better con artist than I think, or it's true that crusaders don't always have a sense of humor. Rebecca Mercuri forwarded my message to several people with the note, "Read and weep!" She also sent me a scathing message about my stunning decision, but happily followed it a few hours later with a sheepish apology. It turned out she had only read the first few lines before going ballistic. Kim Alexander got the joke well enough, but scolded me, saying that of all people I should know words can be twisted and that I should be more careful. My mom suggested that it was perhaps time to stop with the April fool's jokes. Princeton's Ed Felten posted it to his Web log. Others joined the fun and gave me a taste of my own medicine. Our department administrator at Hopkins, Kris Sisson, convinced me that as a result of my e-mail she had removed me from the payroll and notified the dean of my resignation. Will Doherty, the executive director of Verified Voting, sent a note to my colleagues on the volunteer advisory board of the organization informing them that I had been kicked out, owing to my decision. I sent him a worried reply, insisting that it was only a joke, then realizing a split second after I hit the "Send" button that I'd been had. The best response came by e-mail.

From: J.A.Kass@diebold.com
Subject: InterNet Message of April 1, 2004
Date: April 1, 2004 6:36:43 PM EST
To: rubin@jhu.edu

April 1, 2004

To: Professor Aviel Rubin
Johns Hopkins University

Certified Mail, Return Receipt Requested (and via electronic mail)

Dear Mr. Rubin:

I am Assistant Corporate Council for Diebold, Inc. My office is in receipt of an InterNet message from you (dated today, April 1, 2004) in which you make false, misleading and damaging representations regarding your supposed employment with Diebold as its "Chief Security Officer."

Diebold, Inc. has never tendered to you an offer of employment of any kind, nor has it engaged with you in any negotiation that would or could lead to such an offer. Furthermore, the position you claim to have accepted does not exist at Diebold. My client is very concerned about damage to its business and reputation as well as any other losses resulting from your publication and dissemination of the false and apparently malicious information referenced therein.

You are herewith directed upon receipt of this notice to immediately cease and desist from publishing any and all false, misleading, incomplete or defamatory information about Diebold, Inc. or any of its subsidiaries, your employment with Diebold, Inc. or any of its subsidiaries, its products and systems, as well as any other material adverse to Diebold, Inc.'s business or political interests.

You are further directed to publish, via any and all media through which your original false and misleading message was delivered, a full and complete retraction of the false and misleading facts.

Your compliance with this notice is essential to mitigate the irreparable harm you have caused to my client. We reserve the right to pursue additional remedies, including litigation, as deemed necessary by my client.

Finally, you and all members of your family are directed to register and vote in the 2004 Presidential election, for a candidate chosen by my client as communicated to you at a future time. Diebold reserves the right to install software and other monitoring features in its systems to ensure your compliance with this clause.

Please feel free to contact my office if you have any questions.

Sincerely,

J. A. Kass

Assistant Corporate Council

Diebold, Inc.

Enclosure (1)

My wife pointed out that, besides being an obvious joke, the letter had clearly not been written by a lawyer. I managed to trace the message through e-mail headers to a computer owned by Matt Blaze, a former AT&T colleague who was now a professor at Penn. I had to hand it to him.

This kind of clowning around provided comic relief but didn't detract from the time and serious attention I devoted to e-voting security issues. I even incorporated the topic into a course I was teaching, setting up a little experiment to test the relative difficulty of hiding—versus finding—malicious code in mock e-voting machines. I broke the class up into several small groups, and we divided the semester into thirds. In the first third, each group built an electronic voting machine that it demonstrated to the rest of the class. These machines were basically simple programs that allowed a user to make choices among several candidates in different races and that were required to keep an electronic audit log and produce the final tallies when the election was over. The groups then devoted the second third of the term to planting a back door in their voting machines—a mechanism by which a voter could cheat and change the vote totals and the audit logs so that the change would be undetectable. Each team had to turn in two versions of its system, one that worked properly and one that "cheated," with all the code for both.

The groups spent the last third of the semester analyzing the machines and code from the other groups, looking for malicious code. The goal of the project was to determine whether people could hide code in a voting machine such that others of comparable skill could not find it, even with complete access to the whole development environment. Each group was assigned three machines from other groups—one good one, one bad one, and one chosen at random, but none of them identified as such. That was for the students to figure out by analyzing the code and running the machines. Admittedly, this setting was not much like that of a real manufacturer, in which there would be years to develop and hide malicious code in a code base that would be orders of magnitude larger and more complex than in our little mock-ups. Furthermore, the students had all just spent more than a month developing and hiding their own malicious code, so they had a good idea of what the other groups might try. Conversely, in practice, auditors would have considerably more time to analyze and test potential code for problems. Still, I expected the results to be revealing, and I was not disappointed.

Many of the groups succeeded in building machines in which the hidden code was not detected. In addition, some of the groups succeeded in detecting malicious code, and did so in a way that in and of itself was enlightening. In one case, the students discovered the cheating almost by accident because the compiler used by the programmers was incompatible with the one used by the analyzing team. The experiment demonstrated, as we suspected it would, that hiding code is much easier than finding hidden code.

I had described the project to John Schwartz, who came down to Baltimore and sat in on the class in which the students presented their findings. The *Times* ran his story a few days later, with a picture of me and several of the students. The headline— "Who Hacked the Voting System? The Teacher"—made me wince a little, but the article made me immensely proud. It also made me blush a little.

I pursued this avenue of study the following semester in an advanced topic seminar with ten students, most of whom had been part of the voting machine project. Again, I centered the course on the technical issues surrounding the hiding and manipulating of code. The class scoured the computer science literature for papers on the subject, and then using what we had learned, the students built automated tools for hiding code and for finding code. At the end, we put together a paper summarizing previous work in the area, the tools the students had built, and future directions for research and work. I didn't design the class specifically around e-voting, but given my intimate involvement with the subject, it figured prominently in our discussions.

My former co-author Bill Cheswick devised a great class activity to explore this theme further. It was a game, which we dubbed "Programming Balderdash" in honor of the board game from which we borrowed the scoring system, and it seemed so exciting that Bill traveled to Hopkins to participate in the class. The idea was simple. Each student had to write two short, simple programs that could be easily read and analyzed. Working with one program at a time and without revealing the author, I handed each student a copy and gave them three minutes to analyze it and write down what they believed the output would be. At the end of the three minutes, we announced who had written the program and had each student say what he or she thought the output would be; we rated each answer as "high confidence" or "low confidence." The author of the program would then reveal the answer he or she expected the students to give.

The point of this exercise was to devise programs that would fool people about their output without resorting to complex or blatant obfuscation. We kept score on a board in the front of the room. The author of the program got a point for every low-confidence guess that matched the predicted, erroneous output and two points for every high-confidence guess that missed the mark. Students who correctly stated the output received two points for low-confidence answers and three for high-. A student's score wouldn't benefit from writing a program that was difficult to understand; the idea was to *trick* the other players, not baffle them. The game was a huge hit, not least because we were able to fool each other with surprising ease. In fact, word spread, and when we played the game a second time, students from outside the class asked to join in. The exercise brilliantly demonstrated the complexity of software.

If graduate students in computer science can hide bugs in five-line programs that can fool ten other grad students and two senior researchers, imagine what professional programmers can hide in fifty thousand lines of code. Computer scientists are well versed in the mathematics of computability and complexity theory and intuitively understand how easy it is to hide code. But someone who has never programmed a computer, much less studied the intricacies of computer security, simply doesn't have that kind of intuition. And without it, it is impossible to make reasoned and informed decisions about electronic voting policy.

I have been gratified by the ways in which my work in computer science and my work in e-voting have fed off of each other. Just as my deeper understanding of security issues has enabled me to make valuable contributions to the e-voting discussion, my analyses of the e-voting dilemmas have furthered my appreciation and understanding of general computer security matters. Similarly, as my position and expertise facilitated my e-voting work, success and recognition in that arena have helped in my professional career. It has been a challenging and at times arduous journey, but one for which I am very grateful.

19

Matthew Damschroder, director of the Franklin County
Board of Elections, said . . . after Precinct 1B closed, a
cartridge from one of three voting machines at the polling
place generated a faulty number at a computerized reading
station. The reader also recorded zero votes in a county
commissioner race. He couldn't explain
why the computer reader malfunctioned.
—Associated Press, *November 4, 2004*

I f any segment of the population has learned the value and
necessity of speaking up for itself and fighting for its due, it is
the disabled. However, when it came to electronic voting, this
community sometimes surprised people.

For all the activists who were working against DREs, there
were equally dedicated people who came out in force against
paper-based voting. Blind and vision-impaired Americans threw
the weight of their community behind DREs, which could operate in audio mode and which they believed provided the only
mechanism for blind people to vote unassisted. The highest-
profile and most vocal activist for the blind on the issue of electronic voting has been Jim Dickson, the vice president of the
American Association of People with Disabilities. Dickson has
put enormous effort into a noble and important cause, but not

always with the most helpful results. I don't think you will find anyone on any side of this debate, especially among computer scientists, who does not support the right of blind people, or people with other disabilities, to a private ballot and recognize the need to provide it. Many people have worked long and hard to propose voting systems that are verifiable, auditable, *and* accessible to the blind. The state of California even developed standards for an *accessible* voter-verified paper audit trail (AVVPAT). Unfortunately, Jim Dickson has viewed the debate only through the lens of this single issue and advocated measures that would serve the blind but compromise the overall security of the process. He has succeeded in generating widespread support for this position.

At the rally outside the EAC hearing, Dickson did some grandstanding, interrupting the congressman, commandeering the microphones, and passionately declaring his right to a private ballot. He proclaimed that DREs were the only answer. Holt tried to calm things down and to reason with him, but Dickson kept speaking, clearly preferring theatrics over any actual communication. (In fact, on a previous occasion Dickson had challenged David Dill to put on a blindfold and then try to vote.) Kevin Shelley asked Dickson for a word and gently ushered him away from the crowd, prompting someone to shout, "Hey! He's getting you away from the cameras! Don't let Shelley take you away from the cameras!" Dickson knew well that the television crews were his real audience, and they were more than happy to oblige.

Although Dickson presented himself as speaking for the entire blind community, that wasn't actually the case. I learned that some blind people were uncomfortable with Dickson's one-note posture. Late in December 2003, I spoke with Chris Danielson, the director of communications for the National Federation of the Blind. Danielson shared my belief that the country should not jeopardize an entire election so that a small percentage of the population could vote unassisted, but at the same time he felt strongly that my community of computer scientists needed to push harder for accessible voting. We had a lengthy exchange of ideas, going over the possible options for producing a paper trail that blind people could use to verify their votes. I suggested a system in which the machine would print out the voter's choices on a VVPB in a standard format; the voter could then verify the ballot at the polling site on a scanner-type machine (from an independent vendor), perhaps like those used to check prices at a supermarket. The machine would have an audio option so that once the ballot was scanned it could play the selections through a headset. The paper would be kept at the polling site, just like the ones created by sighted voters, for later use. Vendors have since come out with such machines.

The NFB headquarters are in Baltimore, so Chris was able to make a memorable visit to the Information Security Institute at Hopkins in which he helped me more fully appreciate the challenges of blindness. I had never had the occasion to observe a blind person so closely before. After escorting Chris from the elevator to my office, I watched as he effortlessly set up a recording device similar to what a court reporter uses to make transcripts. I was amazed by the ease and dexterity with which he set up and operated the equipment, which had quite a number of parts, cables, and connections. There were questions I wanted to ask, but I didn't know the etiquette and didn't want to insult him. But then it dawned on me that Chris wasn't exactly hiding his blindness, so I asked how he had learned to handle such complicated equipment. I believed that if I suddenly lost my sight, I would have been stopped cold by a simple tape recorder, much less a sophisticated machine like that. Chris seemed to appreciate my interest and explained that when you live as a blind person for a long time—in his case, for his whole life—this sort of thing becomes second nature. He said that many people react as I had, thinking that blindness would be too difficult for them, but that they imagine the situation relative to the way they live in the world—with sight. Chris pointed out that he'd had a lifetime to get good at being blind. He had gotten very good, I thought.

I hoped that the time I spent with Chris Danielson would leave me better prepared to relate to the blind people who often called when I was doing live radio programs. These callers often made very emotional appeals. "Dr. Rubin, you are not blind. I am," the caller would begin. "You cannot appreciate how hard it is to hear someone try to take away machines that allowed me to vote for the first time in my life in private. Why are you doing this?" I always felt at a disadvantage, knowing that anything I said might sound uninformed or callous. I could only trust that my conversation with Chris was as edifying for him as it was for me, since I was able to explain in greater detail the problems created by DREs. He and I agreed that the consequences of relying on these voting machines could be dire, but also that a better solution was still needed.

By contrast, Jim Dickson seemed always to remain belligerent, and I never managed to meet him on common ground. Dickson confronted me after the House administration committee hearing and demanded a copy of the $10 million grant proposal we had written at Hopkins. This was out of the question on the face of it, given that NSF submissions are confidential until a funding decision is made. Dickson didn't want to hear that and taunted me for being a "hypocrite" because I insisted on transparency in voting systems but refused to make the text of my own proposals public. Dickson's comparison sounded like a legitimate challenge, but the two processes have nothing to do with each other. Fairness demands transparency in the process of recording and counting votes in a national presidential election, just as it demands confidentiality in the process of submitting competitive proposals for a government research grant. Although that grant proposal was not funded, we were encouraged to resubmit and ultimately were funded to the tune of $7.5 million to set up A Center for Correct, Usable, Reliable, Auditable, and Transparent Elections (ACCURATE), housed at Johns Hopkins, with me as the center director and Dan Wallach as the associate director.

Dickson's public displays were often irrational. In November 2003, he spoke on a panel in Washington called "Claim Democracy" with Barbara Simons, Marc Rotenberg, and Ted Selker. When he had the floor, he kept repeating the same thing, getting louder and louder each time, almost as if he were starting a cheer at a football game. "What do you do if the paper ballot and the electronic tally don't match?" he cried. Barbara tried to get an answer in edgewise, but he cut her off, saying again, "What do you do if the paper ballot and the electronic tally don't match?" The ridiculous irony here was that he was arguing against his own position. For the life of me, I've never understood how someone could even ask this question and yet oppose a paper trail. The existence of such a discrepancy is exactly why a separate audit trail is needed. It's the discrepancy between the two tallies that alerts officials to a problem with the machines. The truth is that in the case of a discrepancy, neither the paper nor the electronic record can be considered definitive a priori. Selecting one as definitive renders the other completely worthless. The discovery of a discrepancy should trigger an independent and transparent investigation in which the contents of the electronic audit trail and any other evidence, either the paper ballots or the electronic ones, or some of each, are binding. A public confrontation might make for an exciting fifteen seconds on the network news, but it doesn't get us any closer to any kind of resolution of the problem, especially when the argument isn't rational.

The cause of the blind community took a blow in October 2004 when Kim Zetter of *Wired News* brought to light details of a financial relationship between the NFB and Diebold. This scandal, first alluded to in a *New York Times* editorial, potentially explained some of the behavior of the more vocal DRE supporters among the blind. At the very least, it revealed a serious lack of full disclosure, which Diebold had been self-righteous about with regard to my advisory position with VoteHere and which Jim Dickson had berated me about with regard to our NSF grant proposal. Zetter wrote:

> The NFB isn't the only disability group to receive money from voting companies. The government lobbyist for the American Association of People with Disabilities, who has traveled around the country testifying on behalf of touch-screen voting, acknowledged this year that his organization received at least $26,000 from voting companies, but only after first denying it. . . . Dickson didn't disclose the gifts at hearings in California this year, where he tried to convince officials not to decertify touch-screen voting machines made by Diebold and other companies. Nor did he disclose the information in Washington in May when he participated in hearings with the federal Election Assistance Commission.

Jim Dickson and the NFB each showed poor judgment in failing to disclose that they had taken money from Diebold, and I believe that the blind community deserves better. They have a legitimate right to accessible and private voting, which should not be diminished by such an unfortunate episode. I see no reason why future voting systems can't achieve full voter accessibility along with security, reliability, and usability.

Such future systems could look very different from anything in use today. With the notorious exceptions of Ted Selker and Michael Shamos, mainstream computer scientists uniformly agree that paperless electronic voting is a bad idea. However, a small subset of security experts have been developing promising technology for secure and fully automated elections.

One proposed scheme involves no fancy cryptography or protocols. Shuki Bruck, David Jefferson, and Ron Rivest have designed a modular system in which vote generation (marking a ballot), vote casting (turning in a marked ballot, making the vote official), and vote counting are separated and performed by different machines. This avoids the risk that a DRE manufacturer would exploit the complexity of the machine to hide malicious code.

Other novel proposed voting systems make use of complex mathematical properties. The cryptographers who have developed these systems are striving for the seemingly unattainable goal: a system that allows voters to verify that their votes were counted, allows anyone to calculate the outcome of an election reliably, and keeps every vote private and confidential, while ensuring that the system remains transparent to a layperson.

VoteHere has gone after this holy grail, and its designer, Andy Neff, has published his schemes in the Crypto conference. But the best solution, in my opinion, is that of the noted cryptographer David Chaum, a computer scientist–mathematician and former professor who is one of only six scientists to be designated a fellow of the International Association of Cryptologic Research (IACR), an extremely prestigious honor. The IACR is the scientific organization that sponsors all of the top conferences and journals in cryptography. Among other things, Chaum invented digital cash, secure multiparty computation, blind signatures, and many other primitives (the building blocks of computer science theory) that help form the foundation of the field of applied computer security.

When Chaum decided to devote his attention to the problem of electronic voting, he came up with a novel and clever solution, with only one problem, although not a technical one: the voting protocol is exceedingly complicated. When Chaum visited Johns Hopkins as a distinguished lecturer, he gave one of the cleanest and simplest presentations of the material I had ever heard to the computer science faculty and graduate students, yet still managed to lose a good portion of his audience in the technical details. In his scheme, voters receive two ballots with the candidates' names in different order. Voters mark one of the ballots and keep the other one. Since the authorities running the election would not know which ballot each voter marked, the ballot the voter keeps can be used, through some mathematical manipulations invented by Chaum, to keep the election honest. Furthermore, the marked ballot can be stored in such a way that the voter is able to verify that the vote was counted in the final tally, and the tally can be performed by anyone. Chaum's scheme is very good, but not perfect. There are still some technical issues to address, as well as accessibility problems, but I believe that eventually he or someone else will figure out how to perfect the scheme.

The details of Chaum's scheme are too complex and technical to list here, and therein lies the rub. For the sake of argument, let's assume that his system would work perfectly for all elections in the United States, regardless of the candidates or issues on the ballot. A fundamental problem would remain: the public would not understand how the mechanism works. The fact that a system is foolproof does not also make it transparent. The average citizen, not to mention election administrators and government officials, must understand exactly *why* it is foolproof. We cannot condemn election officials for their "trust me" attitude and then turn around and ask citizens to put their blind faith in computer scientists. Over time, both our society and these protocols may evolve to a point where the latter become acceptable. As Ron Rivest explained to me, if every high school math class could write a computer program that verifies election results, the nation could begin to develop confidence in its election system. But I believe we're a long, long way away from the time when schemes like Chaum's are transparent enough for the public to accept them.

20

The true and only true basis of representative government
is equality of rights. Every man has a right to one vote, and
no more in the choice of representatives. The rich have no
more right to exclude the poor from the right of voting, or
of electing and being elected, than the poor have to exclude
the rich; and wherever it is attempted,
or proposed, on either side, it is a question of
force and not of right.
—*Thomas Paine,* Dissertation on the
First Principles of Government, *1795*

As the summer of 2004 turned into fall, it felt like the drama of the previous year and a half since we'd released our Diebold report was about to come to its climax. The time had arrived to see all the abstract issues we'd been debating play out for real. As the nation inched closer and closer to election day, the polls all indicated a virtual dead heat, meaning that even the slightest glitch or disruption in a pivotal state could tip the balance either way—or worse, throw the country back into the kind of confusion and uncertainty we had witnessed four years earlier.

In the week before the election, media coverage of potential problems with e-voting became feverish. I appeared on *The*

Today Show, *60 Minutes*, *World News Tonight with Peter Jennings*, and the cover of the *Baltimore Jewish Times*, in several important big-city newspapers, and on quite a few radio programs. It felt like the media were anticipating a contested election, laying the groundwork ahead of time for problems caused by electronic voting. It seemed to me, however, that the media buzz could actually confuse the issue further. The greatest threat posed by DREs is a software problem—either malicious code or an unintentional bug—that could taint the election in a completely undetectable way, but the media focused entirely on detectable problems. The more attention the media paid to the issue, the more I feared that the election would be viewed as an unofficial referendum on electronic voting. Even if the country overwhelmingly considered the election "successful," the vast majority of my concerns about e-voting would still be valid. Voting machines can perform perfectly normally but remain completely vulnerable to rigging. Perhaps nobody would try to exploit the vulnerabilities this time around. Or maybe they would. Maybe there would be serious error or fraud, *and nobody would know.* The American people would judge e-voting only on the noticeable failures, if any, while the invisible problems would get no attention.

The activist community also shifted into high gear. David Dill's group, Verified Voting, launched several new initiatives just prior to the election, including the high-profile "Tech-Watch," which recruited technically proficient observers to help monitor testing, do poll watching, and collect incident reports during the election. Other organizations arose alongside Verified Voting. The National Committee on Voting Integrity (NCVI) was established as a nonpartisan group of technical experts, lawyers, journalists, and citizens working to promote voter-verified balloting and preserve privacy protections in American elections. Lillie Coney, a senior policy analyst with the Electronic Privacy Information Center (EPIC), served as committee coordinator, and its chair was Peter Neumann, one of America's most eminent computer scientists and one of the pioneers of computer security, a near-mythic figure in the field. Under Neumann's and Coney's leadership, NCVI made a number of valuable resources available to the public, including research tools, news highlights, and a Web page at votingintegrity.org with comprehensive coverage and recommendations.

I had no problem getting up at five in the morning on November 2, election day. I was scheduled to serve again as an election judge in Timonium, Maryland, the same precinct where I had worked during the primary. I shot out of bed totally wired, my adrenaline fueled by a mixture of excitement about the election and anxiety over the possibility of something going dreadfully wrong. In Timonium, the crew of judges was much the same as it had been in March. Gone were the older of the two Sandys and Joy, the former trainer of chief judges who, I learned, had been employed by Diebold before the primary. A new judge named Terry was the security manager for the church that served as the polling place. My fellow judges greeted me warmly, forgoing the silent treatment they had given me the first time. Most of them had read my op-ed piece in the *Baltimore Sun* after the primary and enjoyed my description of our shared experience. They had also seen my op-ed the week before the election, reiterating my concern that, regardless of the outcome, we would never know if the machines behaved properly. Chief judge Marie was quick to point out that Diebold had no hand in setting up the machines this time. She and her husband Bill had come in the night before to open them up. I asked her who had guarded the machines overnight, and she answered that the room had been locked.

Terry, the new judge, had a key to every room in the building and was aligned with the same political party as Marie and her husband. Having judges from each party at each station within a polling site is a key element of the checks and balances built into the election system. Inadvertently, Marie had just told me about an imbalance, a lapse in security. Two judges from the same party had set up the machines alone and then left them in a room accessible only to a person who was also a member of that same party. The threat here was obvious.

The fact that someone had unfettered access to the machines prior to the election raised other possibilities for tampering. A person could have rendered the machines totally inoperable, perhaps with a good whack of a hammer, but that's true of any kind of voting machine. The difference with DREs is the danger of undetectable tampering that could change the vote count. I have no reason whatsoever to believe that my fellow judges did anything underhanded. In fact, I have complete confidence that they did no such thing. I only want to point out the critical importance of noting—and then eliminating—such vulnerabilities in the system before someone less trustworthy tries to exploit them.

The lines formed early outside our precinct, and at 7:00 A.M. chief judge Jim once again cast the first vote, to our applause. Voters began streaming in once the doors were open. The lines of people zigzagged across the room, and the police officer at the door soon started monitoring the flow of voters, letting new people enter only after others had left. In the first hour, we logged more than half as many voters as there had been all day in the primary, and there was no letup in sight. We kept things moving pretty efficiently, and eventually the pace slowed down, although there were one or two minor glitches. Some of the smartcards didn't work too well, and some voters saw unusual error messages on their screens. I didn't see them, but one of the other judges told me they looked like "strange computer messages." By noon more than half the registered voters in the precinct had cast their ballots.

When the pace calmed down in the afternoon, I was able to pay closer attention to voters' reactions to the machines. One voter asked me about the sign we had been required to post, which said that anybody who was eligible to vote on the machines was not allowed to cast a provisional ballot. I explained that if someone's name appeared in our registration books, he or she was required to use the machine to vote. He asked incredulously why anyone would object to voting on the machine, and I explained, with all due indifference, that some people preferred a paper ballot. The voter laughed and said, "People need to get a grip and join the twenty-first century. The world is about computers. Those machines make it so easy." As an election judge, I couldn't take that bait, so I simply nodded politely in response. Again, several voters commented on how enjoyable the voting experience had become, but one couple gave me the third degree. The husband asked me very aggressively why he should have any confidence that the machine was actually recording his vote. Before I could come up with a response, his wife declared her belief that the machines were susceptible to fraud. As calmly as I could, I explained that these machines were what we had in the state of Maryland; if they didn't like them, I strongly recommended that they write to their representatives. I could not have agreed more with that couple, but my role was to help run the election with as little disruption as possible. Despite the fact that these people were expressing my own concerns, I realized that I was hoping nobody had heard them.

We closed the polls at 8:00 P.M. Terry handled the security, since he had all the keys. Every hour throughout the day we had counted the number of people who had voted and then posted the turnout figure on the door of the church. By the time we closed the doors, 725 digital ballots had been cast, and the chief judges decided it would be too much of a hassle to send the results via modem. The protocol was for the results to be sent by modem for use by the media, but doing so increases the vulnerability of the system. The county servers are configured to accept modem communications, which opens them up to several potential attacks. So even though the judges' decision represented a breach of procedure, it helped protect the integrity of the system.

I stared long and hard at the machines, thinking about the little memory cards inside them, not unlike the card in my digital camera, and the 725 votes stored on them. At one point I held them all in my hand while Marie prepared to load them into the machine we had designated as the accumulator. How unimaginably fragile it all was. All of the votes from our entire precinct were right there in the palm of my hand. I could have substituted those five cards with five identical but bogus cards from my pocket, changing all the ballots, because Diebold did not protect the data with appropriate cryptographic measures. I couldn't imagine anyone trying such a thing in Maryland, where the outcome of the presidential race was reasonably certain before the election. But what about the larger battleground states like Ohio or Florida? There were only 725 votes cast in our little precinct, but that was enough to make fraud involving the swapping of paper ballots impractical. At the very least, anyone trying to manipulate 725 paper ballots would run a high risk of detection. The memory cards didn't pose much of a challenge, though, and I shuddered when I thought of the many thousands of votes contained on memory cards in large precincts around the country.

My election day experience was quite different from my first time as a judge eight months before. On Super Tuesday, I had been overwhelmed by the magnitude of my civic responsibility and perhaps a little self-conscious about my unique situation. That had been an awkward and emotional experience, and I had felt uncomfortable. We'd had nine judges at a polling site that recorded a total of 199 votes. There had been media people hanging around, and the president of Diebold Election Systems stopped by. In November, however, everything felt more natural. It was a busy day, and we had our hands full doing what we were there to do.

The most frustrating part of working in a polling place is that you can't find out anything about how the election is going. We were sequestered for the day, denied communication with the outside world, including cell phones, and discouraged even from talking to voters about the election. The moment we closed the polls, I called Ann, who summarized the day for me. There had been some sporadic failures, but the biggest problems were connected to the much higher voter turnout than had been expected, and the long, long lines at many polling stations. Several key states were still too close to call, and the balance of the election was hanging on Ohio. We stayed up late watching the news coverage and eventually went to bed not knowing who had won.

The next day, John Kerry called George W. Bush on the phone and conceded. The Internet was immediately ablaze with conspiracy theories, fueled by the early exit polls, which had Kerry in the lead. I got dozens of e-mails every hour with subject headings like "Bush steals the election!" and "Please help save our democracy." Everybody seemed convinced that there had been foul play, and many of the fraud theories that found their way into my in-box were backed up by very impressive graphs and charts "proving" that the election had been rigged.

I wasn't buying it. My opinion was that Bush had probably won fair and square, or that just possibly some extremely clever and undetectable fraud had given him enough of an edge in Ohio to tip the state in his favor. In either case—no fraud or *undetectable* fraud—nothing was going to change the outcome. People can protest the results until they are blue in the face, but if the fraud is carried out cleverly enough, it can never be proven or disproven. Neither fraud nor legitimacy in the voting can be verified.

The many activists who definitively claimed, with no evidence, that the election had been stolen did a great disservice to everyone who had thoughtfully and seriously criticized the e-voting technology. It was now guilt by association as DRE proponents made great sport of lumping us together with all the crackpots and agitators. Three days after the election, the *Baltimore Sun* ran a story that quoted Michael Shamos. "There are people on Earth who claim they were abducted by aliens and had surgery performed on them on spaceships. They have no evidence of it, but they believe it. If you laugh at those who believe aliens live among us, then you really ought to howl at those who believe there is massive tampering with voting machines. There is no evidence of it." Later in the same article, I was also quoted: "I don't think there is any evidence that the election was rigged. What I think is that we're heading down a dangerous path with the machines, where there's no way to disprove theories like that because there's no paper trail available. We're using a technology that's unverifiable. If you're using machines that can be rigged, then yes, it can happen, but did it happen? I doubt it. The exit polls were still within the statistical norms of the results."

After that story was published, I received many angry e-mails and phone calls from people who thought I was selling out by not fighting the election results. But there was nothing to fight them with. Undetectable fraud doesn't leave any evidence. Shamos argued that there had been no tampering because there was no evidence of tampering, which is like claiming that there are no stealth bombers heading our way because none are showing up on our radar.

While countless wild and undocumented accusations of election fraud kept protesters busy, there were some very serious glitches that demanded attention. In Franklin County, Ohio, an electronic voting system reported that Bush received 4,258 votes against 260 for Kerry in a precinct where only 638 voters had cast ballots. The *Columbus Dispatch* first reported the story, which was picked up by the AP newswire. This is the kind of serious bug that should have been caught in the testing process, but disturbing as it was, it didn't affect the final outcome, since the margin of victory for Bush in Ohio was more than 100,000 votes.

In Carteret County, North Carolina, a machine manufactured by a California company called Unilect lost between 4,500 and 12,000 votes, depending on which press account one read. How was that possible? The large voter turnout generated a volume of votes that exceeded the memory capacity of the machine. Once the memory was full, new votes overwrote old ones, so that at the end of the day the earlier votes cast on the machine were simply gone.

In a number of instances, voters complained about malfunc-
tioning machines. Many independent reports coming out of
south Florida told of voters casting votes for Kerry that the machine registered for Bush. There was also an incident in Indiana
in which an effort to vote a straight Democratic ticket resulted
in some of those votes going to candidates from the Libertarian
Party. Since that location used paper ballots, the problem was
discovered and corrected. Elsewhere in Florida questions arose
in some heavily Democratic counties where the voting had gone
overwhelmingly Republican. Rumors spread on the Internet
that rigged software on the optical-scan machines used there
had counted votes for Bush regardless of how they were cast.
This underscores an important point about security: a VVPB like
those produced by optical-scan machines cannot guarantee security on its own. It must be accompanied by a postelection audit
in which manual recounts in random precincts are compared
with the electronic totals. Auditing must be a part of any system,
regardless of the voting technology used. There's no point in using machines that produce voter-verified ballots if those ballots
are never inspected or otherwise used to ensure the integrity of
the vote.

In all, more than 30,000 incidents of problems with computerized voting machines were reported nationwide by an organization called the Voter Protection Center, which collected
incident reports on the website voteprotect.org. This stunning
statistic was enough to prompt a congressional letter asking the
U.S. General Accounting Office (GAO) to "immediately under-
take an investigation of the efficacy of voting machines and new
technologies used in the 2004 election." The letter cited 265 specific complaints and bore the signatures of eight Republican and
six Democratic members of Congress, including the ranking
members of several powerful committees.

Overall, however, despite the widely publicized glitches and the request to the GAO, the DREs appeared to function reasonably well across the country. Vendors and their supporters—the likes of Linda Lamone and Cathy Cox—claimed that the "successful" election vindicated the machines and should silence the critics once and for all. Harris Miller said in a *Computer World* article that "electronic voting machines took an important test on Nov. 2, and passed with flying colors." The same article quoted me, singing a familiar tune: "If you drive without a seat belt, as we did in this election, and you don't crash, that doesn't mean you should conclude that it is safe to drive that way."

As time passed after the election, I expected the calls from the press to slow down, especially since the winner was determined relatively quickly and there hadn't been any catastrophic problems with the electronic voting machines, but if anything, the press attention intensified. As Doug Chapin from Electionline.com observed, nothing happened in this election to silence the critics of DREs, nor to deter further use of the machines. Those who supported paperless DREs before the election felt that the machines had proven themselves, though I maintain that nothing of the kind happened. As long as the machines remain vulnerable to undetectable rigging, and as long as they cannot generate the audit trail necessary for meaningful recounts, the criticisms will remain valid. Perhaps the media will move on to something else for a while and the attention will die down, but I have no doubt that the debate will continue to flourish and that in 2006, and probably again in 2008, the controversy will erupt all over again.

ON AUGUST 1, 2005, I had the privilege of being an invited speaker at the annual conference of state supreme court chief justices, held in Charleston, South Carolina. It had dawned on me that few people were in a better position to influence state policies regarding voting technology, especially since, as experience had already taught me, this issue was more and more likely to be debated and settled in courts of law. Fortunately, my schedule allowed me to spend a couple of days in Charleston beyond the day of my talk, and I was able to talk with a number of the justices on an individual basis.

The chief justices turned out to be as diverse a group as the state election officials and elected politicians I had encountered over the last few years. Most were open-minded and eager to listen to the case I presented, but a handful, from both sides of the e-voting issue, clearly arrived with strong preconceived notions. Speaking on the afternoon of the first day, I described our study of the Diebold code, the lack of auditability in paperless computerized elections, and my vision of an ideal voting machine. Although no one had asked any questions of the speaker who came before me, I was prepared for my Q&A session to be lively and contentious, and I wasn't disappointed. The chief justice of Utah, Christine M. Durham, challenged me by asking if wholesale fraud was really possible if the manufacturer created a machine long in advance of the election and the local officials produced the ballots later. How could a manufacturer manipulate the results if nobody even knew the names of the candidates when the machine was programmed? I'd heard this question more than once in the past and had thought hard about an answer that could avoid such technical matters as buffer overflows and memory heap management. I explained, as best I could, that the manufacturer that builds a system also controls the data format on the smartcard that contains the ballot. So the voting system can be built to search the data on the smartcard for strings such as the words "Republican" or "Democrat."

There are many ways to design a machine so that it can recognize where on the ballot a particular party's candidate appears; from there, cheating would be easy. It's also possible to configure a machine's code using information about the precinct numbers in battleground states for precincts with known voting patterns. So, if the machine winds up in a precinct that traditionally votes overwhelmingly in opposition to the rogue programmer's political leanings, it can be programmed to simply swap some votes to the other party. If it ends up in a precinct not chosen for cheating, it would operate normally, making it unlikely that the malicious code would be detected in generic testing at the certification labs. My answer failed to erase the scowl from the questioner's face.

The most hostile questioning came from the chief justice of the host state of South Carolina, the Honorable Jean Hoefer Toal, an imperious woman with a drawl thicker than any I'd heard growing up in Nashville. After pointing out that many precincts still used paperless lever machines with no complaints from activists, she blasted paper trails in general, declaring, "Paper is not secure either!" I was grateful that Justice Toal's tirade did not seem to have a lot of support from the other justices and responded politely but directly about the differences between lever machines and e-voting machines. The programming of lever machines is easily observable and in fact is always videotaped, but there's no meaningful, practical way to observe a programmer writing fifty thousand lines of code to run in a voting machine over the millions of lines of Microsoft Windows code. Besides, I was not advocating the use of lever machines, which I agreed are another poor, paperless technology. I made the final point that lever machines are useless in facilitating wholesale fraud in the way that e-voting technology can. Justice

Toal responded testily, and illogically, that "videotaping technology has only been around a short while, but lever machines
have been in use for a hundred years." Later I learned from
some of her colleagues that she had invested a tremendous effort in automating a court. Like so many others I had encountered, Justice Toal seemed to be seduced by the promise of
computers to eliminate the endless flow of paper and was
dumbfounded by the suggestion that paper be reintroduced into
the voting process.

After my session, the justices broke up into smaller committee
meetings. A few of them told me later that the lively discussion
sparked by my talk had continued during those meetings. I received a good deal of positive feedback over the next couple of
days. Some justices, especially those from states that had been
recently rocked by contested elections, like Florida and Washington, talked about their fresh appreciation of the role of paper
trails specifically and of auditability in general in safeguarding
the process. At least one justice even allowed that he had come to
the meeting believing that paper-trail advocates represented a
somewhat radical fringe element, but that his understanding
had been completely turned around. A constant theme was that
these justices were hearing election-related cases with greater
frequency and many of those cases decided who would take office and who would not. The chief justice of Puerto Rico, who
was kind enough to invite me to join him and his wife for a delightful breakfast, told me that in the last election for governor
there he had cast the deciding vote in a split supreme court ruling that determined the result in a race where the margin was
within two thousand votes.

The up-close exposure to the chief justices, the chance to talk
to them face to face as people rather than as the office they held,

was enlightening for me. I was reminded that even these highest arbiters of fairness brought strong feelings and sometimes personal agendas to matters of critical public policy. And yet, I believed that the opportunity to present the case to them in that environment, free from partisan politics, out of the earshot of constituents, special-interest groups, spinmeisters, and camera crews, was invaluable.

BY THE SUMMER of 2005, concerned citizens had been making their voices heard as never before. Even as electronic voting technology was spreading to new locales, the public looked like it was prevailing in some places in the cause of election integrity. In Essex County, New Jersey, where I lived for several years, the county freeholders voted against following through with a purchase of paperless DREs, even though that decision might have jeopardized their eligibility for HAVA funds. In California, citizen groups descended on the state capital of Sacramento to protest unreliable machines—and this in a state that mandates voter verifiability. The word was spreading.

Too often in American life, when it comes to divisive issues, the facts can be less important than the weight of public opinion. It sometimes feels as though we no longer concern ourselves with right and wrong in any objective sense and are too eager to follow after whoever most effectively wins over our hearts and minds. Some issues defy objective decisions and can be judged only according to individual belief, rather than through an accumulation of evidence. Such matters may never be fully resolved, and that is both the blessing and the curse of democracy. The security of electronic voting systems, however, is not, and cannot be, such an issue. There really isn't much room for subjective interpretation. The only way to understand the risk posed by a system is to ask the people who have the expertise and experience to make that assessment. If our local power company had assured us that its new reactor was safe but some scientists came out with a study showing that it was contaminating the water, we would probably wait to drink the water, no matter what the power company claimed, until independent objective scientists said the water was safe. The same principle must be applied to computerized voting, but for reasons that continue to escape me, it hasn't been.

In the never-ending war over public opinion, DRE proponents have found it advantageous to portray critics as subversives, hysterics, irrational conspiracy theorists, or Luddites who instinctively mistrust progress when it comes in the form of new technology. And no doubt some of those who have spoken out against e-voting machines fit that description, at least in part. But what angers me most is when careful, considered criticism—*scientific* criticism—is condemned as undermining democracy. It makes my blood boil when those who argue for paperless DREs claim the high ground of patriotism. Every ounce of energy that I or any of my colleagues have ever put into the e-voting question has had a single motivation: our desire to preserve the integrity of the American democratic process.

In our democracy, dissent is not merely a right, it is an obligation. America was born out of an act of dissent, and it relies on the willingness of an informed citizenry to speak out, without fear, against questionable policies. Ironically, most of my public statements on the subject of e-voting have been made at the request of the government, which has repeatedly called on me to give my scientific opinion. I have been a part of the process, not an obstruction.

Among the cornerstone principles of our government is the

system of *checks and balances*. We assume that from time to time one of the three branches of government is going to get something wrong. Whether it's through honest error or malicious intent, it's going to happen. That's why we've built into the system the capability—the responsibility—of the other branches to check, or ratify, or verify, the actions of the errant branch. In electronic voting, the paper trail provides the check. To reject it is to reject a fundamental protection of democracy, thus placing that democracy in jeopardy.

The ballot is perhaps the single greatest privilege we have. Protecting it must be considered a matter of public interest as important as a threat of national outbreak of disease or any other impending national disaster. There can be no "sides" in the debate over such an issue, only differing approaches to achieving the single common goal. The disease must be cured, the disaster averted. The facilitation and securing of the voting process cannot be left to the private sector, where legitimate concerns about profitability inevitably lead to conflicting priorities. Governments, presumably interested in staying in power, cannot be allowed to act on voting technology without proper public oversight and total transparency. Questions cannot be adjudicated by our legal system, which pits the interests of one side against another in adversarial trials that do not seek to find objective truths. We will find the answers only through a commitment to a publicly funded, nonpartisan, multidisciplinary research initiative in which no individuals stand to gain and yet the entire nation stands to benefit.

America deserves a foolproof voting system. It must be dependable and easy to use. If the machines cannot be guaranteed to be secure, then they must allow for meaningful audits and recounts through a voter-verified record. Whoever designs that system must be able to prove that the system cannot be cheated and be able to explain why to the average eighth-grader. No American should have to trust someone else, someone with obscure expertise regarding the integrity of the system; it must be simple enough that every citizen can evaluate it for himself or herself. The system must be accessible to all Americans, regardless of disability, and every aspect or component of its workings must be available for public scrutiny.

It sounds hard, but I know it can be done. It requires only that all of us agree to hold the same truths as self-evident—that we can leave nothing to chance or wishful thinking when it comes to safeguarding the most precious element of our democracy and that government of the people, by the people, and for the people will survive only if the people can trust that their voices will be heard and their votes counted.

Resources

The organizations, institutions, and individuals listed here have figured prominently in the electronic voting discussion across the country. Also listed are links to some of the reports, testimony, news accounts, and press releases that are cited in the book but are too long to include in their entirety. In some cases, I've utilized the website http://tinyurl.com, which produces very small Web addresses that are easy to type in, in the place of unwieldy, longer Web addresses. The tinyurl redirects your browser to the original page.

Electronic Voting Websites

Brave New Ballot
http://BraveNewBallot.org
The website for this book includes links to the resources cited here.
Verified Voting
http://verifiedvoting.org
This organization, founded by David Dill of Stanford, was established to make sure that election systems are reliable and publicly verifiable.

ACCURATE
http://accurate-voting.org/
A Center for Correct, Usable, Reliable, Auditable, and Transparent Elections (ACCURATE), funded by the National Science Foundation, is a collaborative project involving six institutions. ACCURATE investigates software architectures, tamper-resistant hardware, cryptographic protocols, and verification systems as applied to electronic voting systems. ACCURATE also examines system usability and ways in which public policy, in combination with technology, can better safeguard voting nationwide.

Douglas W. Jones, Department of Computer Science, University of Iowa
http://www.cs.uiowa.edu/~jones/voting
Doug Jones's Web page on voting and elections is one of the most comprehensive resources for information on electronic voting and security and transparency in elections. This is perhaps the best site for someone interested in the issues.

U.S. Election Assistance Commission
http://www.eac.gov/
This commission was established by the Help America Vote Act to serve as a national clearinghouse and resource for information and review of the procedures followed in the administration of federal elections.

California Voter Foundation
http://www.calvoter.org/
The California Voter Foundation is a nonprofit, nonpartisan organization promoting and applying the responsible use of technology to improve the democratic process. It was founded in 1994 by Kim Alexander.

Caltech-MIT Voting Technology Project
http://www.vote.caltech.edu/
This project was established by the presidents of the two universities to work toward preventing a repeat of the problems that plagued the 2000 election. The project has produced several reports that tackle many issues related to electronic voting.

Electronic Voting Documents and Publications

Analysis of an Electronic Voting System
(February 27, 2004)
http://avirubin.com/vote.pdf
Co-authored by Tadayoshi Kohno, Adam Stubblefield, Dan Wallach, and myself, our initial report on the vulnerabilities of Diebold voting machines first appeared as Johns Hopkins University Information Security Institute Technical Report TR-2003-19, July 23, 2003, and was subsequently published in *IEEE Symposium on Security and Privacy* (IEEE Computer Security Press, May 2004).

SERVE Report (January 21, 2004)
http://servesecurityreport.org
Written by David Jefferson, Barbara Simons, David Wagner, and myself, this report, *A Security Analysis of the Secure Electronic Registration and Voting Experiment (SERVE)*, caused the deputy secretary of Defense to cancel the SERVE project, which explored Internet voting for military and overseas civilians.

SAIC Report (September 2, 2003)
http://tinyurl.com/7yvgd
The only version of the SAIC report on its analysis of the Diebold voting machine available to this date is the one redacted by the state of Maryland. Still, the *Risk Assessment Report: Diebold Accuvote-TS Voting System and Processes* highlights serious security problems and calls the machines highly vulnerable to compromise.

RABA Report (January 20, 2004)
http://www.raba.com/press/TA_Report_AccuVote.pdf
Commissioned by the Maryland General Assembly Department of Legislative Services, this "trusted agent report" on the RABA Technologies Red Team analysis of the Diebold voting machine confirms many of the security problems we identified and also points out some new vulnerabilities.

Checks and Balances in Elections Equipment and Procedures Prevent Alleged Fraud Scenarios (July 30, 2003)
http://www2.diebold.com/checksandbalances.pdf
This is Diebold's rebuttal to our report. It is full of technical errors. See our rebuttal at http://avirubin.com/vote/response.html.

"Diebold Election Systems Moves Forward with Maryland Voting Machine Installation" (September 24, 2003)
http://www.diebold.com/news/newsdisp.asp?id=3003
This is the self-congratulatory press release that Diebold put out after the SAIC analysis found serious vulnerabilities in the machines.

News Articles

Not all of the news stories cited in the book are still available online, but here are links to some of the ones that are:

http://tinyurl.com/ahvxv
"Skeptics of Computer Balloting Score Victory" by Mike Himowitz, *Baltimore Sun*, August 18, 2005.

http://tinyurl.com/bguyv
"E-Vote Guidelines Need Work" by Kim Zetter, *Wired News*, July 10, 2005.

http://tinyurl.com/7hrkz
"E-Voting Tests Get Failing Grade" by Kim Zetter, *Wired News*, November 1, 2004.

http://tinyurl.com/97×27
"Diebold and the Disabled" by Kim Zetter, *Wired News*, October 12, 2004.

http://tinyurl.com/yr8r2
"How E-Voting Threatens Democracy" by Kim Zetter, *Wired News*, March 29, 2004.

http://tinyurl.com/8xyoo
"Security Measures Urged for Voting Machines" by Stephanie Desmon, *Baltimore Sun*, January 30, 2004.

http://tinyurl.com/dklv4
"E-Vote Still Flawed, Experts Say" by Kim Zetter, *Wired News*, January 30, 2004.

http://tinyurl.com/7a2sa
"Risky E-Vote System to Expand" by Kim Zetter, *Wired News*, January 26, 2004.

http://tinyurl.com/ae24r
"Pentagon's Online Voting Program Deemed Too Risky" by Dan Keating, *Washington Post*, January 22, 2004.

http://tinyurl.com/onu1
"Maryland: E-Voting Passes Muster" by Kim Zetter, *Wired News*, September 25, 2003.

http://tinyurl.com/77j3l
"E-Vote Machines Face Audit" by Kim Zetter, *Wired News*, August 12, 2003.

http://tinyurl.com/djhau
"Computer Voting Is Open to Easy Fraud, Experts Say" by John Schwartz, *New York Times*, July 24, 2003.

Glossary

ACCURATE A Center for Correct, Usable, Reliable, Auditable, and Transparent Elections
AES advanced encryption standard
AVVPAT Accessible Voter-Verified Paper Audit Trail
DES data encryption standard
DMCA Digital Millennium Copyright Act of 1998
DRE direct recording electronic
EAC Election Assistance Commission
EFF Electronic Frontiers Foundation
EPIC Electronic Privacy Information Center
ES&S Election Systems and Software
FEC Federal Election Commission
FVAP Federal Voting Assistance Program
GEMS global election management system
HAVA Help America Vote Act of 2002
IACR International Association of Cryptologic Research
IEEE Institute of Electrical and Electronic Engineers
ITA independent testing authority
ITAA Information Technology Association of America
JHUISI Johns Hopkins University Information Security Institute
L&A Logic and Accuracy
LCG linear congruential generator
NAS National Academy of Sciences
NASED National Association of State Election Directors
NCVI National Committee on Voting Integrity
NFB National Federation of the Blind
NIST National Institute of Standards and Technology
NSRL National Software Reference Library
RDS reference data set
SAIC Science Applications International Corporation
SERVE Secure Electronic Registration and Voting Experiment
TGDC Technical Guidelines Development Committee
UOCAVA Uniformed and Overseas Citizens Absentee Voting Act
VVPB voter-verified paper ballots
VVPT voter-verified paper trail

Index